HUMANIST REASON

ERIC HAYOT

HUMANIST REASON

A History. An Argument. A Plan.

COLUMBIA UNIVERSITY PRESS

NEW YORK

Columbia University Press
Publishers Since 1893
New York   Chichester, West Sussex
cup.columbia.edu
Copyright © 2021 Columbia University Press

Library of Congress Cataloging-in-Publication Data
Names: Hayot, Eric, 1972– author.
Title: Humanist reason : a history. an argument. a plan. / Eric Hayot.
Description: New York : Columbia University Press, [2021] | Includes
bibliographical references and index.
Identifiers: LCCN 2020030650 (print) | LCCN 2020030651 (ebook) |
ISBN 9780231197847 (hardcover) | ISBN 9780231197854 (trade paperback) |
ISBN 9780231552370 (ebook)
Subjects: LCSH: Humanities—Philosophy. | Humanities—Study and
teaching—History. | Humanism—History. | Reason.
Classification: LCC AZ103 .H37 2021 (print) | LCC AZ103 (ebook) |
DDC 001.3—dc23
LC record available at https://lccn.loc.gov/2020030650
LC ebook record available at https://lccn.loc.gov/2020030651

Columbia University Press books are printed on permanent
and durable acid-free paper.
Printed in the United States of America

Cover design: Milenda Nan Ok Lee
Cover art: Nataliia Kucherenko © Shutterstock

CONTENTS

ACKNOWLEDGMENTS

A UDIENCES: I am grateful to the following places and people for hosting me at various talks, workshops, and events, and for helping me sharpen my thinking and my work: University of California, Berkeley (Colleen Lye, Rob Kaufman, and Namwali Serpall), Northwestern (Chris Bush), Brigham Young University (Matthew Wickman), the University of Virginia (Jahan Ramazani and Rita Felski), the University of Wyoming (Scott Henkel), Stockholm University (Stefan Helgesson), Stanford University (Nelson Shuchmacher Endebo and Jin Yun Chow), University of California, Davis (Sheldon Lu), Calvin University (Jennifer Williams and Gary Schmidt), Cornell University (Andrea Bachner), the University of Heidelberg (Joachim Kurtz and Barbara Mittler), and Concordia University (Omri Moses).

Institutions: Penn State and the National Endowment for the Humanities provided research support that made this book possible. I started working on the project while at the Karl Jaspers Center for Advanced Transcultural Studies at the University of Heidelberg, where I was supported both by the center and by a Fulbright fellowship. Many thanks to Barbara Mittler, Joachim Kurtz, Martin Dusinberre, and Martin Hoffman, my interlocutors there. In Heidelberg and at Penn State, my presence has been supported by the work of administrative and library staff and by administrators and bureaucrats, who form the institutional backbone of academic work. I am especially grateful to Olivia Brown, Becky Bressler, and Laura Shaffer, and to Susan Welch and Eric Silver as well. While looking for support for the book, I also applied for a number of fellowships that were awarded to other people who are not me, a fact I note here to countermand the habit of only registering in public one's obvious successes. Failure and fear and envy were part of this work, just as much as joy and excitement were.

Friends, listeners, critics, the people I trust to tell me when I'm thinking well and when I'm thinking badly, the people whose fingerprints are, directly and indirectly, all over these pages: Sam Frederick, Anna Kornbluh, Jon Abel, Derek Fox, Erica Brindley, Christopher Bush, Christopher Hill, Jack Chen, Rebecca Walkowitz, Mark McGurl, Daniel Purdy, Sarah Cole, Ben Schreier, Chris Castiglia, Chris Reed, Rita Felski, Jahan Ramazani, and Haun Saussy.

At Columbia University Press, Philip Leventhal, the book's editor, has been a trusted guide through several projects, including this one. I am lucky to have had the chance to work with him, as I am to have benefited from the work of all the people at the press who were part of the editing, production, and marketing of the book. I am grateful to two sharp-eyed, anonymous readers, whose suggestions (and encouragement) have made a significant difference to the pages you have here.

No one writes a book alone. This book, more than any other of mine, owes its life to two specific people, who were with these pages from beginning to end, from the first sentences of Kant's that sent me down the road to chapter 2 and the first public airing of its big ideas, to the private reading of pages and testing of concepts, the working-through of doubts and obstacles, fears and small victories, which have led me to these last lines, written in April 2020, some six years after I wrote the first ones. Those six years, and this book, are unthinkable without them, and so I dedicate *Humanist Reason*, with all my love and friendship, to Paul Saint-Amour and Lea Pao.

HUMANIST REASON

INTRODUCTION

FIRST STORY. Spring 2007. I am one of a group of fellows associated with the International Institute at the University of California, Los Angeles. We have talks every couple of weeks, and because the fellows are drawn from both the humanities and the social sciences, some of the talks are by people doing quantitative political science, anthropology, and similar subjects.

On this day our speaker is Romain Wacziarg, at the time an economist and assistant professor at Stanford Business School (he's now at UCLA). Wacziarg introduces his research: he and Enrico Spolaore have been trying to understand the spread of technological innovation. Their null hypothesis is that the transmission of new technologies and ideas should mainly be a function of interpersonal distance. If someone invents something that gives them a technological advantage, that is, others who are rational economic actors should adopt that innovation at a rate that matches their distance from the original invention. So if I invent a new widget and you live next door and Yuanfei lives on the other side of the street, you and Yuanfei should adopt my new widget at the same time; meanwhile, Gerald, who lives down the street, will only hear about it, and adopt it, later on. And the same should be true for nations or other large collections of people.

In the real world, as we all know, it doesn't turn out like this, and Wacziarg and Spolaore are trying to figure out why. Specifically, they want to know why the technological and economic developments that helped drive European dominance during the modern period were not immediately or quickly adopted by Europe's competitors, and why economic development did not diffuse in the way one might expect if it were simply a neutral effect of distance from innovation. To measure this effect, they are using "genetic distance," defined as "a summary measure of very long-term divergence in intergenerationally transmitted traits across populations," as a proxy for cultural, racial, and religious differences; basically, they're assuming that large-scale genetic differences in populations correlate in some meaningful way to cultural and religious differences that would create potential barriers to the transmission of ideas. To see whether this is true, they are mathematically mapping these degrees of genetic distance between populations against rates of technological transmission. And what they conclude is this: the "long-term (and mainly random) divergence" captured by DNA "has created barriers to the diffusion of technological and institutional innovations across societies in more recent times."[1] In other words, differences in human culture affect the rate of transmission and adoption of technology, and this has particularly strong effects during and after the Industrial Revolution. If I'm a Muslim, and so are you, but our neighbor Yuanfei isn't, you're likely to end up adopting my widget technology before Yuanfei does, even though we all live next to each other. The long-term accumulation of such effects, Wacziarg tells us, helps explain the forms of economic divergence that led to the planetary dominance of Europe and its settler colonies.

I am sitting in the audience, feeling a little bit like I am losing my mind. All this work to prove that cultural differences affect how groups of people share the proceeds of their innovation and wealth? Something that historians, sociologists, and scholars of literature have spent centuries trying to explain, and around which they have built tremendously influential economic, political, and sociocultural models and theories? Something that everyone in my field *already knows?*

I calm down and try to ask the question nicely: "Everyone in my field already knows this. Can you tell me what debates in your field, what arguments, make this a relevant research question?" Before Wacziarg can answer, the historian Ron Rogowski, one of the directors of our fellowship program, chimes in: "That's because you're all Leninists!"

Which is funny enough, I guess.

What Rogowski means is that people in the humanities tend to believe, as your barefoot doctor theory of Lenin might tell you, that the social is almost entirely an effect of the projection and distribution of power. Which is true! I more or less believe that. But that's not all that he means. He also means that I think the way I do for a particular kind of reason—namely, that I (like many of you reading this book) am a Leninist. This political affiliation has determined, at least as far as the joke goes, my understanding of the world. It requires no trammeling by actual research.

As a description of me, this is false. If I believe that cultural differences affect the transmission of technological innovation, I do so on the strength of historical evidence: namely, the evidence that has been put before me by the last few thousand years of human history, as they have been described, interpreted, understood, and explained by humanists. It's not a matter of being an "-ist" of some kind; it's a matter of having a coherent, relatively stable theory of reality—one grounded in evidence and susceptible to change on the basis of future evidence.

In this way, I am no different from Wacziarg and Spolaore, of course. They started with a hypothesis: rates of technological innovation should not depend on cultural differences if people are rational economic actors. And then they disproved that hypothesis using tools and evidence that make sense within the institutional context of their disciplines. I started my life without a theory of how people behave, and I ended up, thanks to my teachers in person and in print, with a conclusion that looks a lot like theirs. But I did it a long time ago, and many other humanists did it before me; it didn't take us until 2007. What is striking, therefore, is that for Wacziarg and Spolare, the null hypothesis of rational economic action remains essentially plausible, despite all the evidence on the other side of the equation. It has not yet been, in the case of the spread of technological innovation as the field of economics understands it, effectively disproved.

Why not? My own null hypothesis: humanist work done to disprove the truth of any proposition does not count, if you are an economist, as *in any way true*. All those books, those conference talks, those months and years in archives, the sentences that put these ideas together: all these are, from a certain perspective, just a little bit of Leninism, just some ideological gabble. For Wacziarg and Spolare, only the mathematical relation between genetic distance and technological innovation moves facts into the realm of the true. Only their methods make things true in economics.[2]

Story number two, later that same year. I am writing *The Hypothetical Mandarin*, which follows across a variety of cultural texts a European and American relationship to Chinese suffering. Sometime that spring, I share a draft of the introduction with my writing group. At our meeting, amid all the criticism and praise, one person points to some sentences that appear at the end of the introduction's second section. They come in a paragraph where I'm pointing out that my destabilization of Western knowledge about China ought not to be mistaken for a claim that Chinese knowledge about China is always accurate and correct. I am trying to make sure, in the moment, that my work to understand and undermine the way that Europeans have historically thought about China does not get interpreted by certain people—as it once did at a conference—as asserting that "only Chinese people should be talking about China." I say that in the introduction, and add that I want my work to make nationalists uncomfortable on both sides of the Pacific. And then I write these sentences: "I do this work, however, not to produce this undermining effect but because I am trying to understand what is historically true. That truths occasionally destabilize the self-aggrandizing delusions of patriots is a happy side effect of their pursuit."[3]

So my friend reads these sentences. And he comes up to me after the meeting and says, "Look at these sentences here: do you really want to say that? Do you really want to say that you're saying things that are true?"

I get what he's asking. In the humanities today, the assertion that one is saying true things, or attempting to, is likely to be met with a great deal of suspicion. Why? Well, for good reason: thanks to a broad sense of historical and interpersonal relativism, most humanists believe that there is no such thing as "the" truth; rather, there are only multiple, historically contingent truths that operate in particular cultural contexts and shape the truth regimes that form there. The fact that economists don't think that humanist knowledge produces truth is pretty good evidence for such a claim, but so are the vast number of ways in which the people of the past or of other places confront us with beliefs that seem to us impossible, unreasonable, outrageous, and so on, and present us with worlds that we have been trained not to judge on terms derived entirely from our own situation or our own epistemological self-satisfaction.

Most humanists believe, also, that whatever truth regime exists does so (at least partly) to consolidate the power and worldview of the social group, class, or institution that proposes it, and that it is just as likely that truth is a function of social power, and not the other way around, as most people might like to believe. Humanists of my generation learned this primarily from reading Foucault, whose wide-ranging discussion of epistemological regimes in *The Order of Things* and *The Archaeology of Knowledge* combined with the specific forms of analysis of institutions and their practices in *Discipline and Punish* and *The History of Sexuality* to produce a picture of the social world as striated and organized by operations of power reified and given life not only in the large-scale ideological social institutions like the school or the prison, but also in a wide variety of essentially subconscious ways of being embodied and living in the world, as we do, in time. Foucault's work, along with a great deal of other writing that appeared around and after it, amounted among other things to a significant critique of the ideology of truth and knowledge that stemmed in its secular version from the discoveries of the Scientific and Industrial Revolutions, and in its theological one from the intellectual and diplomatic aftermaths of Europe's religious wars. It is the battle against this particular ideology of truth—the one associated today with a common-sense vision of science, and at its worst with the ideologies of scientific positivism—that helps create a world in which humanists warn one another not to say that they think they are saying things that are true. Truth is historically contingent, and it is almost certainly a vehicle for domination.

Most humanists believe this at some important and fundamental level, which is why it made sense, in spring 2007, for my friend to ask me if I wanted to retain those sentences.

I left the sentences in.

Why? A few reasons. First, the radical critique of truth-claims, like any radical form of epistemological relativism, runs into a pretty serious set of philosophical problems. To argue that all truth is relative, or that truths are inevitably expressions of power and therefore not "true" in a strong sense, involves making truth-claims. You can't possibly believe that these things are true unless you have some sense of what falsehoods they're contradicting. And even though you may well believe, in general, that truth-claims are historically specific, and therefore subject to revision, and also that truth-claims often, if not always, reproduce hegemonic power structures, (1) you do not believe that the claim that truth-claims are historically specific is itself historically specific—you think that all truth-claims are historically specific; and (2) you think that the idea that truth-claims serve mainly to disseminate power does not apply to the claim that truth-claims mainly disseminate power. Both of these beliefs suggest that any kind of epistemological relativism will always be partial, that the validity of the general claim to relativism can only be sustained by an important potential self-contradiction, which can necessarily only be resolved in practice.

You can tell that this is true by looking, in fact, at what people do: people who generally believe that truth is historically contingent and largely a function of social relations nonetheless regularly make truth-claims. Humanist scholarship is filled with a variety of truth-claims of a variety of types (e.g., historical, theoretical, conceptual, or methodological). When you say something like "Reading George Sand this way teaches us something new about the nineteenth-century French novel," you are saying that the things that her work teaches us are true, even if that's not what you say you're doing. You certainly don't think you're saying something false. And so on for all the various claims that you or any other humanist has ever made—all of those claims operate in some system of truth that *also*, and *at the same time*, believes that truths are culturally relative and likely to be motivated by power.

What this means is that humanists live inside an entire intellectual field in which saying that what you're saying is "true" feels risky because there is a very compelling and serious critique, within the intellectual field, of the very idea of truth. And at the same time, they have an entire field composed largely of people making truth-claims, not only about what one might think of as historical facts (a man named Alfred Dreyfus lived at such-and-such a time, and did not commit treason) but also about historical causes and motivations (contrary to what Dreyfus's accusers said, this is why he really was accused), historical processes (abolitionism is partially an effect of the rise of contract capitalism), and historical meaning (this is what we should learn today from a rereading of the work of Stuart Hall).

And at the same time as those two things, outside this intellectual field, you have a culture in general, and certain institutionalized epistemological disciplines in particular, that don't treat the research results produced by the humanities as completely legitimate knowledge. They imagine the field as essentially, as Rogowski did on that day back in 2007 (and probably a few times since), the epiphenomenon of an ideological point of view—as a field that cannot in fact make any kind of truth-claims because all its truth-claims amount to expressions of some dumb (probably Marxist) political preference.

* * *

All this feels like a problem to me, in three ways. It feels like a problem because the kinds of knowledge that the humanities have historically produced are in fact useful guides to understanding and explaining the world. The casual dismissal of that knowledge as only merely possibly true, but not "really" true, restricts the kinds of knowing that can be available to policymakers and voters and institution-runners and union workers and sexual and ethnic minorities as they make their demands on the social. In other words, the critique of humanist knowledge as ideological aims primarily to remove that knowledge from the field of the social and political commons, thereby shaping the realm of the politically possible.

Second, this feels like a problem because the humanist critique of truth seems to lead humanists themselves into a metadiscourse about their own practice that makes it harder for them to advocate for that practice. It makes it harder for humanists to describe what they do as a truth-generating activity whose research results ought to be taken into account by social actors. And third, this feels like a problem because its picture of humanist knowledge is *false*: false as a representation of what humanist work does, and false in its claim that humanist research cannot "prove" that something like "Cultural differences affect rates of technological adaptation" is true.

These three problems are in fact essentially the same problem viewed from two different angles. (1) There exists a widespread, complex metadiscourse about the humanities that aims to marginalize or delegitimize the work humanists do as teachers and scholars; and (2) humanists often participate in that discourse, even when they are trying to resist it.

* * *

All societies have a set of things that count as valid truth-procedures. Most societies have multiple sets of such things, appropriate to various kinds of social or institutional situations or degrees of seriousness. What's striking about modern society is that the epistemological forms associated with one very particular set of truth-procedures have come to dominate the idea of reason as such, that one specific kind of reasoning, the one we call "science," has risen to such prominence that it can occupy the regime of reason almost entirely by itself. This is not a book about the rise to prominence of scientific reason, the history of its tremendous successes across a variety of fields. This is not an analysis of its embeddedness in capitalism or Europe or other social forms that have imposed it on the rest of the planet (or indeed about all the ways in which each of the words in a phrase like "single scientific reason" can be made more complex, undermined, multiplied, and historicized). It is a book, instead, about the strange place of humanist epistemology today, the complex forms of incoherence that frame and surround it, the ones produced by humanists and nonhumanists alike. It is a book that reclaims and redescribes the work of humanist thought and humanist scholarship as a form of reason, as a form of truth-seeking. And it is a book that supports those claims on the basis of the evidence of humanist scholarship.

One could well begin a critique of the current state of reason by remarking on the genuine *epistemological* weirdness of scientific reason's dominance, which in some respects seems to fail the test of reason itself. Is it not a bit strange, after all, that the culturally dominant idea of reason and truth with which we live stems from the steps forward made by a set of institutionalized practices that focused, as they developed this theory of reason, almost entirely on inanimate, nonconscious objects, or on nonconscious parts of animate objects? What would make an entire society think of "reason"—the process whereby one thinks through things and comes to conclusions that can be shared with and criticized by others—as being primarily theoretically derived from such an unusual subset of the available evidence? If I told you this story about another society, or made it a feature of some alien civilization in a work of science fiction, you would see right away how fucked up it is: These folks have an entire ideology of truth that derives from their study of some tiny percentage of the things that make up their lifeworld. And they do not believe that things are true unless those methods derived from the study of that small percentage of things, most of which are inanimate, can be used to prove things about *all the other objects in that lifeworld*, including societies, people, historical processes, and so on. That is not reasonable by scientific standards, for the same reason that a claim about ducks in general cannot be based on the study of a group of mallards. At best, it's a claim about mallards. Similarly, if one were to ask what reason is, one would do well to derive a theory of reason from truth-procedures as applied to a wide variety of objects, and not just to inanimate or nonconscious ones. That the historical attempts to make scientific reason apply to the objects from which it does not derive (to historical or social processes, to events or objects that have minds) have so often turned out to be failures, both as descriptions of actual human activity as predictions of future events, suggests that some epistemological skepticism is in order.

The reason to explore humanist reason, then, is not just that dominant theories of reason and truth tend to dismiss the work of the humanities (though they do); neither is it only that such an exploration might give humanists more ways to creatively organize their teaching and scholarship, or even to profoundly reimagine it (though it will). It is also, much more simply, that the currently dominant theory of reason is unreasonable. Pictures of the history of reason that bypass the humanities (or treat their knowledge-modes as primitive or outmoded) are not true pictures of the world. The culturally dominant theory of reason has not been properly built up from the evidence before it. It does not give us an accurate picture of the way that people have lived and thought in the world and are likely to continue to live and think in the world, regardless of scientific reason's dominance. Against that dominance—but not against scientific reason per se, which shares many features with humanist reason, as I will suggest—I wish to produce a fuller and more complete picture of our society's actually institutionalized practices of reason, to point us toward, therefore, a richer sense of the actual epistemological workings of our collective institutional and personal endeavors and to open to the sphere of political and social legitimacy the kinds of knowledge and forms of truth that the humanities have been producing all along—and which, incidentally, have all along been doing all kinds of social and political work under the shadow of the more general delegitimization of the humanities as such.

Do the humanities really shape the real world? Can the truths that the humanities provide really change the way people act or think? Consider the following question: what percentage of people living today have had their general sense of the workings of gender altered by the history of feminism and queer theory? Most of the readers of this book, to be sure . . . but I would suggest that nearly every human being alive today has had their thinking, and their sense of their own gender, influenced by that work, whether or not they've ever heard of Sue-Ellen Case, or Chandra Tapalde Mohanty, or Leo Bersani. The social practices and institutions that govern the workings of gender worldwide—not to mention the individual experiences of gender

and sexuality that help compose a self—have been completely transformed in the last fifty years for nearly everyone on the planet. This
is a case of the kind of knowledge that humanists produce having
enormous sociopolitical and individual effects, from the passage of
laws to the reorganization of labor markets to the institutionalization
of legitimate insurance claims to individual decisions about what
to wear, how to love, or how to live. These effects are the products
of humanist truth, a truth that results from a combination of philosophical imagination, historical and sociological description and
analysis, and writing, teaching, and advocacy work. What happens if
we attribute these undoubtedly positive (though often rejected and
resisted) changes to the work of new humanist knowledge? What
happens if we try to describe the intellectual protocols, assumptions,
and procedures whereby that knowledge came to be produced, dis-
seminated, and integrated into personal lives and social institutions?

* * *

A book specifically interested in addressing the state of humanist
reason today would have to do a few things. It would have to think
carefully about the historical and philosophical origins of the epistemology of the modern humanities, and to measure those origins
and their claims against the evidence of humanist practice. It would
have to come up with a provisional definition for the ideas of reason
and of truth that corresponded to those practices, while retaining
its connections to existing, evidence-based critiques of the social
use of such terms. And it would have to do so in a way that gave its
readers a vision of the humanities that was simultaneously recog-
nizable and transformed, familiar in its core capacities and beliefs
but unfamiliar in terms of its social position and its long-term
possibilities for expansion. Ideally, such an effort would also occasionally, in the spirit of the plentiful evidence that human life has
provided us that these things matter, even to reason, move its readers, or make them laugh.

Fingers crossed.

* * *

Let me describe the book and answer a few questions.

First things first: it's divided into four chapters. The first two are more traditionally academic—full, detailed notes, close reading, a tone and style at the sentence level that resembles the norms for scholarly work in my field, despite my fondness for the occasional swear word. They're pretty good, and full of fun—I promise! But they're not as open and inviting as the third chapter, which is more polemical and looser in tone and style, more like this introduction. In many ways, that chapter is the heart of the project—the part that lays out the boldest ideas of the book.

Given this difference, for a long time I thought about breaking the manuscript in two. I briefly considered printing the third chapter upside down and backward, so that you'd have to turn the book over to read it from the other direction. I also worried—as did one of the readers of the manuscript—that the more academic style of the first two chapters would drive away some readers, who would never get to the part of the book that matters most. (Another reader of the man-uscript worried that the third chapter was too unfootnoted and too loose to be as convincing as the first two; this is the same problem, seen from another perspective.)

In the end, I left it as you have it here. Part of that decision has to do with what I need, right now, as a writer and thinker—with how I'm feeling about my own work, with my own anxieties about whether the writing and thinking I do is serious enough, or if it's just saying obvious things with a bit of charisma, and loudly. But most of it, I hope, comes from a commitment to the following prin-ciple: that the simple, looser, plainer things that we learn to say in the world often rely, as they do so obviously here, on an enormous amount of humanist labor of the scholarly type, without which the saying of the simpler things, or the simpler saying of these things, would not be ethically or epistemologically legitimate. I wanted to make the difference between those two modes stylistically starker here, and then keep them in the same book. The relatively sharp dis-tinction made between more scholarly books on the *history* of the humanities (like Chad Wellmon's *Organizing Enlightenment: Infor-mation Overload and the Invention of the Modern Research University*) and more public-facing books on the social status and institutional positioning of the humanities (like Kathleen Fitzpatrick's *Generous Thinking: A Radical Approach to Saving the University*) tends to treat the former as though they have little to tell us about the politics of our contemporary institutional life (except as a kind of background), and the latter as though they aren't somehow works of real scholarship. I wanted to make that reaction more difficult to have, in both directions.

So what does the book actually do, then?

Well, chapter 1 begins by working through some of the intellectual history of the late nineteenth century, showing how the philosophical debates of that time anticipate (and indeed found) the basic patterns of humanist metadiscourse, and showing, also, how they responded to institutional and intellectual pressures similar to the ones we face today. The defenses and presumptions about humanist work that were developed in the late nineteenth century carry forward into much contemporary work in humanist history, literary criticism, sociology, and anthropology, where they manifest primarily as intense resistance to hierarchy, pattern, structure, and subordination in sociocultural analysis. My argument will be that this basic pattern of thought corresponds not only to the metadiscourse of humanist reason, but also to the structure of feeling associated with humanist practice; that this pattern not only describes how humanists think about what they do, but how they feel about it, how they position themselves ethically in relation to the world.

Along the way, I will at various moments contrast this metadiscourse with what I know about actual humanist knowledge-practice, as well as with what I know about how most people live their lives. My claim will be, more or less, that no one can actually live out, either in their ordinary daily life or in their scholarly work, the major ethical claims of humanist metadiscourse. I have some thoughts about why this is, as well as about the ways in which that very impossibility has been imagined as a kind of tragic aporia of human existence or of the very workings of thought. I will argue that first, there exists an alternative, *equally plausible* description of humanist reason, and, second, that this equally plausible description has a number of practical advantages if you would like humanist reason to expand its hold on our social lives.

What do you mean by "metadiscourse"?

It's been easiest for me to think that there are two major metadiscourses on the humanities. The first involves claims about the institutional status of the humanities, about their status as departments, majors, graduate programs, and fields. Many such books, written by humanists, focus on the university in general—Andrew McGettigan's *The Great University Gamble*, Stefan Collini's *Speaking of Universities*, or Louis Menand's *The Marketplace of Ideas: Reform and Resistance in the American University*. Such books participate in a broader international discourse on the state of the humanities in modern society and address, for those reasons, two major kinds of topics: (1) the status of the humanities as an institutionalized form; and (2) the value of that institutionalized form for college undergraduates, and, by extension, for society at large.[4]

This book is mostly not about that metadiscourse. That doesn't mean that there's anything wrong with it; in fact, lots of it is quite interesting and good, though I mostly agree with Helen Small (*The Value of the Humanities*) that claims about the social or personal value of a humanities education are first, hard to prove, and second, fairly ineffective.[5] This doesn't mean that the institutional questions don't matter; I have done some thinking and writing about these topics, some of which appears in chapter four, where I imagine about the potential institutional consequences of the kinds of arguments I make about humanist reason here. But for most of the book, that kind of thinking is set aside.

In its place comes an attention to another kind of metadiscourse around the humanities. This one focuses on epistemological questions. Unlike the first metadiscourse, which is nothing if not explicit (as one might expect, it being a metadiscourse), this metadiscourse is more implicit, emerging as a matter of practice or a set of normative bases for the practice of humanist scholarship. Its major features include a forthright dedication to the singular, the nonhierarchical, and the plural; a distrust of vertical causality; and an investment in complexity (as against simplicity, rule, or structure). These are matters of epistemological commitment; but they are also, as I show here, matters of ethics, of a fundamental orientation toward other people, other lives, other things. Such ethico-epistemological principles are metadiscursive in the sense that they constitute a set of overarching agreements about how scholarship in historical and cultural fields should conduct and justify itself. But they are weirdly metadiscursive, insofar as they appear mainly as both general principles—"All work should orient itself to the singular qualities of its evidence"—and as more specific claims—"historical research is based on the archive" and "literary analysis requires extensive analysis of citations"—that are so much the stuff of general agreement that they hardly need to be written down or spoken aloud. Chapter 1 thus spends a great deal of time with a few texts in which those principles have been made explicit, and in understanding what kinds of structures produced those explicitations and why.

So you describe the rise of a metadiscourse around humanist epistemology, and follow it through to the present. Then what?

Chapter 2 goes back to the philosophical roots of humanist reason in the modern period, which the book winds up discussing with respect to the work of Immanuel Kant, whose philosophy lies at the origin of much of how the late nineteenth-century defenders of humanist reason, and their inheritors (including us), think. The Kant section aims not only to expose some deeper roots of modern humanist metadiscourse, but also to begin the work of moving through and past it. I generate, in good humanist fashion, a rereading of Kant that ends up having the text (or Kant himself, if you prefer) say more or less the opposite of what others (including Kant himself) have believed that he said. My argument is not, however, that I understand Kant, and that others have not; it is that I am in this moment producing a specific *reading* of the Kantian text that allows us to think differently about the problems before us. That reading basically says: Here are the roots of one major strain of humanist discourse, and here is why, if we reread what Kant wrote, we can come up with a completely different, but equally plausible (and ideally more compelling), set of roots, which will them ramify into a very different metadiscourse about humanist reason.

The Kant section, therefore, sets us up with more work to do. That work appears in chapter 3, where I lay out a series of overlapping principles that underlie the teaching and scholarship that humanists do—principles, that is, that develop theoretically from aspects of humanist practice and that derive from imagining those aspects as

expressions of underlying ideas about how human life, human society, and human knowledge work. Preceding these is a short definition
of "reason" itself, conceived in a way that resolves, I hope, much of
the discomfort that one might (on evidentiary, reasonable grounds)
feel about a concept that has been so intimately tied to epistemological disrespect and colonial and capitalist violence. There, as well as
throughout the book, my argument is neither that "contradictions
are bad and must be resolved" (in fact, contradictions are socially
necessary and useful; see chapter 3) nor that "practice is living and
abstraction is dead; therefore, we should just look at practice" (in
fact, there is no practice of the social without conceptualization and
theorization from the beginning; abstraction is foundational to language and social life). It is rather that the practice of humanist reason
and humanist teaching and scholarship can be redescribed in ways
that will serve the humanities by allowing them (1) to produce more
compelling self-justifications; (2) to develop a richer and more epistemologically productive metadiscursive self-reflexivity; and (3) to
radically expand the fields of their research and expertise—all of this
within the particular social context that currently frames them.

All that sounds nice, but . . . are the humanities really worth saving?

The humanities in their current institutional configuration . . .
that's complicated, and the stuff of a different book. But humanist reason, absolutely, yes. Because *sometimes* that reason, which
emerges from the extensive study of human lives, cultures, and
environments (and all the nonhuman things, living and nonliving,
that such cultures and environments include)—and which therefore
understands all proposals for the political or social future of a human
group of any size, local, national, or global, as constrained by what we
know of the history of the planet and the species, and also open to
the vast array of actually existing possibilities that the planet and the
species have shown us so far—has helped move societies closer to
the creation of a democratic social welfare planet, in which health,
well-being, and the opportunity to explore one's full capacities as a
being (human or otherwise) do not depend as much on the exploita-
tion and diminishment of others as they do now. *Sometimes.* That is a
truth-claim. Its evidence appears, to my epistemological satisfaction,
in both the historical record and in the humanist scholarship that

has explored, interpreted, explained, and theorized it.[6] A true description of how such work thinks, of how it puts into practice principles of reason that create knowledge in common, knowledge that can be shared with and taught to others, is thus the major goal of this book.

Let me be clear, therefore, about the kinds of historical claims I am making here, and about the kinds of value-claims I am making on humanist reason's behalf. The so-called crisis in the humanities, a crisis which, in epistemological and social terms, dates quite clearly back to the late 1800s (as chapter 1 will show), has taken an especially grim institutional turn since the 2008 financial crisis. A book on humanist reason might be taken to say that this crisis can be resolved (or could have been avoided) had humanists had a better theory of their own reasoning practices. I do not think that that is true. I do not ever intend to suggest that the wounds suffered by the humanities today—the funding cuts, the precariousness of employment for many humanists with PhDs, the adjunctification of teaching, the sociocultural disdain that attaches to our programs and our majors, the political hostility that comes from social conservatives and neo-libertarians—are either self-inflicted or the product of this epistemological problem They're not. For my money, the best way to restore the institutional humanities in whatever form (though ideally in a new form) would be to restore or increase public funding for primary, secondary, and university education.

That said, the history of humanist-generated metadiscourse about the humanities—by this, I mean language about how the humanities work that is produced by humanists themselves—has boxed humanist institutions and scholars into a rhetorical and political corner that has not served them well. More specifically, the gap between the metadiscourse of humanist reason and the practice of humanist scholarship has made it difficult for humanists to (1) properly understand their own work; (2) fight back against stupid characterizations of it; and (3) free the humanities from a set of institutional and intellectual constraints that limit the scope of their attention, their ambition, and their labor.

What, then, is this "humanist reason" that solves all these problems, and what is its relation to humanist metadiscourse and to the institutional state of the humanities? These are the topics of this book. But let us anticipate a bit, so that we enter the historical record of chapter 1 with a definition and a sense of value in hand, with a sense of where we're headed and why: Humanist reason is a way of thinking that uses a variety of epistemological and evidentiary practices to study the lifeworlds of beings with minds. Such studies necessarily include vast historical and physical contexts, as well as fine-grained analyses at the smallest of scales of the linguistic, cultural, aesthetic, social, institutional, and political output of those beings, as well as all the environments (geological, artificial, and living) that construe and constrain them. Humanist reason makes truth-claims; it builds models; it tests models against evidence; it considers, carefully and at great length, the way in which the nature or natures of its evidence (as understood in any given historical moment or epistemological context) make demands on, and shape and are shaped by, the methods with which they interact. On these grounds, and on the strength of its research, humanist reason builds models of causation, of meaning, and of life, that aim to explain pasts, understand presents, and imagine futures. Such models are *reasonable*, insofar as they can be the product of shared methods and shared conclusions, all of which are self-reflexively modifiable in common. And they are *realistic*, in that they provide the grounds for pragmatic decisions about how to interact with the social in ways that can be effective in the actual world. Making their case—tracing the history of their emergence, working through the patterns and problems of their reasoning, and imagining the possible future of their development—is the task of the pages that follow.

I

THE RISE OF IDIOGRAPHISM

Or the Origins of Humanist Metadiscourse

1. WILHELM WINDELBAND'S RECTORIAL ADDRESS

Kaiser-Wilhelms-Universität Strassburg, May 4, 1894: the university's commemoration day.[1] The philosopher Wilhelm Windelband, speaking (one imagines) from behind the same majestic black beard he wears in the photographs we have of him today, was delivering the "Rede zum Antrittdirektorats," the university's Rectorial Address. Windelband was a week away from his forty-sixth birthday; he had published, two years earlier, *Geschichte der Philosophie* (The History of Philosophy), a book that would cement his reputation as a major figure of the neo-Kantian school and the leader, until his death in Heidelberg in 1915, of the southwestern branch of that particular philosophical outlook.

The talk's subtitle, "Geschichte und Naturwissenschaft," (History and Science), by which it is now generally known, gives us its organizing principles. Its immediate target is the division of the university into disciplines. The then-conventional disposition, which distinguished between the *Geisteswissenschaften*, the sciences of mind, and the *Naturwissenschaften*, the natural sciences, was, Windelband told his audience, "unfortunate." "Nature and mind is a substantive dichotomy"—one based on the substances that researchers study, maintained, "with absolute rigidity" in modern philosophy, from Descartes to Hegel.[2] But the difference between mind and nature is not as clear as that rigidity has made it seem. We have reason to doubt, Windelband said, that the mind is purely *in here*, and never *out there*; we cannot assume that something like "inner perception" functions as a "special, autonomous mode of knowledge," detached entirely from the world "outside" the mind. What's more, the traditional division between nature and mind cannot account for the mysterious place of psychology, because the latter studies the mind *as* nature. Neither can it explain the way that it separates philosophy from mathematics, even though both disciplines, building their arguments with logic, eschew real-world observation and therefore have more in common with one another, Windelband says, than with either the mind-oriented disciplines or the nature-oriented ones.

In other words, the entire system of knowledge is bunk. Windelband would spend the rest of the address, and indeed much of the rest of his career, trying to set it right.

Needless to say, he didn't. But to understand what Windelband thought he was rectifying and why, to understand how his solution emerged from the longer history of nineteenth-century German intellectual life, to understand how his position was taken up and modified by others, including relatively obscure figures like Heinrich Rickert or Emil Lask, as well as the leading lights of German philosophy and social science in the years between 1890 and 1933, including Wilhelm Dilthey, Edmund Husserl, Martin Heidegger, and Max Weber, and indeed to understand the ways in which these problems and their solutions went to—and still go to—the heart of what scholars and scientists could and can mean, then and now, when they talk about or do science, social science, or the humanities, what it means to think, then and now, of the interaction between regulative and law-oriented forms of knowledge, especially ones that rely on the analysis of large numbers of pieces of evidence, and those forms of knowledge that tend to focus on single, especially interesting objects—to understand, even, the basic patterns and structures that govern and underlie how we know, and how we think and feel about how we know—is to acquire a grasp not only of the history of the late nineteenth century, but on the entire modern history of intellectual and university life.

This book is not about either Wilhelm Windelband or the intellectual history of German philosophy. Rather, it is about the contemporary state of human knowledge as it is theorized, practiced, and institutionalized in the modern university system and in the modern divisions of the disciplines—which is to say that it is, perhaps like all books, about the conditions of its own production. My argument is simple: first, that there is a better way to describe the basic justifications, both epistemological and ethical, that govern the work of humanist reason today; and second, that changing the way that humanists describe and justify what we do could have significant consequences for both the future of humanities departments and the university more generally, as well as, in the long run, for the entire pattern that organizes the way we think about knowledge.

The description of those consequences, and the laying out of the advantages and disadvantages that accrue from abandoning some of the most basic ethical justifications for humanist reason, including the centrality of the human to it, will have to wait for the end of the book. Before we can get there, we must understand both where we are, epistemologically and institutionally, and where we came from. To do so, we will spend some time with Windelband and company. That means stepping back into the history of late-nineteenth-century German intellectual life and into the conditions to which Windelband's Rectorial Address most intimately, and with a sense of great urgency, responded.

* * *

The decades from 1850 to 1890 saw philosophy in Germany threatened on a number of fronts. The dramatic midcentury decline in prominence of German philosophical idealism, partly prompted by the deaths of its two major figures (Hegel in 1831, Schelling in 1854) played some role in fomenting a general sense that philosophy was out of ideas. But the more prominent factors were institutional and disciplinary as well as epistemological, tracking broadly across a variety of related cultural and scientific fields. The rapid rise to prominence in the middle nineteenth century of scientific naturalism and positivism, which claimed that only knowledge derived from the natural world could be legitimate, was abetted by the explanatory triumphs of Darwin's theory of evolution (and its social Darwinian cousins, which seemed to explain society as well), by the effectiveness of advances in material sciences and medicine, and by the rise of psychology, which promised, on the medical/Darwinian model, to take over from philosophy the explanation of the workings of the human mind (and thus the answers to basic questions about why or how we know or feel).[3] The new developments in the social sciences, especially in economics and to a lesser extent in nascent sociology, aimed to elucidate economic and social laws that could serve both as explanations for the history of the species and as modes of social and political control. Both tasks were abetted by the new science of statistics, which developed in parallel in France, England, and Germany whose modern name derives from the German word *Staat* (state), reminding us of the field's original motivations and goals.[4] This attack on philosophy, coming on what Herbert Schnädelbach has called a "double front" of idealism and the natural sciences,[5] produced a need among historians and other humanists to defend and justify their field, to mark out its particularities and to separate it from its competitors, to "sharply and fundamentally delimit the sphere of history against related fields of knowledge, and above all against the general sciences of man, for which the name 'anthropology'—though some might prefer 'sociology'—still seems like the right one to me," as Eduard Meyer wrote in 1902.[6]

This need to defend humanist reason interacted with (and contributed to) the midcentury rise of German historicism, whose major figure was Leopold von Ranke. Ranke's work, with its heavy reliance on archival sources and its quasi-relativist take on forms of historical and cultural difference, took aim at both the idealist philosophy of history developed by Hegel and the more positivist, pseudoscientific models of history typical of works like H. T. Buckle's two-volume *History of Civilization in England* (1857–1861)—a positivism emblematized later in the century by Karl Lamprecht's claim that to "work scientifically means . . . to bring the infinite world of singularities under general concepts, and to thereby rule them."[7] In a series of lectures

"On the Study of History," given from 1868 onward, Ranke's student Jacob Burckhardt argued, against such historical positivism, that the new history ought to "reject all attempts to be systematic: we make no claim to 'world-historical ideas,' but are content with observation; we make cross-sections through history, and in as many directions as possible; above all, we do not provide a philosophy of history."[8]

At the "core of the methodological critique of Hegelianism" that Burckhardt shared with the entire historical school lay a strong, ethically motivated "rejection of subordination," a refusal to describe historical events as effects of some transhistorical process of teleology or progress, or to subsume such events to some general structure or principle that would in effect determine them in advance.[9] Already in 1836, Ranke had made of this rejection of subordination a basic epistemological principle: "From the particular you may ascend to the general; but from general theory there is no way back to the intuitive understanding of the particular."[10] A similar resistance to general laws, abetted by a strong sense of historical relativism, also appeared in schools of German historical economics, particularly in the work of Karl Knies, who argued from 1856 onward against the idea that any such laws could be developed in his field, since economies and economic behavior are historically bound. "The idea that permanent 'laws' of economic behavior can be based upon the generality of 'private egoism' struck Knies as pure 'fiction,' " writes Fritz Ringer; Knies rejected the idea on "ethical as well as methodological grounds."[11]

This shift toward historical relativism and an emphasis on local detail (abetted by Ranke's emphasis on the use of original documents and sources, including texts in so-called ordinary genres or written by everyday people) can be thought of as having common cause with the critique of Hegelian idealism as it emerged from the field of philosophy proper. The historicist critique of Hegel abetted the general decline of philosophy as a field for two reasons. First, idealism was, in the middle of the nineteenth century, essentially synonymous with philosophy itself, so any critique of idealism functioned as an attack on philosophy more generally. Second, relativism's apparent reduction of philosophical questions to historical ones stripped from philosophy much of the territory it had claimed for itself in previous centuries, including the capacity to answer basic questions about right and wrong, about how or why we know, about the nature of friendship and of political organization, or about the guiding principles of human life. All these were, from a historical point of view, matters of cultural context, and from a particularist point of view, not generalizable into common or universal lessons in any case. If all knowledge and all aspects of human culture come down to matters of context and every moral decision grounds itself in the particular and unrepeatable circumstances of its situation, then one has little need for a certain kind of philosophy at all.

The situation of German philosophy in the late 1800s was therefore dire. Buffeted on one side by the successful certainties of natural science (which contrasted sharply with the failed Hegelian ones), on another by the rise of historicism, on a third by the new work being done in psychology, and on still a fourth by positivist claims about historical laws, philosophers felt the need to carve out a place for their field. They wanted to lay the groundwork for a common theory of humanistic knowledge that would unite the disciplines lying outside the natural and observational sciences and provide institutional and social support for their continued work. In this context, even the most basic questions about what English speakers today call the humanities were up for debate: What do we call the kinds of knowledge that do not rely on observation of nature? Are they in fact actually sciences, and if they are, what are they sciences of—or are they of anything at all? How might one describe the humanities' epistemological difference from natural science, and justify their epistemological legitimacy, without giving them over fully to the dream of positive social science and the development of natural laws of humankind, or simply turning them into a form of relativist empathy-development or self-improvement? In short, how might one describe the human sciences' relation to value, either individual or social, and in so doing cause others to value them?

If these questions feel as fresh, as relevant, and as connected to our circumstances today as they did for Windelband's listeners in 1894, it is because we contemporary humanists are very much the inheritors of the debates of the late-nineteenth-century German *Methodenstreit*. Like Windelband and his colleagues, we face a startling loss of epistemological prestige of the humanities relative to the science, technology, engineering, and math (STEM) disciplines. Like them, we are challenged by the decades-long swerve toward quantification across all the social scientific fields, a swerve now making incursions into the literary and historical disciplines via the computational analysis of texts under the umbrella of "cultural analytics" or the "digital humanities."[12] And like them, we live in an epistemological lifeworld at least partially defined by a substantive dichotomy (the study of nature versus the study of the human), even though, in our case as in Windelband's, such a dichotomy fails to account for the place of the social sciences, which are treated either more or less like the study of nature (because quantitative) or more or less like the study of culture (because qualitative)—without anyone asking whether these January faces reflect anything more than the intensity of the dichotomy that precedes them. The general organization of the American university, borrowed heavily from the Humboldtian model that influenced the German system from the beginning of the nineteenth century onward, reifies these problems at the institutional level in the form of departments, colleges, and schools, even as the public debate about the value of the various disciplines and the level of state support for them produces a continuous state of anxiety and crisis. Even the terms "idiographic" and "nomothetic," for which Windelband's address is mostly remembered, have made a comeback in recent years, with the result that Windelband's nomenclature now seems to be permanently associated, at least in literary studies, with the debate over quantitative and computational methods, with the digital humanities, and with all the other features of our contemporary method-strife.[13] We are facing his problems. We are speaking his language. And he is speaking ours.

∗ ∗ ∗

Let us return, then, to Strassburg in 1894, where Windelband has only begun his address. He opened, you will recall, with a basic analysis of the conceptualization of the disciplines: the division between nature and *Geist* defines, mistakenly, the scientific fields by virtue of the substances to which they attend. And here is a preliminary solution: we should think of the disciplinary dichotomy not as a matter of substance, but as method.[14] To describe this difference, Windelband introduces two figures of speech: the words "nomothetic" and "idiographic" (175). Each term names a way of thinking about and understanding the world. The nomothetic, he says, orients us toward "the discovery of the laws of phenomena"; the idiographic, by contrast, seeks to "reproduce and understand in its full facticity an artifact of human life to which a unique ontological status is ascribed" (174–75). In other words, the nomothetic sciences "are concerned with what is invariably the case," while "the sciences of process," as Windelband calls them, "are concerned with what was once the case," with actual historical people and events as opposed to natural or scientific regularities (175).

Windelband's immediate target here was the 1883 work of Wilhelm Dilthey, whose *Einleitung in die Geisteswissenschaften* "is considered to have provided the classical formulation" of the term *Geisteswissenschaften*, today widely considered to be an uncontroversial equivalent of "the humanities" or "the human sciences," as they might encompass the fields of history and literature as well as psychology, sociology, and economics.[15] As Windelband's introductory remarks suggest, however, the idea that the humanistic fields ought to be thought of as united by their interest in things *Geist*-ish could be challenged on any number of grounds—particularly given the word's association with Dilthey's work. Dilthey's choice of *Geist*, which can mean "mind" or "spirit," attempted to rebrand a word deeply associated with Hegelian idealism for a novel purpose; for this reason, Rudolph Makkreel argues that in this context, it ought to be translated into English as "human," as it largely is today.[16]

But that did not stop Windelband (or his student Heinrich Rickert) from objecting to the term on antimetaphysical grounds, and accusing Dilthey of drifting dangerously close to psychologism, of treating reality as an effect of mental processes.[17] Against Dilthey, Windelband sought to affirm "that nature and history are not two modes of being, but the logical objects of two different modes of investigation." This dichotomy is not "ontologically grounded in differences between two kinds of entities" (nature and human life), but rather "axiologically defined by differences between two types of interests."[18] Hence Windelband's reference to "sciences of process."

Hence also the unlikely pairing in the title the address: "History and Natural Science." Grasping the logic of that unlikely coupling is crucial to understanding both the goals and the grounds of Windelband's efforts. The opposition between *Geisteswissenschaft* and *Naturwissenschaft*, each one a substance paired with a nominalizing descriptor, is obvious enough. The same might be said for other similar oppositions, including the one between the natural sciences and the sciences of concrete reality (*Wirklichkeitswissenschaften*; Georg Simmel), or the one between the natural sciences and the cultural ones, favored in later years by Rickert. But history and natural science? How do these two concepts stand in for the organizing dichotomy of modern knowledge, and what justifies their opposition? On what grounds, in particular, can history occupy the other side of a dichotomy from natural science, as though what were being opposed here were not merely two ways of producing knowledge about the world, but a mode of knowledge-production (on one hand) with a concrete, existing substance (on the other)?

The answer lies in Windelband's conceptualization of history itself. He explains to his audience that the disciplines "that are usually called sciences of the mind [*Geisteswissenschaften*] have a distinctively different purpose [from those in the natural sciences]: they provide a complete and exhaustive description of a single, more or less extensive process which is located within a unique, temporally defined domain of reality" (174). Their goal is to "reproduce and understand in its full facticity an artifact of human life to which a unique ontological status is ascribed. It is clear that, in this sense, the sciences of the mind comprehend the entire domain of the historical disciplines" (174–75). The word "unique," which Windelband repeats across these two sentences, describes both the "domain of reality" that surrounds the "single . . . process" that is the epistemological target of the non–natural scientific fields, and the "ontological status" ascribed to the "artifact of human life" so studied. It is this uniqueness that gives rise to the word Windelband proposes to describe these methods: "idiographic," with *idio*- from the Greek for "particular" or "individual." Idiographic disciplines, he writes, "are concerned with the unique, immanently defined content of the real event"; they focus on "what was once the case," on an unrepeatable and singular object—one that cannot merely be the instance of a more general principle or the case of an overarching rule. In this way, they contrast with the other disciplines, which Windelband calls "nomothetic" (from the Greek *nomos*, relating to the law). These latter focus on "general laws" and "general, apodictic [if-then] judgment" that seeks to define what is "constant" and "invariably the case" (176).

At the heart of the idiographic/nomothetic difference lies a fairly simple observation: events considered historically are unique, in the sense that *they take place only once*. They are incomparable, fundamentally particular, unrepeatable. They cannot, therefore, be subject to any law, or indeed any methodology, save one that emerges from their particular uniqueness. Each of the objects of idiographic attention, Windelband says, "requires a mode of investigation which conforms to its own special properties," whereas the objects of nomothetic science are governed by the modern equivalent of the Platonic ideal—namely, the "natural law," which treats their individuality as a symptom of some larger, governing generalization (174). The nomoethetic/idiographic distinction, he notes, thus goes back to the "relationship which Socrates recognized as the fundamental nexus of all scientific thought: the relationship of the general to the particular" (176).

It is on these grounds that history can stand alone against natural science: the very substance of history (or of things historically considered) is in and of itself—within a certain framework—simply incompatible with the natural-scientific method. Years later, both Windelband and Rickert would use "historical sciences" (*Geschichteswissenschaften*) to stabilize the dichotomy, but in this early moment, the willingness to make history alone bear the pressure of opposition directs us to something fundamental in their thought. What makes the objects historically unique as such is that every historical occurrence happens, in the stream of time as humans experience it, only and precisely *once*.[19] In this sense, history is (ontologically) a kind of bed or garden for the development of ontological uniqueness (so far as humans are concerned), throwing up at infinitely small intervals sets of circumstances, events, attitudes, and collections of physical and mental phenomena, each of which will never appear in precisely the same way again. Windelband calls this the "domain of reality" surrounding the "single process" that guarantees the "ontological status" of the idiographic as a unique thing, and therefore as something worthy of idiographic treatment. (You will notice that we are veering, despite Windelband's emphasis on method, dangerously close to another substantive distinction. More on this later.)

The danger of this uniqueness, in both the field of historical study and the study of the work of art, is that it leads the scholar to an extreme relativism or nominalism: if everything is absolutely unique, in all of its properties, then no general or comparative category could come to abuse it; no category developed from an outside, no language that did not belong precisely and fully to the thing under investigation, could properly be used to understand it. Such an object of investigation would be fully monadic, withdrawn from abstraction, paraphrase, or description. Scholarship could, in such a scenario, aim only to repeat the thing exactly as such. And even such a repetition would be a falsification, since the circumstances of such a repetition would be nonidentical with the circumstances of the first occurrence. The southwestern neo-Kantians, including Windelband, his students and collaborators (Heinrich Rickert, Emil Lask, and Max Weber), and their differently neo-Kantian antagonists (Dilthey and Husserl), would worry at this problem for the next several decades. It continues to haunt historical and aesthetic study in our time, and we will address it again later on.

For now, however, I simply want to observe in our current intellectual and institutional practices the traces of our inheritance of the Dilthey-Windelband debate. From one point of view, Windelband was clearly prescient, and correct: humanistic research today does not confine itself to questions of mind, spirit, or culture, but ranges broadly across the history of physics, economics, and biology, teaching and writing about Galileo, Darwin, Adam Smith, the impact of cellular life on human culture, and other subjects, with all of this subsumable under the general rubric of history, a history challenged a heightened awareness of the roles played in human historical culture by nonhuman living beings, from ecosystems to *Escherichia coli*, as well as by nonliving machines, objects, and things of all types. This catholic relation to the objects of research does not impinge on method; no one would confuse a book in the environmental humanities with "doing" biology, even if some of the objects are the same. The methodological difference remains:

observation, calculation, general laws, a focus on reproducibility and predictability, heavily abetted by the aggregation and manipulation of large sets of data (nomothetism, in other words), belong on one side of the epistemological and scientific divide, while the idiographers, on the other, focus on their single cases, their fully contextualized instances, their things organized in patterns of formal relations that make their own laws. Many of our deepest disciplinary divisions emerge in the ways that we use and make claims about evidence, the patterns and methods whereby evidence can lead us to theories, and the kinds of theories that can legitimately result from them. (That is why the arrival of quantitative research to literary shores feels like such a crisis and provokes such intense and emotional reactions.)

And yet Dilthey, with his division of disciplines by substances, was right as well. For all the calls to interdisciplinarity and all the shifts brought about by the expansion of the humanist canon (via cultural studies, science and technology studies, and other fields), disciplinary topics still produce sharp institutional and professional distinctions. It is one thing to say, as Windelband did in Strassburg, that there are two major ways of looking at the things of the world, and that much depends on how you look. It is quite another to produce, as his professorial successors have done, an entire institutionalized system whose structure suggests that in fact, these two ways of looking at the world stem not from ways of looking, but from the nature of the things themselves—that the integrity of knowledge depends not only on a series of methodological choices, but also on their application to, and indeed symbiotic relation with, the objects they purport to explain or understand.[20] For all the foofaraw about methods, one might say that at the end of the day, the institutional justification for the disciplinary divisions most often comes down to simply this: nature for the natural sciences and culture for the humanities.[21] Certain things—people, works of art, historical events—are widely believed to be understandable only via what Windelband would call idiographic approaches. Other things—chemical processes, the internal biology of cells, or the movements of the stars—can be grasped only, if the institutional apparatus is to be believed, via nomothetic approaches, which explains why the chemistry department has no truck with close reading.[22] In this way, the division of disciplines by the ontologies of their objects turns out to have had a remarkable, Diltheyian staying power. The idea that certain objects demand certain kinds of methods, and vice versa, continues to be fundamental to the organization of our institutions, and to our professional self-understanding.

What does such an idea imply? At bottom, that nature and the mind are fundamentally different orders of things, and that the differences that *lie inside them* and *belong to them as such* produce a set of epistemological demands, to which the *Geistes-* and *Natur-wissenschaften* respond in turn. It is not just that the methods correspond, in some strong sense, to their objects, but also that the difference in the objects produces—or seems to produce—the dichotomized difference in the methods needed to understand them. If we have different methods, then, it's because the objects themselves demand it, because of something that is, after all, substantively in the real, to which our methods respond.

Such a conceptualization of the real is incompatible with Kantianism, as Windelband well knew. And so at its most revolutionary, the 1894 Rectorial Address rejects that logic wholesale. The difference between the idiographic and the nomothetic, Windelband says, is not a matter of the objects of one's attention, but of the way one thinks about or treats them: "The same subjects can be the object of both a nomothetic and an idiographic investigation," so long as one moves from one perspective to another by shifting the frame or timescale of analysis (175). Although, for instance, "all of the single instances of the use of a language are governed by its formal laws . . . on the other hand, this same distinctive language as a whole, together with the totality of its special formal laws, is nothing more than a unique and transitory phenomenon in the life of human languages as such" (176).[23] If you're writing about the history *of* English, that is, you treat it as a unique particular within a general system of languages; if you're writing about sentences *in* English, then you treat those sentences as the particulars, and the language as the system. This is Ferdinand de Saussure's *langue/parole* distinction, so long as we remember that for Windelband (as for Saussure), it was not a matter of there being some sharp distinction between the instance and its generalization, but rather a question of the *application* of that distinction at a certain point within a broader system. The determination of the elements of that system as either idiographic objects or nomothetic ones happens, from this perspective, not in advance, but at the moment at which the distinction gets made—by some scholar who has a reason to make it.

This same observation extends in principle to all the natural sciences. If, after all, the relation between seeming idiography and apparent nomothetism is merely a matter of time span, then the process of evolution, though it takes place over a very long time and can be described on that scale by any number of rules or laws, nonetheless cannot be considered as eternal or universal in the strong sense. "There is neither evidence nor even a likelihood that this same organic process has been repeated on some other planet. In this case the science of organic nature is an idiographic or historical discipline" (176).

The same goes for physics or astronomy: we have no idea whether the laws that apply to our universe, which has after all a lengthy historical existence about which we know a great deal, would apply to other universes, too; even the "physiology of the body" can be treated idiographically if one considers that no two bodies are ever exactly alike (176). In this way, the entire dichotomy of nomothetic and idiographic with which Windelband opens—and for which the Rectorial Address is almost entirely remembered—trembles at its foundations. The difference between nomethetism and idiography lies neither in the ontological status of the examples chosen (laws of phenomena versus unique ontological facticity) nor in the absolute relation to a fixed temporality (eternal and invariable versus particular and historical), but in the *historical* (and thus *epistemological*) perspective that one adopts toward any given object. In this way, the logic (and philosophy) of scientific investigation moves from a set of decisions about the nature of the objects studied to a work of philosophical epistemology, framed entirely by the apparatus and needs of human culture.

I find this idea electrifying. Among other things, it threatens the dissolution (or resolution) of the science/culture dichotomy that organizes the modern university, and opens an entirely new field of intellectual responsibility. It reveals, at the same time, the degree to which our institutional reifications, and the financial and cultural politics that shape them, have kept us from seeing alternatives to the ways we think now. Windelband was neither the first nor the last scholar to push back against those reifications, nor was he the only one to have done so at a moment of particular stress for historical and cultural studies. But many twentieth-century visions of the total conciliation of the knowledge-field include a good dose of humanities-bashing (the *locus classicus* for most English-speaking academics is C. P. Snow's "Two Cultures" essay of 1959), or amount, at worst, to extensions of the legacy of nineteenth-century positivism that complain that humanists are conspiring to deny the realities of human nature.[24] What makes the *Methodenstreit*, and Windelband's address, so exciting is that, in coming from within the humanistic tradition—and therefore with a knowledge of, and respect for, the fields that variably make it up—they showcase a deep and sustained engagement with the basic philosophical questions governing (the possibilities of) humanist reason, and attempt, over and over again, to think about how such reason emerges from institutional and disciplinary practices, how it might be epistemologically justified, and how it might explain its value to a society dominated by science and technique.

At some level, the collapse of the nomothetic/idiogrpahic distinction, or its rewriting as a sliding scale, permits a fairly radical reimagination of the task of a "historian" or "biologist": we could imagine an idiographic biologist working on the unique history of a single cell, or a nomothetic historian analyzing theories and problems of the *longue durée*. And indeed this seems to be one end point of Windelband's address.

But in fact the address does not end here. And in what follows, weirdly and sadly, Windelband seems to step back from the radical undermining of his own opposition. Instead, he reifies it. As close as he comes in these moments, that is, to suggesting that the entire nature/culture dichotomy is a matter of attitude or degree (and therefore not a dichotomy at all), he continues for the rest of the Rectorial Address to treat it as a difference in kind—not simply as a convenient and modifiable reification of institutional practice, but as a distinction between two fundamentally irreconcilable ways of looking at and thinking about the world. Having shown, that is, that matters of evolution, astronomy, and physics can be treated idiographically (and that language and literature might be discussed nomothetically), he proceeds to describe a world in which natural scientists and historians never do the same things. The natural scientist turns out to be purely a nomothetist, treating an individual "datum as a type, a special case of a general concept which is developed on the basis of the datum," and focusing only on "the properties of the datum which provide insight into a general nomological regularity." The historian, on the other hand, aims idiographically to "breathe new life into some structure of the past in such a way that all of its concrete and distinctive features acquire an ideal actuality or contemporaneity. His task . . . is similar to the task of the artist," which explains, Windelband says, the intellectual and social kinship between the historical sciences and the *belles lettres* (178).

If the scientist and the historian in these descriptions seem to be back to their old jobs, let us agree at least that one of those jobs sounds a lot better than the other: the idiographer's involves life, actuality, and artistry, while the nomothetist's focuses, somewhat pedantically, on the developing general concepts out of data. History, Windelband tells us, "produces images of men and human life in the total wealth and profusion of their uniquely peculiar forms and with their full and vital individuality preserved intact"; it allows the languages and nations of the past "speak to us" through its voice, "resurrecting what is forgotten into a new form of life." Meanwhile, the natural scientist describes "a silent and colorless world of atoms in which the earthy aura of perceptual qualities has disappeared completely" (179).[25] This division of labor, which carries through the rest of the speech, amounts to nothing less than the division between life and death.

The difference between cold physics and warm history does not merely reflect a happenstance of scholarly production. Things could not have been the other way around: warm physics is an oxymoron. Because what is at stake, Windelband says, laying out a general philosophical justification for the work of historical research, is a question of the very value of human life.

And here we arrive—because in this discussion we have been following the text in order—at the Rectorial Address's emotional peak.[26] "Every ascription of human value is based upon the singular and the unique," Windelband says. Think about how "our emotions abate whenever their object is multiplied or becomes nothing more than one case among thousands of others of the same sort. 'She is not the first,' we read in one of the most terrifying texts of *Faust*. Our sense of values and all of our axiological sentiments are grounded in the uniqueness and incomparability of their object." And is it not, also, "an unbearable idea that yet another identical exemplar of a beloved or admired person exists? Is it not terrifying and inconceivable that we might have a second exemplar in reality with our own individual peculiarities?" (182). The *Doppelgänger*, after all, terrifies for just those reasons. And indeed life in general "is debased," he says, "when it has already transpired in exactly the same way numerous times in the past and will be repeated again in exactly the same way on numerous occasions in the future." The entire historical process has value only if it is unique—if the past, "in its unique and unrepeatable reality," is part of the common carriage of humankind (182). We cannot be doppelgangers all, ticking our way through the factories of time like the hapless workers of Fritz Lang's *Metropolis*. We cannot be, if we are alive, if life is something to be reckoned with, merely the twinned and tripled reincarnations of what has come before.[27]

The world happens once. Whether or not that fact is true, as Windelband seems to have believed, it is worth at least recognizing that the idea that the world happens only once does indeed create special philosophical problems for historiography. It suggests, first and foremost, that no general laws of historical development can be valid at all historical scales—if every moment in time is unique, it cannot in theory be the subject of the kind of repetitive testing that would be required by the rules of natural science; what's more, since the moment that would immediately follow any such moment would itself be unique, there would be no guarantee—no matter how much one knew about the first moment—that the second moment could be predicted from it. (In fact, one may think of strong prediction as a kind of ontological threat to uniqueness; if a series of subsequent moments can be fully derived from a previous moment, then the essence of those later moments, their historical being, can be said to be located in the earlier one rather than in themselves.) Similarly, even absolute knowledge of the actual events of the past could not guarantee—on the condition that everything happens only once, without strong ontological repetition—any capacity to fully understand their causes or to adumbrate the historical reasons for their having taken place (as might be possible, ha ha, for a collection of billiard balls on a table). In such a scheme, the laws described by natural science are not *real*. There is no law of gravity in the real world; there are only things falling, one at a time. This is why Georg Simmel had already, in 1892, described history as a "science of reality as such" (*Wirklichkeitswissenschaft schlechthin*): because "historical science has to describe what has really happened . . . it enters into the sharpest possible contrast to all science oriented towards laws (*Gesetzeswissenschaft*)."[28]

To what degree the orientation toward a unique—and hence temporally, if not axiologically or technologically progressive—history, common enough in the contemporary West, owes anything to the history of Christianity, is a topic for another book. But let us at least observe that plenty of folks theoretically included in Windelband's description of "our" affective horror of personal or historical doubling have believed in reincarnation or historical cycles, have undergone extensive therapy to discuss their own repetitive behaviors (think of all the Freudian cases that turn on the unconscious repetition of a forgotten, misremembered, or retrojected act), have treated their holiest book as the figural and typological repetition of the holy book written by another culture a millennium or more earlier, or have been fascinated enough by repetition's possibilities to produce and consume the voluminous literature, fictional (the Gothic novel, Asimov's *Foundation* trilogy) and nonfictional (dystopian theories of historical decline and violence like Oswald Spengler's or Samuel Huntington's), written on the subject. We don't have to seek out some obscure tribe to find the weirdos who believe that history sometimes repeats itself, even if the difference between repetitions is merely, as some like to think, a matter of tragedy or farce.[29]

Nonetheless, there are a few things to pay attention to here. The first is Windelband's emphasis on historical uniqueness. Notice how much that uniqueness matters to his theory of historical epistemology and, more broadly, to his argument for the very possibility of idiographic science. That an idiographic study can count as knowledge happens partly because that knowledge orients itself toward something fundamental in the being of the object that it addresses (namely, its status as a historical particular). The second is Windelband's courage in addressing the simplest possible question one could ask of this quasi-ontological claim: how do we know that history is unique? Or rather, in what sense does history contain only uniqueness? Windelband grounds his argument not in facts about history itself, but in examples of ordinary, everyday human behavior, in a description of the common revulsion or terror that "we" feel at the prospect of personal and historical doubling. The claim is that *for human beings*, the uniqueness of history—both as a experienced sequence of events and as a structure giving rise to "personalities" (i.e., historical individuals)—has an inherent value. This value does not rest *in* historical uniqueness itself; for all we know, what we call "history," seen from the point of view of a god or an alien, may not be unique at all (if the word meant anything to such creatures). It lies, rather, in a (species-level?) relation to the historical, in which "every dynamic and authentic human value judgment is dependent on," as Windelband says, "the uniqueness of its object" (182).

This is what permits us to make a distinction between the two modes of repetition that characterize the nomothetic and idiographic approaches. The nomothetist's focus on the universal law comes as a result of the fact that their experiments are repeatable, whereas the uniqueness of the idiographer's "structure of the past" means that it cannot be repeated as such, but only reanimated. The temporal structure in each case is folded over or doubled: the idiographer deals with a unique event, yes, but makes it breathe new life: this reanimation is *not* a repetition. Whatever idiography is, it involves this double movement between the past and "an ideal actuality or contemporaneity"; the final object of its attention is the production of this doubledness on the basis of a historical event whose uniqueness paradoxically legitimates it—not to mention the "dazzling leap across scales of description, connecting an instant of personal experience to collective historical time," which Ted Underwood has called "one of the distinctive achievements of modern criticism."[30] As for the nomothetist, their work is to ground analysis in the repeatable components of events—to focus on what events have in common. The repeatability of these experiments is not, as a matter of practice, a pure repeatability, but an attempt to control local contexts such that the repeatable elements of a situation come to the fore. As with the idiographer's uniqueness, this repeatability is not inherent in the object—it is not a property of the world beyond human culture. It is made; it is a matter of claiming that the manipulation of the experimental situation produces a true-enough repetition, a sequence of actions that may as well occur *at the same time* (i.e., the time of the universal and the eternal, insofar as it is possible for humans to know it).

Let's review the chain of claims here. It's critical to recognize that Windelband's argument so far is at heart anthropological (this is why he's a neo-Kantian): it bases its philosophical claims on a description of actual, ordinary human practices, behaviors, and feelings. The argumentative chain goes like this:

1. Humans value things; this value emerges only from social, anthropological action and is a matter of both individual freedom and social consensus.

2. Humans value things—this is an anthropological claim—in their uniqueness. The economy of value, like all economies, emerges in a situation of scarcity. Uniqueness is, therefore, a fundamental aspect of the human experience of history, personality, and culture.

3. To discuss events or personalities without treating them as unique would be to treat them not as *human* events or *human* personalities, but as events or personalities determined from outside the anthropological sphere of culture, from the point of view of an alien, or a god, or a thing.

4. To consider objects in this way is impossible since all scientific human activity (and indeed all activity) is embedded within the anthropological sphere.

5. A science that considers human life must be idiographically oriented; this reflects its orientation toward the human production of (and need for) value, and therefore recognizes that value as fundamentally embedded in, and of, the objects of culture, of them such that to dismiss or forget it would be to cease considering the object in its human reality.

Before going on, let us register here a resistance to all these quasi-universalizing claims, even if they restrict themselves to the realm of humans in general. Statements about how "we" all feel a certain way, references to "authentic human value": these things raise hackles, and legitimately so. It is probably not the case that some nineteenth-century German guy spoke for the entire historical population of the planet.

Nonetheless, Windelband has a point. A certain revulsion against repetition remains, at least in the twentieth- and twenty-first-century world that I know, a pretty standard operating procedure for ordinary life.

Imagine this situation: You go to your therapist to complain about problems in your relationship. You and your partner aren't getting along; you're tense all the time; you don't have sex as much as you used to; when you try to talk about it, you just end up repeating the same old arguments, and things get better for a day or two but then go back to the way they were. Oh, don't worry, your therapist tells you: you're just having the seven-year itch. No, no, you say—I've heard of that, but our problems are specific to *us;* you know, Chris changed jobs a few months ago, and I've made some new friends, and then, sometimes I just feel like I've outgrown the relationship, and I try to talk about it but it's really hard to be honest. Yep, your therapist says. Sounds like the seven-year itch to me! Your happiness doesn't have anything to do with all that stuff; it's just the product of a natural cycle. That's the way things are, it's not your fault, and there's nothing you could really have done to avoid it.

Now, it seems to me that you would have a legitimate case to feel aggrieved about this conversation. The therapist doesn't seem to be taking your problems seriously; they have offered no real solutions; they have not empowered you to imagine how you could change what is going on. You seem to be getting treated as an instance of a more general principle, not really as an individual; the things that make your problem *yours*, that make it unique (both historically and affectively), seem to be getting subsumed under some theory that treats those features as mere epiphenomena of some larger, predictable process. I don't like to be treated this way, and most people I have known don't like it either.

Why? What protocol is being violated here? What is missing in this conversation, which after all does a pretty good job of proposing a causal mechanism that would explain your unhappiness? Why does it feel like the therapist has failed in some basic responsibility of interpersonal attention? Mainly because, I think, the therapist has not treated you as a historical individual; they have discussed the particularities of your situation, and your experience of that situation, as though they were epiphenomena of a larger, repeatable process. Rather than feeling supported and empowered, you feel ignored. "Our sense of values and all of our axiological sentiments are grounded in the uniqueness and incomparability of their object," Windelband told his audience in 1894. Perhaps especially so when that object is ourselves. No one likes to think of themselves as yet another example of a process (or, for that matter, as a generic member of a social group). No matter that sometimes, of course, we are the products of processes and social groups. Most people don't like to be *treated* that way because it makes us feel unvalued, unrecognized. It makes us feel unattended to, in our being.[31]

This feeling results, in Windelbandian terms, from a certain philosophical insight. Even if a general law applies in a given case, as Windelband noted, it doesn't apply causally in an idiographic sense. Consider an explosion. From the nomothetic point of view, the cause of the explosion "lies in the nature of the explosive material itself, expressed as physical and chemical laws." But in another, idiographic sense, the explosion's cause lies in a "single event or motion, a spark, shock, or something similar." The two causes are not derivable from one another: the general law does not cause the person to light the match, and the person lighting the match does not cause the general law. Only "both together . . . explain the event," and no explanation focused solely on the generality will address the historical particularity of the instance it addresses.[32] Nomothetic explanations of causes are therefore forever incomplete.

This insight leads Windelband to a definitive, quasi-metaphysical conclusion: "in all the data of historical and individual experience a residuum of incomprehensible brute fact remains, an inexpressible and indefinable phenomenon" (184). The sequence of negations tells the story: what remains when the nomothetist leaves the room is *incomprehensible (unbegreiflich), inexpressible (unaussagbar), indefin-able (undefinirbar).*[33] Idiographic space is, in this conceptualization, a kind of negative of the law, a place for and host of the residual, the leftover, whatever material lies outside what Windleband calls the "cosmic formula." What passes for ordinary historical reality from the human perspective is, in this conceptualization, always a kind of Bartelbyian refusal, a holding back or withholding of the event from the law, an unbreachable integrity that cannot be explained, only understood.

The event and the law thus define the limits of philosophy in the modern era. We know from the history of failed attempts to derive "the particular from the general, the 'many' from the 'one,' the 'finite' from the 'infinite,' and 'existence' from 'essence'," Windelband says, that these two juggernauts—the unique and individual historical particular and the reproducible, eternal, colorless rule—constitute the ne plus ultra of human thought. We cannot think beyond them. The law and the event remain as the ultimate, incommensurable entities of our world view, he writes. "This is one of the boundary conditions where scientific inquiry can only define problems and only pose questions in the clear awareness that it will never be able to solve them" (185).

On this epistemologically tragic note, applause. Windelband closes his address: we have reached the end of the road and must stand, mutely, before the gray wall of silence imposed by the real. As it may or may not exist outside the human capacity to know it.

Rest.

. . .

. . .

* * *

But. Is the awareness that we can never solve certain problems really *that* tragic? Or rather, isn't the tragedy partly (or even mostly) rhetorical? Because what has been rescued, in this anthropological ontology of history, is the quasi-metaphysical realm of the humanis-tic sciences, constituted as and through a brute, impenetrable kernel of reality, one as inaccessible to the general law as the divine is to the profane. The epistemological impenetrability of that kernel is not just a matter of philosophical interest; it preserves, rather, the entire undebased, authentic realm of human life. In defending the particular from the general, it guarantees nothing less, Windelband says, than the possibility of human liberty: "The ultimate and most profound nature of personality resists analysis in terms of general categories." This resistance "appears to our consciousness as the sense (*Gefühl*) of the indeterminacy of our nature—in other words, of individual freedom" (184, translation modified).

Freedom! That it is at stake in these methodological debates at all has been long known and understood by anyone familiar with the history of positivism, with utopian or dystopian fiction, or with the fever dreams of their local Chicago-school economist. The humanist resistance to general law can be described—generally, I admit—as a resistance to logical, historical, or causal subordination or subsumption: a rejection of the idea that the law that umbrellas the particular not only shelters it within the framework of a pattern or a tendency but determines it in advance, explains it away as something other than itself, and locates its essence in something other than a historical moment, a momentaneity construed again and again as the site of the law's most intense application, and of its deepest rejection. For the time of the law cannot be the time of the moment, as the law, in gathering moments together, strips from their historical eventfulness the very timeliness that makes them historical as such.[34] We must resist the work of those, Eduard Meyer wrote in 1902, who pretend "to discover the eternal laws of all historical, human life, and who use individual events to illustrate the force of those laws, by subsuming the former under the latter."[35] The illustration of laws by events, the interest in developing complete or total forms of understanding that "subsume" life under the law: this is what all the antagonists of the neo-Kantians, from Hegel and the philosophical idealists to the scientific positivists and social Darwinians to the theorists of economic and historical laws of development, had in common. Meyer says that such historical lawmakers attempt to erase, or at least move into the background, "all the purely individual moments that we have heretofore treated as decisive factors in the march of history"—namely, the operations of chance, the workings of free will, and individual or collective "ideas" and representations. In such a history, all individuals are treated as "types," he writes, and the "endless manifold of real life" disappears.[36] Within this context, Windelband's "idiographic method, this practice of intelligence in comprehending full and factual particularity, is nothing other than the exercise of autonomy," an autonomy whose epistemological and methodological freedom mirrors precisely the autonomous dimensions of its particularized, unique objects.[37] It was in this way that Windelband and his colleagues sought to preserve, under the guise of history and the cultural sciences, "the possibility of a genuinely human, that is, rational and ethical, life."[38]

It would be a mistake, I think, to see this concern with freedom as the "real" cause or source of the *Methodenstreit*. The demands produced on the philosophy of epistemology by the rise of the new observational sciences, the development of statistics, and the elaboration of ideal historical or economic laws were compelling and profound. They created all sorts of institutional pressures to which the intellectual activity of the Heidelberg neo-Kantians responded. If the study of history, literature, and art were to continue as it had before, and to take place within the university, it would have minimally to explain what it thought it was doing, and answer to the double demand for knowledge that was both socially useful (meaning that it could be held in common) and intellectually legitimate (meaning that it resulted from a set of shared, explainable procedures). Nonetheless, it is impossible to avoid noticing, either in the late nineteenth century or indeed in the entire history of humanistic methodological claims since that time, the consistently simultaneous appearance of ethics and epistemology, or the intensity of the little knot that binds the problem of particularity and generality to the problem of necessity and freedom. Which at least allows one to ask whether in fact the institutional defense of the historical sciences could have taken place (or could take place one day) without the ethical imperatives—the respect for singularity and uniqueness—that has historically come along with.

That the basic problems the ethico-epistemological crisis of the *Methodenstreit* belonged then, as they do today, to the philosophy of knowledge, that they belonged yesterday to theology or to the realm of folktales, makes no substantive difference to the argument here.

Does history happen once, or many times? Do we make our own decisions, or does someone or something else decide them? The problems are fundamental and bigger than theology or philosophy, bigger than the modern era, bigger than the classical one; they are as big, and as long-standing, as the history of human self-consciousness. That they were caught up in questions about the value of the humanities, about the epistemological and social legitimacy of the study of events-as-particulars, that they are still caught there, should come, therefore, as no real historical surprise. Like a lot of big problems, they appear and are refracted in any number of the realms of social life.

That said, it is nonetheless interesting, and important, that these problems become imbricated in the defense of the humanities in a particular historical moment, and that that moment coincides with the emergence of the modern, tripartite division of knowledge—the humanities, social sciences, and sciences—that now characterizes the entire world university system, as well as the apparatus (journals, conferences, etc.) that surrounds it.[39] And it is interesting, and important, that these problems become imbricated in the defense of the humanities at a moment at which the humanities, which until something like 1700 might well have laid claim, under the headings of philosophy and natural philosophy, to the entire field of knowledge-production in the European West, come under intense epistemological scrutiny as a result of the challenges to their intellectual and social legitimacy from those other fields. The modern defenses of humanist reason, and indeed our contemporary understanding of, and ethico-epistemological justification of, the intellectual work humanists do were all formed in this nineteenth-century crucible.

Drawing once again on Windelband's work, which brings to these issues an admirable and sometimes quite beautiful level of self-conscious intensity, let me outline some of the basic features of that justification:

1. It relies heavily on a strong distinction between the particular and the general, which it then maps onto the relation between freedom and necessity; thus epistemological issues are always to some extent ethical ones.

2. It is anthropologically substantive: it justifies the kinds of attention it pays to its object of interest on the basis of features of that object as it operates in the sphere of human knowledge and life. It is *because* the historical or cultural object is unique (as far as humans are concerned) that it must be treated with methods that are unique to it, that it cannot be simply treated as an instance of a pattern or an example of a system.[40]

3. This second justification implies, at its core, that all unique objects deserve to be interrogated or researched by methods that require some knowledge of that object—that the object can only be approached respectfully, seriously, if one already treats it in ways that are generated from within by the object itself. That is why humanistic work has less to do with *explanation* (which comes from without) and more to do with *understanding* the object of research (this is where Dilthey's emphasis on *Verstand* comes together with Windelband's on idiographism; we see that the two descriptions of method are in some sense merely mirror images of one another.)

4. This set of principles produces a second set of ethical imperatives, heavily coded in a language of resistance to the possibility of total knowing (think of Windelband's residuum), as well as a lexicon of dynamism, authenticity, and vitality, all opposed to coldness, technicity, and death. Together, these languages imagine the object of humanist reason as in and of itself inherently opposed to scientific totality and control. The humanities in such a model address, and preserve (or testify to the inherently self-preserving, self-withholding qualities of) nothing less than the essence of living life.

5. All of this is accompanied in turn by a series of dominant metaphors, all of which are strongly antivertical, emphasizing horizontality, connectedness, embeddedness, groundedness, situatedness, and so on, against the general, the systematic, the legal, the overarching, the structural, against anything that would *subordinate* or *subsume* the particular to some broader or more general understanding.

These claims have a strong moral and rhetorical appeal. But to understand humanist reason in this era, you must see that this ethical appeal is the other side, not only of the coin of humanist epistemology, but of aesthetic practice as well. On the first count, remember

Ranke: "From the particular you may ascend to the general; but from general theory there is no way back to the intuitive understanding of the particular." And on the second, in slightly more Romantic terms, remarks Goethe once made about allegory: "There is a great difference, whether the poet seeks the particular for the general or sees the general in the particular. From the first procedure arises allegory, where the particular serves *only* as an example of the general; the second procedure, however, is *really* the nature of poetry; it expresses something particular, without thinking of the general or pointing to it."[41]Real poetry, like real history, only moves from the particular to the general, the small to the large; the rest is parable, allegory, in short, and from the limited but obviously fairly influential perspective of a certain modernity in literature, bullshit.

In Goethe's lines, the affinity Windelband imagined between "historical accomplishment and aesthetic creativity" appears in full flower (178). And in that affinity, we understand, also, the rarely discussed choices for the second halves of Windelband's neologisms, the nomothetic and the idiographic. For while the nomothetist makes laws (*nomos*) and puts or places them, arranges them (*tithein*), the idiographer treats particulars by drawing them, or writing them down (*graphein*).[42] In this way, the idiographer's treatment of the particular finds itself bound to the particularity of its own markings or words. In bringing the past to new life, the idiographer animates in the present not only some ideal actuality of the past, but also the contemporaneity of its own appearance—an appearance, particular in all respects, that might one day become, as Windelband's work has here, fodder for some future idiographer, member of an endless chain of particulars and love, all of it tied eternally and in all its idiosyncratic and unrecoverable resistance to the specificities of its forms of expression.[43]

We may thus imagine that the difference between the sciences and the humanities, from the perspective of the description of humanistic reason, has something to do the former's distanced relationship from its object of research: the law of gravity is not itself a falling object.

And so a final feature of the general justification of humanist reason:

6. Humanistic knowledge, in this conception, is the kind of knowledge that shares properties with its object. This is true not only because both knowledge and object are bound together as historical particulars, but also because the very ethos of humanistic knowledge declares that to understand the object properly requires borrowing from it the fundamental structures by which it will be evaluated, and therefore valued. In a world increasingly persuaded that objective observation—sustained, of course, by the textual and institutional apparatus of science itself—defined the parameters of knowledge as such, you can see why an entire field devoted to the intimate work of idiography would have some explaining to do, if it were to count as knowledge at all. Much of the history of modern literary criticism, including, for instance, the development of the New Criticism, has been rightly understood as an attempt to manage that situation by turning the study of literature into something more like a natural science. In this way, we have remained fully absorbed within the problems of humanistic reason registered in the *Methodenstreit*; in this way, we remain, both consciously and unconsciously, in a whole series of complex and interconnected ways, framed, bordered round, by the double limit of the law and the event, even if it is possible now to understand, better (I hope) than Windelband did, that the frame itself may well be the projected generality of an immediate particular: a symptom, masquerading as a cause, of an imprisonment that gives humanist ethos and scientific desire their deepest meaning, precisely insofar as it creates the conditions for their restricted, self-enclosed existence, thereby fulfilling what Ben Etherington has called, in another context, the "world-historical wish for the reunification of immediacy and reflection."[44]

2. AGAINST WINDELBAND, EVEN SO

The description and theory of humanist reason that I am putting forward in this book suggests the impossibility of reaching the stoppage of history implied by the perfect stability of totalizing practice of a universal law, or the infinite freedom of infinite particularity that characterizes the Windelbandian event. Neither of these, taken as a

whole, seems compatible with human social life. They make, therefore, poor guides to political or epistemological practice at most
scales. No one wants to live in a society without general structures
and patterns, habits and conventions; and no one wants to live in
a society organized by an unchanging law even if, in a wide variety
of smaller matters of daily life, or indeed in the resistance to either
seemingly endless particularization (as of capital) or seemingly infinite stability (as of the state apparatus), one might want to deploy,
pragmatically, a strategy attuned to the opposite pole of the spectrum
that ordinarily cleaves law and event, general and particular, abstract
and concrete.

Strictly speaking, however, the dichotomy cannot hold. The law,
the generalization, the abstraction: none of these can exist without
their concretized, particularized counterpart, just as the moral, physical, or actual law cannot exist without their examples, their cases,
or indeed their practice. J. Hillis Miller demonstrates as much in a
reading of Immanuel Kant's *Groundwork of the Metaphysics of Morals*, showing that the status of the moral example in the face of the
infinite and nonutilitarian general law comes down to a matter of
linguistic play in the text.[45] This catachrestic transformation, this
shift in levels of explanation, remains true for all generalizations, all
examples: the movement from particular to general happens on the
basis of a principle that *cannot be included*, strictly speaking, in its
own system (for the principle of inclusion would have to involve some
claim about the nature of inclusiveness, which would have in turn to
address in advance the nature of the included object or the including
sphere)—even if the histories of both moral philosophy and statistical analysis are full of attempts to do so.[46]

Short of a universal accounting of all the instances of your general proposition—which would, of course, take too much time and
miss the point of making generalizations in the first place—there is
no real solution to this problem except, at least as a matter of practice, to make sure that you adjust your general claims properly to the
range of your examples. What it suggests, however, is the degree to
which all theories or conceptualizations remain bound to the history of the examples used to reify them. The example perpetually
haunts the idea; the datum cannot disappear as it is made in part

by the theory that seeks it out; the fact that grounds the principle is, and must be seen on the basis of, a set of principles before it can do any grounding.[47] What we call a "particular" is the social product of a great deal of abstract, generalizing work, and vice versa. The relation between event and law is not—I am arguing against Windelband here, attemping to push his anthropology a few inches farther—a matter of a total irreconcilability, but rather of the operation of the intimate parameters of a socially produced and socially modifiable thought-system.

The study of a given culture's modes of particularization and generalization, concretion and abstraction would, therefore, also amount to a history of its epistemological practice. Anyone wanting to study the epistemological parameters of the present moment might begin, for instance, with a schema that included all the various names and practices that aim to manage the relation between concretion and abstraction, including binaries like example/concept, particular/general, part/whole, singular/universal, concrete/abstract, instance/theory, iteration/process and so on, as well as a variety of ancillary concepts like quality, quantity, sample, event, synecdoche, structure, schema, system, network, totality, or world, all of which create the general epistemological atmosphere in which we use the word "particular" to do a specific kind of work. And all of which have equivalents, or near-equivalents, in other languages. (Could there be a language with no such equivalents? Or a society with no such conceptualizations? Probably not, unless such a society or language operated without what we think of as words, and only used names.)

What language can describe this set of relations as a whole? None of the pairs can itself serve as a master term, since to make "concrete/abstract" (for instance) the most general of the terms governing the field of generality and particularity would be to assume in advance the very theory of generality being described. But in that case, how can one know, when one talks of pairs like particular/general, member/set, part/whole, example/theory, object/method, concrete/abstract, quality/quantity, and freedom/necessity, that one still is talking about the "same" thing? An analysis deriving from the insistence on the pure ontological particularity of the individual concept puts paid to the entire project. It would say, first, that each conceptual pair ought to be treated as a particular of its own, expressing some unique shade of meaning different from that of any other pair; and, second, at the limit, that one cannot assume identity across any two uses of the terms. Not only should we not say that something like particular/general is the same as example/theory, but we also should not say that any single example of example/theory is the same as any other example of it; to make something into an example of something is, from a certain perspective, already to do violence to its ontological singularity, its appearance inside a history that happens only once.

You will recognize this critique as a strong version of idiographism. We can acknowledge the critique and still continue thinking, so long as we accept its insight and its force. We can agree that everything in the world, including conceptual or imaginary things, has a historical or actualized particularity that cannot map exactly onto anything else (in other words, there is no two of anything; resemblance never achieves identity). But we can also see—and this is especially true for concepts, though it may well be true of anything—that no object withholds itself fully from other things. Things interact. And what they interact with is other things in a social lifeworld, which frames and grounds their field of potential activity. For something to be apprehensible by a human being "as" anything at all, to have any kind of social effect, it must be "in" the social. This means that it is not withholding itself fully from comparison, relation, or activity. If it did, you simply could not interact with it; you would not be able to see it or notice it at all. (Art is fascinated with the asymptote of this possibility; but even Bartleby's preference not to appears *in the social* as an understandable sentence in English, and indicates, by its appearance, both the impossible limit beyond the asymptote and one actually expressible limit to it.)

It is the force of such interactions that allows us to speak of connection, homology, and resemblance. What this means is not that anything goes—that everything comes down, or rather up, to the general law—but that in the case of categories like particular/general, example/theory, and so on, we cannot establish a prophylactic against cross-contamination. How could you ever know that your sense of what an "example" was did not depend in some way on your sense of what "particularity" is? How would you, or could you, disaggregate the two? Surely anyone can try. But anyone could come in afterward and take apart whatever difference gets imagined in the process. There is no "true" meaning of particularity that we could distinguish once and for all from exemplarity; there is no specific, unique and calculable difference between the general and the universal (or wholeness, or the worldly) that belongs to those categories outside of any interaction that they have with one other. This kind of overlap affects many kinds of words, but it especially affects words that describe concepts, and that themselves amount to figures of speech. They describe the very intellectual processes that one would have to use to make distinctions among them—giving examples of examples, say, or arguing that abstraction is more general than generality. "The example," J. Hillis Miller once wrote, "is said to be like that of which it is an example."[48]

Pause for a moment to marvel at the work that "like" is doing in that sentence, and realize this: the best we can do is establish rough guides to existing practice. Because concepts develop together, interpenetrate, and modify one another, they change historically and conceptually in response to one another. To fetishize their "proper" or "precise" use, to insist on absolute distinctions, is to carry the deconstructive critique of similarity only to the point of a pure (Leibnizian) monadism, and not beyond it, to the concept of the monad, of self-similarity, itself. In this way, we escape the critique of pure idiographism, but not by a retreat to a general rule; rather, we see how the social life of concepts creates the possibility of generality without needing to abstract anything nomothetically at all.

My interest in testing concepts against their social use draws on the post-Kantian insights of the American sociologist Harold Garfinkel and the German philosopher Peter Janich. I begin with two basic ideas: first, that there is no ontology except in social practice, and therefore all objects or concepts are socially produced and maintained reifications (Garfinkel); and second, that all social practices function to meet explicit human needs, making these latter, therefore, their ground or cause (Janich).[49] What is primary, then, in the example-concept relation, is first, the need that humans have to concretize and abstract in order to manage and/or talk about the world; and second, the set of social practices that reify those needs into concepts like "example" or "concept," which emerge into being only as the result of the social practices that generate them.

Seeing things this way has the effect of getting away from ontological questions, or of moving ontological questions into the social and anthropological realm. From that perspective, we might say that the primary act governing the particular-general relation is the actual declaration "X is a particular of Y," or, to be a bit more sophisticated, the complex, socially agreed-upon process and history of practice that governs the legitimacy of the claim "X is a particular of Y" at any given social moment. This process is entwined with other processes and other reifications, including the reifications of concepts like "abstraction" or "concretion," as well as of the habits of argument, discourse, and mind that govern their use in the social. What this all suggests, finally, is that there is no such thing as an example as such. The act of particularization-generalization not only defines something as a particular for local purposes, and in so doing solidifies or destabilizes, as the case may be, the wide variety of conceptual reifications (example, instance, iteration, sample, but also theory, pattern, concept) that govern it and are governed by it.

Some sense of the extent of the labor required in the social to maintain these practices emerges if you consider how much time we all spend discussing things like whether a single act defines the kind of person someone is, whether historical records can predict future results, or whether one has fairly characterized some group, some cuisine, some region, on the basis of a limited number of experiences. All of these amount to practices governing the actually existing social ontology of particularization, and all of them are subject, as a matter of course, to the problems of historical relativism, and therefore of generalization or universalism itself—meaning that the analysis of particulars cannot happen without involving the metadiscourse that would theoretically identify or name those particulars as particulars in the first place.

This description of the complexity of living social practice comes up, inevitably, against the realities of common structures of social perception. Take, as one instance of this problem, the social status of examples. A theoretically sophisticated description of how examples work immediately encounters the fact that one way that examples work is through the production of a metadiscourse that reifies all that theoretical complexity into a set of binary oppositions: example versus theory, concretion versus abstraction, life versus thought, and so on. That we have such a simplifying metadiscourse at all suggests that it meets, in its very simplicity, a particular human need—the need to be able to organize things so that we don't have to expend neurological or social resources paying attention to them. Given that humans have probably never lived without basic practices of generalization and abstraction (every word is a generalization), it makes no sense to lament the existence of simplified metadiscourses, about examples or about anything else; as Krishnan Kumar and Herbert Tucker have argued, a ban on generalization, "so basic to human intellection," would only serve to drive the practice "underground."[50]

Indeed, we may well recognize that simplification as a form of theorization/abstraction, a generalization of what happens usually enough in the way examples and abstractions are used, such that it makes sense to adopt it as a kind of rough guide to practice. This suggests that writing the history of exemplification—or the (more general?) history of epistemological practices that would include it—would have to take account not only of the actual complex use of examples, but also of the metadiscourse that describes and generalizes those uses, which itself, inevitably, can become the subject of a further discourse, a meta-metadiscourse, that argues about how we should think about abstraction, concretion, particularity, generality, and the like, all of which might in the long run get reified into a series of institutional structures or even personal beliefs, and each of which might have either a strong or a weak relation to the actual practice that it purports to narrate and describe, all of which might be theorized on the basis of the evidence they provide us.

But even writing that what results from "evidence" is a "theorization" is disciplinarily tendentious. The very name of the thing that results from looking at evidence—theory, understanding, system, law—forms part of the evidentiary relation that Windelband described as central to idiographic or nomothetic thought, as does the very word "evidence," for which one might wish to substitute words like "example," "case," "facts," "data," "text," "archive," or "experiment," depending on disciplinary training. Indeed, an entire set of logical and rhetorical protocols govern the patterns of disciplinary legitimacy, the movement between what one might think of as the first stage in the production of knowledge, where its raw material is gathered, the second, where it is manipulated in some way, and the third, where it becomes the stuff of some larger set of claims.[51] Steven Connor has argued, in an essay that deserves to be read and reread, that all this disciplinary work can fall under the name of "exemplification," using that term as a general figure for the process of moving from the first stage to the third. Connor defines the characteristics of the evidentiary protocols that characterize disciplinary integrity, refining the Windelbandian grain by describing subconcepts that govern epistemological methods in practice. He defines these practices along four lines, including (1) exemplificatory ratio, "how many examples are needed to make any particular argument plausible"; and (2) exemplificatory substitutability, "the degree to which examples may tend or be held or be required to be interchangeable with one another, and therefore to enforce conviction through their accumulation."[52]

Ratio and substitutability are, in this conceptualization, linked: if you have 5,000 examples of something, you can lose a few or replace a few while doing very little harm to the entire collection (in other words, you have high substitutability), while if you have only one or two, adding a third or taking one away makes a real difference to the whole. Likewise, with fewer examples, examples will tend to be seen as more intimately linked to their argument (low [3] "separability," as Connor would say), and will therefore be thought of as more significant within it (higher [4] "priority"); and vice versa for large numbers of examples. In other words, the complex parameters of exemplification among the disciplines, and the degree to which they sustain such concepts as evidence, data, theory, proof, argument, and so on, come down in many cases to matters of scale, following naturally from the number of examples in play. Intense, intimate investigation of a small number of examples versus extensive, superficial analysis of a larger number of examples: that's one version of how we get the disciplines.

But here, it is worth making two fairly simple, even stupid, observations. The first observation: even our scales have a scale. No single person does an idiographic analysis of 10,000 novels. Why not? The reason is hardly epistemological. No single person does it because it would be institutionally inefficient, because it would take up too much human time; no one could live long enough to complete the task. If you want to look at 10,000 novels, you can't, as Franco Moretti once observed, really *look at them*.[53] You have to look at something about them, and that something has to be abstractable and manipulable at a scale that allows you to produce some kind of research output within a specific time frame. (The same is true of cancer cells!) The socially experienced and institutionally reified difference between idiographism and nomothetism is, by this account, not only scalar in general but scalar in particular, and the particular scale at which it operates lies at the intersection of institutional and biological time. It is a function of the demands of tenure, yes, but those demands are also partially a function of the life cycle of the species.[54] The work that we do, and how we understand it, depend on the relation between our manipulation of analytic scale on one hand, and our institutional and biological scales on the other.

Observation number two: no one knows where quality ends and quantity begins. We all agree that 10,000 examples of something are not the same as ten. But at what point does quantity acquire, as Stalin was allegedly fond of saying, a quality of its own? At what point, that is, does the sheer aggregation of examples tip us into quantitative analysis? At what point does the difference in degree become a difference in kind? All this presents us with versions of the old sorites paradox—how many grains of sand make a heap?—in which the social and neurological vagueness of qualities is projected onto quantities that cannot manage that same vagueness, and can be resolved only by a retreat to descriptions of human practice.[55] But thinking about these terms does make clear that what we call "quantitative analysis" does not rely, or rely exactly, on quantities. Someone doing a close reading of 10,000 novels (if they lived that long) would not be doing quantitative analysis. In contemporary research, the quantitative has more to do with the ways in which certain structures of abstraction orient themselves toward the object, largely by virtue of altering what Connor would call the ratio and the priority of its exemplarity. Which means, in other words, that the social function of the words "quality" and "quantity"—themselves figures in the great chain of being that includes particular/general, example/concept, and so on—does not actually depend on a strict understanding of the meaning of those terms. The quality/quantity distinction is not a cause of the difference between the sciences and the humanities, but rather an effect of it, and as subject as any other institutional formation to the possibility of transformation and change.

Two conclusions follow: (1) Windelband's intuition that all research is, from a certain perspective, idiographic, is true—even if he himself never follows through on its implications. There is, in the study of this universe, no such thing as nomothetism. Everything is historical. There is only idiographism—only qualitative work, at different time spans, and on different scales.[56] (2) The felt difference between nomothetism and idiographism, the sciences and the humanities, therefore, has to do not with an orientation toward the particular or the general as such, but rather with the *relationship between particularity and generality*—with analytic scale—as it is established in each discipline's rhetoric and practice of knowledge-formation—with, that is, a complex of attitudes and signaling mechanisms that describe a particular relation established between the particular and the general, not the precise number of particularities or generalities involved.[57]

Almost no one thinks this way. To do so would, among other things, require abandoning any sense of the absolute *methodological* distinction between the sciences and the humanities, an abandonment that would require, among other things, letting go of the strong ethical claims for the humanistic approach as such. But it would be a mistake to describe the resistance to such an abandonment as merely a matter of institutional self-preservation. Humanist scholars value their self-conceptualization as defenders of the living, free, and idiographic against the morbid nomothetic on grounds other than institutional stability. They think, like Windelband, that their method describes something true about the world. For them, for us, this way of thinking makes both social and intellectual sense—it helps build a world picture, and insofar as lots of people agree about this picture, it makes it easier to get things done, to get along. But also: humanists are *moved* by this belief. The Windelbandian characterization of the work of the humanities not only describes but also affirms how humanists like you and me see the world; it lays out, beyond its truth claims, an entire political and moral program for human life—a program that describes a vocation, a calling, a task whose socially sacred or deeply political necessity is a matter not just of thinking, of scientific knowledge, but of feeling, of—let's just say it—a political commitment to the protection of certain forms of being from the rapacity of the state, or of capitalism. The metadiscourse of humanist reason expresses an ethos, and that ethos has been the source of a great deal of the humanities' moral, pedagogical, political, and epistemological energy. This is so even if (or perhaps because) that metadiscourse does not adequately or accurately describe the kind of reasoning that humanists do.

3. THE HUMANIST ETHOS TODAY

Windelband's Rectorial Address thus contains *in nuce* much of the history of description and justification of humanist reason that follows it through into our present day. There is, as Windelband correctly perceived, no humanities without the intense focus on particularities, no humanities without the ethical-cum-epistemological emphasis on the method-object relation, no humanities without a strong resistance to universalizing, totalizing, generalization, or simplification . . . and no humanities, therefore, that is not prone to a great deal of anxiety about the status of its own knowledge-production, nor to making heavily moralized claims about the nature of its epistemological relation to its objects, and about its general "value" to civil or democratic society.[58] No humanities, also, without the inheritance of the basic idea that such a view must be "defended," no humanities without the "aura of conservatism and defensiveness . . . inherited" from the reaction to the "imperial claims of scientific positivism" that led to their modern birth.[59] And also, because knowledge operates as a system of modes and institutions, no sciences or social sciences as they are today without this particular version of the humanities, because all three regions of our intellectual-epistemological-institutional lives have formed themselves within the same ecosystem.

As a result, a description of the work of humanist reason will count as evidence toward a more general theory of the entire apparatus of modern knowledge-production (social and institutional), so long as we recognize that the specifically scholarly habitus of that apparatus, though it matters quite a lot (especially to scholars), does not constitute the entire system in which categories like particularity and generality, or evidence and theory, are produced.

Humanists are of course not alone in making value claims about their work; scientists and social scientists routinely advocate for the value of their epistemological approaches and their research results. The question before us as we begin to move to the next chapter is not, therefore, Why do humanists make epistemological value-claims?, because everyone does, but rather, How do the specific forms of such claims emerge, what do they say or mean, and how do they relate to the historical work of humanist scholarship?

We can begin—we have begun—by tracing one especially influential articulation of those claims in Windelband's 1894 address. But it would be a mistake to call these ideas "his," because (1), he did not invent them, and (2) they have at this point spread so widely across the humanities as to acquire that particular anonymous and universal status that belongs to the realm of ideology. The orientation of the humanities toward certain forms of value is not only a matter of practice, or even of rhetorical force and power; rather, it is a matter of affiliation and identification, of self-production and of other-oriented actions, including the actions of teaching and writing. It produces both a *raison d'être* and a *raison d'agir*, a politics or a stance that maps onto a whole host of other social attitudes that define a way of being and acting in the world, of relating to quantity and quality, to economic and preeconomic or paraeconomic life, to historical modernity and primitivity, to power and oppression, to social freedom and social control, and so on.

All of these appear already in the Rectorial Address and across the *Methodenstreit*; all of these carry on through the entire metadiscourse of the humanities from 1894 forward. You see it in the emphasis on close reading in the New Criticism, or in psychoanalysis or deconstructive criticism, in the New Historicism's love for the "incommensurable specificity of the anecdote,"[60] in the historical or sociological case study, in biography, in the "microhistory" of Carlo Ginzburg or Jacques Revel, and especially in the inheritances of French postructuralist theory, with its emphasis on the uncategorizable, the unsystematizable, that which violates without cease the integrity of any captivation: the Kristeva of *Revolution of Poetic Language*, Lyotard's rejection of metanarrative, the constant emphasis on play, paradox, catachresis, and undecidability, in Badiou's "event," Derrida's neologistic avoidance of his own regularization, Foucault's emphasis on epistemological and sexual singularities, on that which cannot be captured by the laws and rules of social organization, and so on.

This preference for idiographism has been accompanied, perhaps especially in the United States, by an equally persistent distrust of nomothetic approaches to humanistic topics, from the suspicions expressed against the generalizations and syncretic methods of Joseph Campbell or Northrop Frye, against structuralism and systems theory, against the "totalizations" of Marxism, against cliometrics or the *longue durée* in history, and, today, against the so-called digital humanities, particularly the modes of quantitative and computational approaches that threaten, or seem to threaten, the final dissolution of humanistic, idiographic analysis.[61] Think of Cleanth Brooks writing against "the heresy of paraphrase"—the *heresy* of not repeating something *exactly as it was*—and you have some sense of how deeply runs the humanist faith in idiographism as a moral and epistemological good, and how deeply this self-proclaimedly anti-Romantic, antitheological faith is expressed, and experienced, in language that borrows from the fields of theology and romance.[62] Or consider Derek Attridge: "The singularity of a cultural object consists in its difference *from all other such objects*, not simply as a particular manifestation of general rules but as a peculiar nexus within the culture that is perceived as *resisting or exceeding all pre-existing general determination*."[63]

The sacred status of our evidence, whether it be literary text or historical circumstance, the intimate appeal of the idea that we speak of that evidence "on its own terms," the belief that our critical voices can ventriloquize "the voice of the dead, for the dead had contrived to leave textual traces of themselves,"[64] the power of claiming to give the text, rather than the theoretical apparatus, the "last word" in the analysis,[65] the fundamental idea that our idiographic interpretations constitute a form of respect and "listening to the other":[66] all these are the affective and moral underpinnings of the hermeneutic progress that moves from a close and respectful attention to the singular, the minute, the detail, to claims about generalities, theories, concepts, and ideas, to an idiographism hostile to nomothetism in general, one that has embraced—at least in its ambitions, its master concepts, and its self-descriptions—a limit at which all that is left is the raw, untouched, pure particular, the particularity that generates without mediation its own exemplarity and thus grants us, if we engage it well and deeply enough, access to another kind of generality. In other words: Life.

Why does this way of treating things feel so powerful, so right, so true? Why, that is, does the idiographic approach have such power, not simply as a matter of epistemological choice among other choices, but as a matter of politics, of ethics, of what is right and good for the world? What set of ideas or values girds up its emotional and rhetorical strength, makes it possible for humanists to experience their daily scholarly work as a form of political intervention in the world?

The next chapter of this book answers those questions with a simple argument: that the forms of epistemological protection arranged around humanist examples—the literary texts, the works of art, the sociological or historical cases or events—essentially treat those examples as an expression of "beauty," as Kant defines it in his *Critique of the Power of Judgment*. In other words, the object construed by idiographic analysis has the implicit ontological structure of a Kantian work of art. The force of my argument relies on a reading of Kant that shows a consistent overlap between the way that the text talks about works of art and the way that it talks about persons. The definition of both as coming into their being only when recognized as self-sufficient "ends," I argue, grants both the person and the artwork an inner dignity that exempts them from transactability—from having what Kant describes, in a gesture that is far from metaphorical, as their "market price."

This overlap between beautiful art and ontological persons constitutes one major justification for the implicit object ontologies of

humanistic methods. It also explains, I suggest, the ethical structure of humanist resistance to large-scale modes of analysis. The
chapter therefore closes with a rereading of certain moments in
Kant that, if twisted in useful ways, can produce an alternative theory of humanist scholarship—one that extends the ontological and
ethical privilege afforded to human beings to all possible objects
of our intellectual and moral attention, and reads that attention,
therefore, as a matter of interest, politics, and care. All this then
opens the door to chapter 3, where the new metadiscourse of
humanist reason that such a rereading makes possible comes into
its first and fullest description.

II

THE FUTURE OF SINGULARITY

Sentimental Value After Kant

IMMANUEL KANT begins his *Critique of the Power of Judgment* by dividing, for the first time in his career, the general realm of judgment into two types. "The power of judgment" in general, he writes in the introduction to the book, "is the faculty for thinking of the particular as contained under the universal."[1] Judgment, however, has two types: determining judgment, which turns out to be the kind of judgment that Kant had used in his first two critiques, those of pure and practical reason; and reflecting judgment, the one Kant would be using (and defining) for the first time in this book. The difference between them is essentially directional: in determining judgment, we move from the universal to the particular, while reflecting judgment "is under the obligation of ascending from the particular in nature to the universal" (67).

Just to be super clear: as Kant arrives, in the late 1780s, at the third text in his trilogy of critiques, and specifically begins to approach the human relation to the aesthetic, he discovers that he needs to describe a new kind of judgment. This kind of judgment, although it shares with other kinds of judgment an interest in universal-particular relations, effectively begins with the unique or singular object and then moves from that object to universal principles, rather than the other way around. And it stems from, or is particular to, the general field of the aesthetic.

I hope that you already see how interesting and exciting and weird this is. It suggests, among other things, that an understanding of the social function of art as a site for the kind of universal-particular relation that Wilhelm Windelband and other neo-Kantians defined as idiographic existed well before the institutional situation of the *Methodenstreit*. And it gives us a philosophical starting point for the kinds of language that they used to understand it.

Here is what Kant says happens when someone sees something and judges it beautiful. That judgment includes the "necessary pre-supposition" (as Kant put it in the discarded first introduction to the text [19]) that there exists some universal pattern, a "unity of all empirical principles" (67) that allows an individual judgment about a single aesthetic object to move from the feeling that "I like this" to the feeling that "This is beautiful." For, Kant says, when I say a thing is beautiful or sublime, I do not mean that it is beautiful or sublime just for me; I mean that it is, or at least could be, beautiful or sublime for everyone. The potential universality of that apprehension—the idea that anyone could find this object beautiful, so long as I do—is what constitutes the specific act of reflecting judgment "as a law" (67).[2]

The possibility of such a universality is assumed, for Kant, by the fact of judgment itself; without it, we have no laws and no universals, just something like preference ("vanilla ice cream tastes good to *me*"). Because of the universalizing tendency, aesthetic validity, the belief that something that is beautiful is, or could be, beautiful for everyone, Kant says, is "subjectively universal validity, which does not rest on any concept" (100). And because of this rejection of conceptual frames, "all judgments of taste are **singular** judgments," that is, not judgments about (say) roses in general, but about one rose in particular. That's because judgments about things in general tend to be determining and nonsingular: roses *in general* are good for giving on Valentine's Day, or roses *in general* are an important part of the life cycle of bees. Each of these will tend to be about the concept or idea of roses, not about a single rose and a single experience of its beauty—and therefore not about aesthetic experience or judgment at all.[3] In other words, aesthetic judgment begins from a singular object and experience and arrives, unmediated by conceptualization or deductive (determining) judgment, at subjective universality, without passing through any other stages on the way.

There is, therefore, something in the singular object as it gives itself to be aesthetically judged that emphasizes, or indeed relies on, a complex relation between singularity and particularity, conceptualization and universality. The aesthetically judged object opens onto a judgment, or is opened onto by a judgment, that leaps from its singularity to the possibility of universal assent in a single bound: "That is **beautiful**," Kant writes, "which pleases universally *without a concept*" (104, my italics). This frictionless transaction—frictionless in both directions—between the singularity of the aesthetically considered object and the universal validity that such a consideration appeals to defines, for Kant, the aesthetic experience as such.

This frictionless and immediate transition between the singular and the universal finally explains why, for Kant, the object of aesthetic judgment cannot be considered in relation to its utility in some social space or mental process. This is the famous "purposiveness without purpose" of disinterested Kantian contemplation:

> Thus nothing other than the subjective purposiveness in the representation of an object without any purpose (objective or subjective), consequently the mere form of purposiveness in the representation through which an object is **given** to us, insofar as we are conscious of it, can constitute the satisfaction that we judge, without a concept, to be universally communicable. (106, translation modified).[4]

Only insofar as the object is considered without any purpose (*Zweck*) can it be potentially beautiful. Such a consideration creates an awareness of what Kant calls here the "mere form of purposiveness in the representation" (*die bloße Form der Zweckmäßigkeit in der Vorstellung*): the purposiveness that exists only in the representation and only for it, the orientation of the representation toward itself and its own goals, and not any external ones, activates the free play of the mind, the "occupation of the cognitive powers without a further aim," in a manner that "does not produce an interest in the object" (107).

Imagine, for instance, that you would appreciate a picture of a stick figure almost falling onto the train tracks, not because it usefully teaches people to "mind the gap" between the train and the platform, but because the contrast between the figure's geometric blackness and the yellow background created within you some aesthetic experience that emerged only from the purposiveness of the representation as such, from a cognitive relation to the representation as a representation rather than as a warning sign. The free play of the mind oriented toward the formal purposiveness of the object is a general play; it is not "restricted to a *particular* cognition," which would immediately focus it on an end of some sort and thereby cease to contemplate the object aesthetically (107, my italics).[5]

So we see that aesthetic contemplation in the *Critique of Judgment* involves an experience of the representing object that neither reduces it to a use, nor generalizes it as an example of a concept or a member of a class. One aesthetically judges *this* rose, or *this* representation of a rose, in a manner that refuses to connect the rose to any conceptual or pragmatic framework, any final purpose. The presumptively universal pleasure simultaneously enjoyed and theorized by aesthetic judgment stems from the evaluation of the object in withdrawn, purposeless singularity—a singularity that pulls back from the realms of the pragmatic (aka practical reason) and the conceptual (aka pure reason) exactly insofar as it approaches the realm of reflecting, aesthetic judgment.

It is through this singular quality that the aesthetic judgment involves the universal. The apprehension of the singular without concept or purpose essentially drives the perceiver to imagine their experience of the beautiful as not only satisfying but *necessary*. The necessity is strange, because it neither invokes an a priori law nor a practical one. Rather, Kant writes,

> as a necessity that is thought in an aesthetic judgment, it can only be called **exemplary**, i.e., a necessity of the assent of **all** to a judgment that is regarded as an example of a universal rule that one cannot produce. Since an aesthetic judgment is not an objective and cognitive judgment, this necessity cannot be derived from determinate concepts, and is therefore not apodictic. (121)

Aesthetic judgment is not apodictic, not subject to the derivations of an if/then structure. It makes a tiger's leap from the instance to the universal. In so doing, it sheds the problem of the example—this latter a mere illustration of something, ontologically reduced to conceptual servitude—and dons the mantle of the exemplary. Exemplarity, like singularity, expresses the ingathering possibility of the bound across vertical or logical scales, a transference that happens in no-time (or now-time) as an impression or a feeling. Held there, exemplarity oscillates endlessly, in the free play of aesthetic cognition, between the thing's uniqueness and its universalizability. This universalizability is predicated on, and universalizes, only the thing's *uniqueness*, and nothing else. Otherwise, it would be reduced to an example, and organized around a concept.

Aesthetic judgment thus paradoxically constitutes, in Kant, both the law and the possibility of freedom from the law. Everything that comes out of the concept of taste "as a faculty for judging an object," he writes, does so "in relation to the **free lawfulness** of the imagination" (124). The seeming contradiction of "free lawfulness" illustrates perfectly the catachrestic logic that exculpates the object from the law at the same time as it allows the object to follow its own rules: the lawfulness that organizes a concept of the object is "free," insofar as it does not subsume the object under the concept, so long as it gives its own law to itself, and thus matches its concept perfectly to its being. For these reasons, Kant continues,

> only a lawfulness without law and a subjective correspondence of the imagination to the understanding without an objective one— where the representation is related to a determinate concept of an object—are consistent with the free lawfulness of the understanding (which is also called purposiveness without end [*Zweck*, also purpose]) and with the peculiarity of a judgment of taste. (125)

A lawfulness without law! The thing is consistent with, Kant says, "the free lawfulness of the understanding," which equals, which "is also called," he says, "purposiveness without end." This all amounts to a description—a redescription, in fact—of the judgment of taste. And it recalls a sentence that Kant had written in the discarded first

introduction to the text, in which the entire practice of aesthetic contemplation was connected with the concept of reflecting judgment
that grounds the aesthetic from the beginning:

> The reflecting power of judgment thus proceeds with given appear-
> ances, in order to bring them under empirical concepts of determi-
> nate natural things, not schematically, but **technically**, not as it were
> merely mechanically, like an instrument, but **artistically**, in accor-
> dance with the general but at the same time indeterminate principle
> of a purposive arrangement of nature in a system, as it were for the
> benefit of our power of judgment." (17)

We do not need here to develop an entire theory of Kant's reflecting
judgment—a type of judgment that Kant distinguished, remember,
for the first time in his career in the introduction to the third *Critique*—to observe that both its method and its object thus coincide in
the aesthetic, whose very process of judgment operates, as Kant says,
"artistically" in its labile transfer from the particular to the universal.

To be clear, Kant's claims about these forms of judgment are essentially anthropological: he believes that he is describing how people
actually think and what they actually mean when they say that things
are beautiful. These are not claims about the way things should be;
they are claims about the way things are in human life, about the
way that humans organize mental categories and make claims, and
about how they judge the world and the objects in it. In a world in
which people regularly call things "beautiful," and in which a whole
series of social apparatuses and forms—museums, the art industry,
the general production of aesthetic objects by "artists," but also by
craftspeople, patronage systems, an interest in color, decoration, or
cognitive pleasure in objects that is over and above their necessary
social utility—works to organize and create such things, then, Kant is
saying, that people will exercise a kind of judgment that moves from
the singular to the universal, and the claims that such judgment
makes can be best described just as they are in the third *Critique*.

We do not need to believe that Kant is right, nor to believe that the
Critique of Judgment constitutes the origin of this kind of idiographic
logic, in order to see some larger cultural connection between his

work, on one hand, and the history of humanist metadiscourse, on the other. Just put together three things: (1) Kant's description of the very *process* of reflecting judgment as proceeding "artistically," (2) Windelband's claim that the task of the humanist scholar is "similar to the task of the artist," and (3) the more general humanist principle that one ought to borrow one's methods from one's objects and treat them on their own terms. Together, these describe a kind of cognition that thinks not only *about* things, but *through* them. And all of them have a strong tendency to find, as a model for that kind of thinking, the kind of experience that humans have when they look at—or make—art.

One final connection: remember Steven Connor's essay on the epistemology of example-formation? There, Connor makes a strong distinction between exemplarity and exemplification. The former, he writes, is more or less what we think of as the classic example: an instance that directs us toward a generality, and whose status as evidence is effectively subordinated to that generality. Exemplarity, on the other hand, is "the use of examples to retard or even resist the passage between" the epistemological spheres normally traversed by the example. The difference between the example and the exemplary is "the difference between a model that provides a general rule and one that exemplifies its own unprecedented and inimitable exemplarity." And the source for this concept of exemplarity, which dominates Anglo-American literary studies, is, Connor writes, "the Kantian doctrine of the non-conceptual nature of the aesthetic."[6] (Remember Kant: "as a necessity that is thought in an aesthetic judgment, [the judgment of beauty] can only be called **exemplary**"). The rest of Connor's essay (published in 1993) is an exploration of the specific tensions between exemplification and exemplarity that characterize poststructuralist literary theory, in which he observes, as we have here, a strong tendency to prefer exemplarity over exemplification, both as a matter of epistemological honesty and as an expression of the desire for an "escape from the necessity of exemplificatory relations," which constitutes what Connor calls the "cult of exemplarity."[7]

It is that humanist cult(ure) of exemplarity, and the epistemological and discursive habits that stem from it, organize it, and shape its self-descriptions and its pedagogies, that I aim to pass through, and supplement or supersede, in this book. My claim is that this kind of thinking—the logic of idiography in general—corresponds neither to what one might think of as philosophical reality nor to the actuality of humanist scholarly practice.[8]

To do so, however, I need to spend a bit more time with Kant. Because, let's be clear: the problem with the Kantian theory of the aesthetic object, or the logic of exemplarity in general, is not that they're obviously wrong. The problem is that they feel so instinctively appealing and right. Like Brooks's claims about the heresy of paraphrase, or Greenblatt's desire to speak with and give voice to the dead, the Kantian logic of the idiographic singularity of the beautiful stages a powerful kind of disciplinary knowledge—a deeply satisfying ethos of knowing that happens, perhaps not by chance, to coincide with the romantic justification of the humanities as a cultural institution.[9] But like the romantic defense of the humanities, the idiographic logic of the singularly beautiful object only goes so far in its attempt to resist larger cultural forces that would seem—as the new forms of scientific knowledge had already done in Kant's age—to dismiss the value of the singular or the particular in favor of the pursuit of general laws (to turn things into examples rather than perceive the exemplarity in them, as Connor might say). The emphasis on the irreducibility of the singular, as well as its modern inheritance in the insistence that all general knowledge must begin with, and elevate to a universal status, the radical singularity of the unique historical or literary case, too bluntly reverse the scientific epistemological paradigm that they battle. The result is, among other things, a set of humanistic disciplines that have a hard time describing their actual practice, and developing theories of their objects of analysis that do not sound like so much special pleading.

Why, then, is the theory of the artwork's singularity so compelling? What is the source of its apparent rightness? Much of its force has to do with the feeling that the singular resists not only generalization, but also a certain kind of monetized, or even capitalized, transactability, and that as a result, it has become—especially in the privileged avatar of the artwork—a figure for a more general resistance to modernity. Both the artwork and the object of humanist research figure, in their resistance to subordination or generalization, the possibility of their being exchanged for other objects of the same type, even as they also resist, simultaneously, the notion that they are being considered merely in relation to their utility in some economy that is not their own. They are neither exchangeable (for other things of equal value, or, in a group, for things of greater value, as in the exchange between a series of examples and a general rule) nor useful (they are not concepts, as Kant says; they are not directed toward some purpose that passes through them and sheds or dismisses them after the fact).

Once again, Kant's work gives us a strong elaboration of the philosophical grounds of this position, which can be summarized, perhaps, in the idea of "art for art's sake," but which in fact, as we will see in Kant's own work, refers not simply to art, but rather to a radically extensive theory of anthropological value, of which art constitutes only one small, intensively privileged instance. I am referring here to the strong structural and lexical overlap that takes place between Kant's theories of the person and his theories of the work of art. This conjunction or homology between the person and the beautiful work, which in both cases amounts to a theory of the self-legislating lawgiver, relies on—or develops en passant—a tremendously powerful understanding of the relationship between singularity and universality, which lies at the core of the Kantian mode of thought, and generates so much of its ongoing appeal.

Are persons and beautiful artworks the same? Not exactly. Although the highest archetype of aesthetic judgment can reasonably be described as an "ideal," as Kant tells us, such an ideal cannot be represented through concepts, but only through (necessarily imperfect) instances. Any ideal of beauty we generate will have to be a product of the imagination, and thus will have to be the product of a "partially intellectualized" judgment rather than a purely aesthetic one. Such an ideal could be described ideally in relation to a "fixed" beauty, one defined by a "concept of objective purposiveness." Things with variable purposes, with only a "vague" beauty, cannot generate an ideal. For instance, "an ideal of a beauty adhering to determinate ends," like the ideal of a beautiful home or a beautiful tree, "is also incapable of being represented" because the ends of such objects are "not adequately determined and fixed by their concept." Only one thing, Kant writes, can have a clear enough end to determine a beautiful ideal, and that thing is the thing that has "the end of existence in itself"—namely, the human being. "This **human being** alone is capable of an ideal of **beauty**," he says (117).

Here, the gap that Kant opens up between the beautiful object and the person—the former incapable of generating an "ideal" of beauty, the latter the only thing able to develop one—would seem to settle the question of the *identity* of the person and the artwork: they are not the same. The human being has an unusually intense relation to the concept of beauty because only the human being can, via the rational consideration of its fully concretized status as an end in itself, generate an ideal of beauty through a double vision that combines aesthetic judgment with critical reason. Beautiful objects, by contrast, are beautiful under only some considerations, some partially intellectualized judgments, which means that their law cannot, finally, self-legislate, even if it can come asymptotically close to that achievement.

To take the distinction Kant makes here as "proof" of the ineluctable difference between humans and artworks would privilege a reading of Kantian logic at the expense of a sensitivity to Kantian thematics. I want instead to read the other way around, attending to the ways in which Kant's language undercuts the sharpness of the logical distinction that he draws.

With that in mind, let us turn, for a clearer understanding of the Kantian human being, to a few sentences from the *Groundwork of the Metaphysics of Morals*. *Groundwork*, published in 1785, five years before the third *Critique*, includes the first elaboration of the Kantian categorical imperative, which Kant justifies on the basis of an ontology of the rational being. This ontology appears in the well-known discussion of the absolute worth of the rational being, the main subject of the *Groundwork*'s second section. At this point, Kant has laid out the basic theory of the categorical imperative, which tells you to act only in ways such that you could imagine your action becoming a universal law. But, Kant says, how can we know that the demand for the imperative itself is universal? Is it necessary *"for all rational beings* always to judge their actions according to maxims of which they themselves can will that they serve as universal laws?"[10]

You cannot argue that it is so on the basis of "relative" claims, Kant says, since claims that relate to the will of only a single person have worth only insofar as they are deductions of that person's individual will. You need something that can furnish a principle that would be valid for everyone.

The only thing that could so function, Kant argues, would be something that had "absolute worth," that could function "as an *end in itself*." Such a thing could not be directed toward any particular goal or arise from any particular situation; rather, it would have to bear within itself its own inherent directionless direction. And that thing, Kant argues, is "a human being and generally every rational being," which "*exists* as an end in itself, *not merely as a means* for the discretionary use of this or that will" (40). People (rational beings) are not merely "subjective ends," having a worth only for the other folks around them; rather, they are "objective ends, i.e. entities whose existence in itself is an end, an end such that no other end can be put in its place" (40–41).

Whatever resemblance exists between the person and the artwork will depend on the strange status that both have of being fundamentally self-oriented, of needing to be considered in and of themselves, rather than in relation to some other purpose or use. This resemblance is affirmed by the repetition of the central word *Zweck*, which gives us both the word "end" in the phrase "end in itself," used in the *Groundwork*, and the word "purpose" in the phrase "purposiveness without purpose" (or "purposiveness without end," in newer English translations) in the *Critique of Judgment*. It's as though the Kantian intuition regarding the self-legislating capacity of the human being, first articulated in the 1785 *Groundwork*, found a kind of junior partner in the third *Critique* five years later—when, as we have seen, the fundamental difference between the object and the person Kant elaborates relies on the idea that the former are ends in themselves only temporarily, while the latter are so a priori. This fundamental distinction notwithstanding (is it really so fundamental? we will see . . .), we may well want to focus here on the strong thematic overlap between the nondirected quality of the rational person—the fact that it is not being used for a particular purpose, as a means (*Mittel*)—and the nondirected attitude that one takes toward the beautiful object, which must be considered in its absolute singularity and not in relation to some purpose it might have or its exemplification of a general principle.

We can bring the two "ends" closer together by observing that the practical imperative that Kant describes in *Groundwork* entails acting "so that you use humanity, in your own person as well as in the person of any other, always at the same time as an end, never merely as a means" (41). One relates to the human being (including oneself) through no specific end—not for a singular purpose—but rather through a general, open-ended endedness rooted in the human capacity for the rational. At this point, we're much closer to a kind of subjective "purposiveness without end" appropriate for the aesthetic contemplation of the object. Like the person in contemplation of the artwork, reason relates to the universal qualities of the legislation of the will "not for the sake of any other practical motivating ground or future advantage"—as a means-type end, in other words—"but from the idea of the *dignity* of a rational being that obeys no law other than that which at the same time it itself gives"—that is, as an end in itself (46).

It is because it makes this unique demand on others that the will, the rational being, lies simultaneously inside and outside the law. The will "is not just subject to the law, but subject in such a way that it must also be viewed *as self-legislating*, and just on account of this as subject to the law (of which it can consider itself the author) in the first place" (43). The human being is thus simultaneously subject to its "*own* and yet *universal legislation*," since in acting in conformity with one's own will, one conforms also to the will's singular universalizability. Kant calls this "the principle of the autonomy of the will" (45). Its description leads directly into his discussion of the inherent dignity of the rational being as such—its inner worth, as opposed to its "market price"—that allows us to see how the singularity of the person also constitutes an inherent, ontological resistance to transaction, assimilation, and exchange.[11] Inasmuch as it remains disconnected from any particular obligation or circumstance, this ontological ground, this inexchangeability, is another form of purposiveness without end, or the end in itself, that lies at the center of the metaphysics of morals. Kant describes the paradox: "that the mere dignity of humanity, as rational nature, without any other end of advantage to be attained by it . . . is still to serve as an unrelenting prescription of the will." It is precisely in the "independence of a maxim from all . . . incentives," Kant writes, "that its *sublimity* consists" (50, my emphasis).

You see how the human being theorized in the *Groundwork* of 1785 prefigures some aspects of the aesthetically perceived object described in the *Critique of the Power of Judgment* in 1790. Like the aesthetically considered object, which engages in a paradoxically "free lawfulness," the person operates in the sphere of simultaneous freedom and unfreedom, itself establishing the universal law to which it submits as a subject. The person belongs to a universal "kingdom of ends," Kant writes, as subject and object, as both a "member" and as "its head" (45); the beautiful work of art vibrates between the singular and the universal, exemplifying the latter without being an example of it. This is, in the case of the subject, what Slavoj Žižek has described as the Kantian "paradox of the universal singularity, of a singular subject who, in a kind of short circuit, bypassing the mediation of the particular, directly participates in the Universal."[12] You find that that same Kantian language applied to the work of art in remarks of Gayatri Chakravorty Spivak's: "Our concern is . . . to ask what makes literary cases singular. The singular is the always universalizable, never the universal. The site of reading is to make the singular visible in its ability."[13] In such a program, the work of humanist scholars (and perhaps particularly the literary ones) amounts to an exercise in the illumination of the singular—a task for which humanists orient themselves specifically against the kinds of nomothetic, difference-collapsing approaches that would subsume the phenomenon under anything other than its own unique being.[14] In this way, the work of art demands nothing less from us than does a person; they both ask us to approach them as, among other things, illustrations of the very possibility of singularity, and thus as resolutions of the larger epistemological, ethical, and social questions of how we relate particulars to generalities, phenomena to concepts, or individuals to society.

At this point, it becomes possible to address more clearly the logical objection, first addressed by Kant himself in the third *Critique*, to any claim of total homology between the person and the artwork. Among other things, one sees easily that the two differ philosophically, since the paradox of free lawfulness governing the person occurs a priori, as a condition of its being, while the contradiction of the work of art results from synthetic, a posteriori judgment. This difference explains the dissimilar motive impressions thrown off by the two forms: the person's end-in-itself-ness feels superimpositional, structural, and synchronic; the artwork's, on the other hand, vibrates, because it depends very much on how it is seen, and on the possibility of its being considered at any moment in another way. When Kant argues that only the human being generates an ideal of beauty, he allows the human's capacity for rationality to produce an ontological rift between itself and all other objects; this justifies the argument against homology.

But what if we deny, first, the unique rationality of the human being? Minimally, one might say that we do not know what rationality is, and that the arguments that seek to generate its justification are easily enough undone. They are undone on one side by evidence that animals have many of the features we think of as rational— evidence that has historically produced an endless search for new or finer justifications of ontological human difference (e.g., that only humans think recursively, although one can never show that this difference is one of kind rather than degree); they are undone on another side by everything we know about human psychology, which suggests that whatever rationality we have operates alongside a series of instincts and unconscious reactions or structures, as well as within complex social and biological contexts, that determine for any given historical moment at all a range of possibilities for human minds and human thought.

More maximally, we may well want to observe that though many human societies have in fact operated with a theorized metadiscourse of human mental superiority that renders the species different in absolute kind from both other living things (with or without minds) and inanimate objects, human beings have nonetheless always lived—now speaking from an anthropological, historical perspective—in a world in which nonhuman animals, nonanimal living beings, and inanimate objects (whether natural or artificial) have participated actively in the making of the human lifeworld, and indeed of the lifeworld of those other beings that live alongside humans on Earth. In other words, the metadiscourse about humanity's special ontological status has always existed alongside a human experience of life that denies that ontological distinction, since it not only relates to but also requires and relies on environments and other living and nonliving things. Thinking anthropologically, then, one might really want to resist the idea that our philosophy of the human ought to focus on what seems to make humans absolutely special, rather than on the various features of human life that make humans just one of any number of types of beings and things that exist side by side and act upon one another to make human social life meaningful and real.[15]

We can also push against the strong distinction between the person and the artwork, or indeed between persons and things more generally, if we remember how human beings actually live their lives. We may then remark that in fact, like the artwork, the person can *always* be treated as a means; it is precisely because of this possibility that we must assert that they should not be. From a material point of view that builds up arguments from human practice, we may well want to say that though humans are an interesting case for the production of ontological rifts between things treated as means and things treated as ends, they are hardly completely protected from the general tendency of all things to treat all other things, sometimes, as means. In fact, ordinary social life would be impossible without our treating one another, occasionally, as means—even the people we love the most serve as means at times (to pick up the kids, for instance); sometimes we even treat ourselves as means, even if we go to therapy to help us stop doing so.

If it is difficult to imagine a human world in which humans do not treat other humans or themselves as means, it is because that world has never existed. And even if Kant knew this—and he probably did—and was simply proposing something that he might call a "regulative ideal," one might ask in response: why should the ideals that regulate our philosophical categories (or even our political ones) be, on the strength of the historical evidence, completely incompatible with the life of the species as we have known it so far, or, for that matter—here now speaking really only for myself—ideals that, if put into practice, would make our lives absolutely impossible and unbearable? How can it make sense to organize ourselves, or our utopian dreams, around an ideal of mutual interaction that we will inevitably fail to achieve?

Of course both people and artworks are sometimes treated as means. This claim is supported by the historical and personal evidence before us, by our own lived experience. Hegel knew it: "The individual man," he wrote, "in order to preserve his individuality, must frequently make himself a means to others, must subserve their limited aims, and must likewise reduce others to mere means in order to satisfy his own interests."[16] He went on to describe this concept as "the prose of the world"—a world of "entanglement in the relative" and "the pressure of necessity, from which the individual is in no position to withdraw." What this poignant reminder suggests is that the status of humans or artworks (or really anything) as *singular* in the Kantian sense is a matter of social and historical practice and action rather than a quality of the thing as such (not even the human thing); it is not *in* something, but rather in the way that something is treated or seen.

In such a conception, the total ontological quiddity of either the person or the artwork would emerge, not from a Kantian, self-legislating kernel, but from the system of different perspectives, from full means-use to full ends-use, that others can take toward them. Things in the world can be treated in different ways: this is ontology. Treating those things as ends, addressing them in their fully contextualized being, and in terms that borrow from the thing itself: this is singularity. This is idiography. In practical terms, then, the being of the person or the artwork would lie not so much in this or that perspective, but instead in the possibility of being interacted with or responded to with one attitude or another, with these attitudes considered as possibilities in the system of all perspectives through which they might be interacted with or observed, and through which they tend, historically and socially, to be interacted with or observed. The distance measured in the gap between these perspectives could illuminate, as in the description of a distant planet, some crucial features of an object's social and ontological being.

Let us contemplate the possible implications of this argument. To do so, we need to remember that concepts do not—even in Kant!—preexist their deployment in analysis. This means that rather than thinking of this discussion as merely being about the person and the artwork, we have to imagine that it is a discussion in which a certain understanding of the relation between the person and the artwork depends, or is presented as depending, on the already-established categories of the singular and the universal. At this point, one can, for the sake of a different perspective, simply reverse the structural priority and ask: what if the debate about persons and artworks exists *in order to* provide a determination of the relationship between the singular and the universal (and through them, by extension, of generality and particularity, theory and example, and so on)? What if the person and artwork are merely vehicles for the production of a certain certainty regarding categories whose actual meaning has *not* yet been established?

Such a reversal does not reveal, as it might seem, what Kant's work was *really* or *secretly* about the whole time. Rather, it illuminates, through parallax, the entire field of play of the argument. Placing the concepts that act as methods on the same plane as the concepts that act as phenomena or objects allows us to recognize the dynamic qualities and interactive structures of an entire thought-system. Such a system divides itself into levels, to be sure, holding some of its concepts steadier than others, but this is an effect of the rhetoric and values of the dynamic process whereby the system constructs itself, and not some outside prior to it. Once we see that all the categories are dynamic, we can argue that the discussion here includes *four* major, mutually determining terms—person, artwork, singular, and universal—as well as a variety of partially or metonymically related concepts, including the example and the exemplary, the concrete and the abstract, freedom and necessity, and, finally, the idea of self-legislation, which acts as a kind of dialectical springboard that permits the leap from one side of the singular-universal binary to the other.

I'm not saying all these things are the same. Mutual influence and imbrication, collocation within a system, do not mean identity. The point is rather to show how the theorization of the person (or the artwork) permits a simultaneously ethical and epistemological resolution of the relationship of the universal and the singular, and also to suggest that there can be—at least in Kant—no consideration of what the human or the artwork is that does not resolve around that *seemingly* more general problem. And then to confront the fact that the knot that the Kantian text establishes describes fairly well the ways we continue to think today about things like close reading or archival research, that this group of concepts and the problems they manage, and seem to resolve, organize many of the ways we continue to think about the production of knowledge across the humanistic disciplines. The entire Kantian discussion of aesthetic judgment is a kind of figure, or passageway, through which one becomes conscious of the actually existing singularity of certain aspects of the real, and thus, in a second stage, comes to understand one's epistemological responsibility to the objects that bear that singularity. Idiographic logic thus names a particularly strong resolution to the related problems of the particular and the general, the concrete and the abstract, the object and the method: the "singular," which, as Žižek observes, "in a kind of short circuit, bypassing the mediation of the particular, directly participates in the Universal."

If that solution is correct—if "Kant" is more or less right about these things—then the method particular to the human sciences is also correct, in the sense that it is a method appropriate to its object.[17] The idiographic method stems, in such a world, from the immediate ontological properties of its objects of inquiry—humans and works of art (it is, therefore, "substantive" in Windelband's sense). To interpret human culture requires approaching its elements with an ethical posture directed toward, and drawn from, their ontology; to read them is always to locate one's work in the general ontological sphere of the singular's mediation between the individual and the universal. As a result of such a practice, the more general task of the humanities would be—assuming that "Kant" is correct—to expose the unique singularity or self-legislating properties of the artwork or person, to encourage others to recognize that unique presence, and possibly to militate for policies and forms of the social that would register, and respect, their special forms of being. This would in turn require humanists to resist any attempt to consider works or people as "means," because to do so would be to consider them not as actual people or works, but rather as weird phenomenal facsimiles of works (or people). To read a novel through quantitative analysis would be merely to read something *like* a novel; the true, singular novel would remain untouched by the generalization of its particulars. Likewise, to suggest that the work of art is *merely* the effect of its circulation as a commodity would not be to discuss the work of art at all, but merely to address one aspect of its social being.

I am going to propose, however, that almost no one actually believes this, or acts in this way. For such a person would have to reject wholesale as "not the study of literature" not only the quantitative analysis of literary texts, but also any work in the sociology of literature that points to the institutional forces that help produce literary activity and meaning (so, work by Pascale Casanova, James English, or Mark McGurl, for starters, but also anything in the general field of, say, the modernist study of little magazines); and also any work in the history of media studies that points to the coproduction of the literary and the mediatic (away with Friedrich Kittler, Laura Mulvey, Vilém Flusser, Lisa Gitelman, Katherine Hayles); any work that would direct us toward the interference of historical or biographical activity with the work of art; or indeed any scholarship that believed in such overbearing and unsingular categories as the poem, the novel, the period, the school, or the genre. At the limit of the ethical relation to the singular, each object would produce a completely singular method, even a singular language, a singular work of scholarship uniquely attuned to its singularity, which would be interpretable (or treatable as a "pure" end) only within the self-sustaining system that it produced entirely from within. That's never happened. And it never will.

The same goes for scholarly work on human lives and social activity. No cultural or social criticism proceeds without a significant amount of generalizing, grouping, and so on, each instance of which technically violates the singularity of the object, which not only fails to address the actually existing complexity of that object but actively ignores some aspects of that complexity to make useful epistemological generalizations about it. What we mean, therefore, when we talk about respecting the object of humanistic inquiry—when we talk about matching the method to the object for both epistemological and ethical reasons—is something other than what we actually do when we study it. The regulative ideal of idiographic attention applies, yes, but *only part of the time*: actually grasping the singularity of an object requires, in fact, putting it into categories, groupings, and other social and contextual contexts that help us understand it. Even a question like "What kind of a revolution was *this* revolution?" suggests, by virtue of the category, that whatever complex set of events under examination has already been grasped and understood as a "revolution," and that a full understanding of that complexity proceeds necessarily from the larger concept. This is true even when the study of the events turns out to change the theory of revolution that was applied to it at the beginning of the analysis.

These are, in any case, the first general grounds on which a strict "Kantian" idiographism does not apply to the actual work of humanist scholarship. Insofar as they reproduce a more general critique of epistemological nominalism, they will be familiar from chapter 1. Alongside the criticisms raised above, my objections at this point can be summarized as follows: first, the idiographic position as "Kant" (and humanist metadiscourse) define it establishes an untenable ontological rift or divide between kinds of objects (persons and artworks on one side, and everything else on the other); and, second, this position confuses a mode of consideration with a property of an object.

Let's start with the first claim. You cannot reasonably restrict the capacity to produce a direct leap from the singular to the universal (let's call this capacity "singularity") to certain kinds of objects when it is clear that with careful thought, one can see or find singularity in a much wider variety of things than artworks or persons: as we have seen from decades of scholarship in humanistic fields, in a wide variety of social forms at a number of scales (so that one can say that each person is singular, but also that each family is singular, but also that each neighborhood is singular, and so on, without the singularity of the "larger" grouping disrupting or undoing the singularity of the "smaller" ones); in any semiotic space of culture, from the highly aestheticized at a variety of levels (including the level of "art" itself) to the completely ordinary and mundane; in any historical moment or process, whether considered in a strong sense as a "singular" event or as a potentially singular instance of a more general process whose generality does not fully capture the singular quality of each instance that it includes. More entities have the capacity for singularity than persons or artworks.[18]

One can turn this inductive insight into a general methodological principle if, following Graham Harman, one argues against "assuming that basic ontological divides can be identified with specific *kinds* of entities"—that is, against assuming the existence of any strong or unbridgeable difference between any kinds of things, in this instance especially between humans and nonhuman animals, but also between, say, objects and concepts (the latter can be singular too!).[19] This is not to say that there are not differences among things, but simply to insist that we do not have any evidence that these differences amount to a fundamental ontological difference in *kind*. This preference for seeing things, when possible, as matters of degree is of a piece, I think, with the general poststructuralist preference for transactionality, or perhaps for the more generally anthropological point of view that opposes to the work of sociocultural nominalization and concept-formation the evidence of actually existing human practice.[20] What it suggests is that though humans and artworks may be especially intense sites for the becoming-visible of singularity, they are by no means the only kinds of things that either *have* singularity or make it visible. We do not owe them any special ethical or epistemological consideration on the grounds of their relation to that concept—there is no moment at which their degree of singularity crosses over to make them uniquely ontologically related to the singular, such that they become not merely different, but radically or finally different, from everything else. It is not, in other words, that ontoloigically unique persons originate self-legislation and then share a diminished version of it with other things; rather, it is that as humans, we tend to see singularity in certain places rather than others, and that we apportion that singularity—the right or the capacity to be treated in a certain way, some of the time—through a variety of social, cultural, and political processes.

As for the second claim, the previous remarks on ontological rifts suggest that we make a mistake when we try to make any feature (but perhaps especially singularity) belong to a certain class of objects and not to others. And here Kant himself offers us a way out of the problem. As you'll recall, the third *Critique* describes the difference between persons and aesthetically considered objects as stemming from the fact that human beings self-legislate a priori, while the beautiful object bears within itself merely the possibility of being understood as self-legislating. I have been suggesting that this sees things wrong, that because both people and artworks are subject to consideration as means rather than as ends in themselves, what appears to be an ontological property of the object may well be a property of the mode or posture with which one relates to the object.[21] In such a schema, singularity appears, or becomes visible, at a moment when one *relates* to something in a particular way, when one treats it as a self-legislating being, as something capable of generating from within the laws that govern its happening before us. Such a mode of consideration cannot be limited to works or persons. Indeed the idea that the phenomenon should generate the mode of analysis proper to it is, at its root, a reexpression of this basic idea. What's good enough for beauty is good enough for people is good enough for the social organization of protest movements, because in each case, the capacity for something to be treated as self-legislating and singular resides neither in the object nor in the method, but rather in a mode of relation that is perpetually possible, and possible for everything.

If singularity is not a matter of the special rational capacities of the human animal, or of the potentially disinterested regard made possible by the beautiful object, but rather a question of how humans or their things relate to other humans and things in their lifeworld, then neither people nor artworks are as ontologically special as we would like them to be. We see that Kantian text brushing up against this conclusion in a very odd moment in *Groundwork*. "In the kingdom of ends everything has either a **price**, or a **dignity**," Kant writes. "What has a price can be replaced with something else, as its *equivalent*; whereas what is elevated above any price, and hence allows of no equivalent, has a dignity" (46). All this is fine, and familiar to anyone who's lived in the post–human rights era. In the next paragraph, however, this comfortable binary suddenly acquires a third element:

> What refers to general human inclinations and needs has a *market price*; what, even without presupposing a need, conforms with a certain taste, i.e. a delight in the mere purposeless [*zwecklosen*] play of the powers of our mind, has a *fancy price* [*Affektionspreis*]; but what constitutes the condition under which alone something can be an end [*Zweck*] in itself does not merely have a relative worth, i.e. a price, but an inner worth, i.e. *dignity*. (46)

Where we had two categories, suddenly we have three: a thing that "conforms to a certain taste" enters the picture, and it has a "*fancy price.*" What is a fancy price? A price that one places on something one fancies; a mark of sentimental or affective value that elevates a particular object over its replicas, that imbues it with a historical or personal aura. Intervening in the gap between the market price and the unsaleable dignity of the human, the fancy price's mediation turns on the difference between *zwecklosen*, the adjective Kant uses to describe the play of the powers of our mind, which is translated as "purposeless," and the noun *Zweck*, the "end" that something can *be* on its own (*etwas Zweck an sich selbst sein kann*). The human difference emerges from the distinction between the adjective and the noun, between a possible condition of the mind and a state of being, with the potential work of art acting as a kind of stepping-stone by which one arrives, finally, at the human. With the question settled, the term *Affektionspreis* does not appear again in either the *Groundwork* or the *Critique of Judgment*.[22]

And yet. What if, rather than raising the question of "fancy" and allowing it to become the supplementary and excluded third term in a system of price relations, one imagines it as the centerpiece of an entire relational system? Taking *Affektionspreis* as a model not only for human dignity—which, in the absence of an ontological justification, would simply be the product of a certain *care*—but also as a model for all those objects that have only a "market price," we may remember that even those marketable objects are rarely as perfectly or cleanly exchangeable and untransactable as the dream of pure and total equivalence would make it seem, and that capitalism too, after all, is subject to what John Maynard Keynes called its "animal spirits."

Such a model would have the advantage of restoring to the process of evaluation—*all* evaluation—a sense of the force of affection and care (or disaffection and distaste, for the emotions are not only positive). It would also focus our attention on relationality as the central feature of the evaluative process because the status of an object as exchangeable or possessed of inner worth would depend entirely on the relation one had adopted to it, to the degree, more or less, of interest one had in allowing it to engage us as singularly universalizable, or in imagining it, as one does, as a partial means to a partial end, at least at certain scales, even as one attempted to account for the perpetually receding horizon of its singularity, at others. Not so much for its purposes, or our own, but for the purposes of the relation constructed thereby, whose name would be, in certain social arenas, "scholarship," but might just as well be "interest," or "attention," or "care."

Can any object really be the subject of singularity-attention, of some expansion of its social self beyond its role as pure and interchangeable commodity? Yes. Not only in the eyes of a certain mode of scholarship, which can, given enough attention, allow the individual history of a particular object—a rock, a hamburger, and so on—to make that object complex, individual, unique, and thus worthy in some respects of the modes of social care that we associate with all the other sentimentally valued objects that make up our lifeworld. More simply, consider the chairs in an auditorium or a classroom, which are fashioned to be identical and from some essentially inhuman perspective, are. But imagine that you sit in a such a seat at the beginning of a lecture or a class, and that at some point, you get up and leave, and later come back. And when you get back, your neighbor has moved into your chair. No one I know would think of this as anything but, minimally, weird, and probably rude as well. Why? Because it was *your* chair, however temporarily, and it was made so by your sitting in it for a while. (How long does this process take? Five or ten seconds can be enough.) You have developed a relationship to this chair that distinguishes it from all the other chairs in the room, even if someone might point out, quite correctly, that your chair is (from a physical point of view) exactly the same as all the others. From this point of view, the chairs do not simply have an exchange value; they have *Affektionspreis*, and this *Affektionspreis* is a matter of their circulation in a social context *over time*.

The combination of social life and the passage of time constitute the being of human experience as such; together, they produce the distribution of value, attention, and care across the vast spheres of the social, on any number of temporal scales. Care, a kind of attention that addresses an object in its social relations and recognizes that object's history and social relation as valuable in their own right, as establishing some set of guidelines for an ethical relation to that object, thus constitutes a kind of relational counterpoint to singularity-relation, a more ordinary and expansive way of thinking about humanistic scholarship as itself, sometimes, a kind of care, and also as a social process dedicated to increasing both our capacity to care and our general recognition of singularity in the world. Not *only* that, but at least partially and importantly that, as we shall discuss in chapter 3.

If—to return now to our main thread—neither a human being nor anything else is ontologically special and unique, and if everything (human beings included) nonetheless has a capacity to participate in a relation that makes singularity happen, then both the idiographic prejudice and the scientific/nomothetic one would need to be abandoned. In such a world, researchers would minimally have to recognize that the conceptual or the methodological—indeed, anything that we might conceive of as "above" the level of the real—would not constitute an unusual violation of the integrity and singular quiddity of an object in order to accept the idea that first, the object also violates the method, and second, that all relations among things produce such violations constantly. At that point, calling them "violations," as opposed to just "relations," would serve primarily to remind us of our solely epistemological obligation to remember that there are many ways to know something, and that any act of knowing is therefore partial. This would militate against any kind of hardcore nomothetism of the positivist or deterministic type—the kind of aggressive and controlling knowledge that has constituted the enemy of humanist metadiscourse since at least the 1880s.

At the same time, since all knowledge of something is partial, different ways of knowing things can contribute to (rather than destroy) an appreciation of the singularity of an object of knowledge by revealing the various modes to which it can be related. No mode of knowing, at any scale, would be inherently unethical or unsound; rather, we would need sound theories of how objects (or persons) look from the perspective of different modes or scales of knowing—recognizing that the capacity to be known via different modes or scales is, finally, an expression of the system of singularity and non-singularity that organizes any given object in the social. Or, rather, that it is the series of possible relations between the object and the method, the variety of ways that the object gives itself to be understood by methods and that the methods call objects to themselves, constituting them as apprehensible domains of relation, useful to a given human community that activates them (either individually or institutionally), that constitutes singularity in practice. In this way, singularity becomes an expression not only of all relations, but of the relations among the possible relations between or among methods and objects, theories and examples, generalizations and particulars, ideas and things, and so on.

(As I have said, and will say again: this argument, framed here as a series of ought-claims, does not need to constitute a "critique" of humanist practice; in fact, and quite conveniently, it mostly describes it. But here, recall Richard Rorty's argument that a pragmatist feminist "will see herself as helping to create women rather than attempting to describe them more accurately"; it is the case that any description that does not imagine itself to be unmasking an essence will also participate, politically and rhetorically, in an act of creation—one that makes sense only in a particular context.)[23]

Just as, in such a schema, any primarily nomothetic/quantitative analysis would have to account epistemologically for the impact on its research outcomes of the forms of ignorance and ethical violation produced by its method, so any primarily idiographic project would have to remain aware of the forms of ignorance produced by its over-privileging of any single instance it interpreted. At that point, calling something "too" nomothetic or "too" idiographic could make sense only as an epistemological claim about the outcome of a *specific*

research project, not as a blanket statement about the ethical or epistemological inappropriateness of a method applied to an object or
vice versa, or of any specific disciplinary mode for that matter.

The final outcome of that practice would be an increased awareness, in both humanistic and scientific disciplines, of the ways in
which method and phenomena shape each other—and, ideally, an
opening up of the varieties of method and the amount of cross-talk,
both within and between disciplines. Such a situation would defuse
much of the tension between the idiographic and the nomothetic
in literary and historical studies, especially once literary critics
and historians recognized that their political commitment to the
idiographic does not match the kinds of thinking and writing they
have been doing all along.

Nothing about the recognition of their mutual imbrication in
questions of generality and particularity requires the humanistic and
scientific disciplines themselves to collapse into a single university.
Although the ontological possibility of singularity may be evenly distributed among things, the social recognition (and even production)
of singularity happens more unevenly. Beginning with that understanding, one could argue that one of the major social functions of
artworks in the post–Scientific Revolution period is to produce an
increased social awareness of the singularity of all things. This function finds itself supported, the argument would continue, in a number of institutional forms, including the museum or the university; it
feeds into both the consumption and the production of works of art,
with all sorts of interesting systemic effects, including, for instance,
the patently negative effect of convincing us that singularity resides
exclusively in artworks or persons, thereby obscuring the basic ethical
responsibility to singularity elsewhere—or even allowing us to forget
the possibility of seeing it.

Here, I am reminded (as I often am) of Jean Baudrillard's claim
that Disneyland exists only to convince Americans that the rest of
their country isn't an amusement park. One might say the same thing,
with more regret, for art museums—they exist not only to collect
"sentimental value" and teach us to recognize it, but also to restrain
or restrict our awareness of the ways in which sentimental value operates outside the museum, and indeed organizes much of our daily

experience of life, not just among humans but among all sorts of human artifacts, including those that operate at timescales more or less removed from "ordinary" human life spans, including institutional ones.

The preferentially idiographic study of the general field of the aesthetic, then, would respond not to an ontological fact, but to a social one. Having displaced the ontological onto the social, one could argue that the current status quo—idiography for the humanities and nomothetism for the sciences—reflects something of the social structure and distribution of the *concept* of singularity (but not singularity itself). In such a world, the differences among the disciplines would be merely contingent, responsive to social shifts, products of different traditions of orientation toward the method-object knot. At that point, the object-methods of humanism would no longer be ontologically protected from the depredations of science. But neither would the object-methods of science be protected from the insights of humanism—from an ontological perspective, the presence of singularity, or circumstance, in the traditional objects of science would generate its own legitimate call to method, or rather to a variety of methods, whose collective coherence would have to be produced through another set of relations to it.

Let me return, finally, to the fundamental claim at the heart of the idiographic defense of humanist reason, to the specifically ethical or moral claims that attend it, and to the ontological claim upon which they all rely—namely, that the specific properties of the objects of humanist analysis demand, by virtue of their uniqueness, a form of scholarly attention that makes them the legislators of their own evaluation. Against all this, I have argued here—on the basis of a reading of Kant and on the basis of arguments grounded in the anthropological actuality of human behavior and practice—that no ontological priority is owed to the object over the method, in the sense that the object self-legislates its method rather than the other way around. In fact, this is an impossibility, and it produces bad theories of the object as passive, inert, or needing to be protected from theory, from the subordination or domination of "bad" kinds of knowledge. In this way, we remove the putative ontological priority of the second half of binaries like general/particular or theory/example, reducing differences of kind to differences of degree, or, better, thinking of them as organized relations into a coproduced network or system.[24]

At that point, activity and passivity cease to be ontologically distinct, meaning that there is no reason to privilege either the subject or the object in an epistemological/scholarly relation. This frees us to stop fetishizing the unique singularity of the object, but also to cease worshipping the unique power/capacity of the observing, nomothetic subject (science or the law); no fetishization on either side, as the possibility of the particular resides everywhere and vexes the most banal generalization—just as the possibility of generalization haunts, even in the latter's deepest originality, every particular.

All of this suggests that if one believes that methods and phenomena must relate to one another (the position with which idiographic logic begins), then one needs a more serious theory of the method *as a phenomenon*, and of the phenomenon as a method. Or, rather, one needs to see that the perpetually amazing recognition of their ontological proximity and relatedness—the methods determine the objects! the objects determine the methods!—qualifies as amazing only if we decide in advance that method and phenomenon are fundamentally opposed things. But in practice, the terms produce themselves mutually, like everything else. It's not that there's no such thing as a theory or an example (or method and phenomenon), but that each of these can be turned into its opposite via a shift in the level of analysis (I can have a theory of theories [which would then be examples of that more general theory], or use an example to exemplify another example, treating it thereby as a theory). The distinctions between theories and examples stem from the relation they're placed into rather than from anything in the ontological quality of the theory or the example considered on its own. There is no "own," at least none to which we have any access. There is just *Affektionspreis*, all the way down.

None of this means that literature (or human social or political life) is not a socially unusual object, worthy of special kinds of attention. It does mean, however, that *all* social objects, including the objects that are databases or strings of numerical observations, as well as the objects or partial objects that give themselves to be measured in those numerical ways, are worthy of particularizing kinds of attention. And it also means that *all* objects, though they may generate (socially) preferred modes of attention, nonetheless can be potentially considered and known (i.e., related to) through a wide variety of such modes, including, perpetually, the mode of the singular, whose most fundamental task is to relate the particular to the universal in a certain kind of way. No ontological barrier, then, between methods and objects, thoughts and things. Nothing, either, that makes any object inimical or inappropriate to method, because there is no phenomenon outside of a mode of apprehension for it (*il n'y a pas de hors-texte*). And, likewise, no mode of analysis inherently inimical to the integrity or dignity of a phenomenon: it is simply a question of seeing what comes of any given object-method relation, of asking to what extent we recognize the object that it appears to produce, and of deciding whether or how we can integrate that new perspective on the object into a more "general" picture of the object-method as something that—however singularly—produces itself in relation to a *variety* of universals, from a number of different spaces, or perspectives, or levels. And takes those spaces, perspectives, and levels for a substantial picture of the world.

III

ARTICLES OF REASON

How Humanists Really (Ought to?) Think

THE REREADING of Kant above aims to make available, via the usual methods, propositions about the kinds of work humanist reason could entail and the kinds of scholarship it could produce. As it does so, it sets itself against the mythologized meta-discourse of humanist reason, and shows—I think—the following: (1) We can conceive of singularity not as a feature of a thing, but as a *relation* between a person and a thing, sometimes chosen for a specific purpose by a specific person, sometimes institutionalized in various social forms; singularity is not a property of either a method or an object that preexists the relation that attention (and affection) create. (2) In doing so, we collapse the absolute boundary between human and artwork, on one side, and the rest of the social life-world, on the other, and collapse, accordingly, any *ontological* justification for the protection of certain classes of objects from the depredations of capitalism or knowledge. This is a small price to pay, since it is the cost of a confrontation with the actual world we live in, and thus the payment we must make in order to address it, know it, make laws or communities within it, in common. Conceiving the Romantic/idealized notion of the human or the artwork as fundamentally a social product—and therefore as being as susceptible as anything else to the work of the social—thus calls us, collectively and together, to labor, to the institutionalization of our modes of care around whatever objects we deem careworthy, and also, therefore, to the development of social forms of protection, democratically achieved, that would require no Romantic or otherwise idealized justification.

What remains now is to describe the principles that would figure and describe the work of the humanities in such a situation. Call them "articles of reason," a set of organizing epistemological practices and beliefs compatible with both the actual practice of humanist scholars and with the generalized, post-Kantian vision of a world in which all relations are affectionate, and therefore the products of human interaction and choice (including interactions with and choices about the nonhuman world, living and nonliving).

Before we get started, however, a couple of questions: Given its ugly history, its allegedly direct oppositional relation to the kinds of thinking that humanists do, and its domination by science, why use the word "reason" at all to accomplish this task? And what could one usefully and legitimately mean by "reason" in the humanities today?

1. WHY REASON? WHICH REASON?

Reason is, simply, a subjective procedure for producing objective, shareable knowledge.

I take the words "subjective" and "objective" from Max Weber's 1904 essay on objectivity in the social sciences. There, Weber is trying to figure out how to address the basic critique, which emerged from the scientific discourse of the time (and which we still know today), that because humanist reasoning seemed to be highly dependent on its individual producer and tightly bound to its analytic objects and contexts, it was necessarily "subjective," and therefore not capable of producing the kinds of truths that the natural sciences produced. (A scientific experiment, for instance, turns out, at least in theory, the same way no matter who does it or when or where they do it, whereas two humanists addressing the "same" question in different places and times, or even in the same place and time, will produce different answers; hence, the humanities are "subjective." QED.) At the same time, Weber was attempting to respond to the work of Wilhelm Windelband's student Heinrich Rickert, who had claimed that although the origins of humanist work were subjective, they aimed finally to express universal, and therefore objective, values. (Rickert would go on, sadly, to argue that the pursuit of allegedly universal values justified, as it did in the Germany of his time, the removal from society, and the murder, of those who stood in the way of that universalism. Sic semper universalists.) Weber, a cultural relativist, wanted to avoid axiological universals, so he needed to separate the question of universal values from the question of scientific research. He was attempting to imagine an objectivity that would be fundamentally social and cultural, an objectivity determined by the actual work and thinking of the human beings occupying social and cultural space.

Weber therefore argued that humanist work (but really all scientific work) was both subjective and objective. The questions historians seek to answer begin subjectively, he claimed, with some kind of interest generated in the present and with things that are culturally significant to them. From the vast selection of possible research questions before them, historians choose ones that reflect some measure of their own historically, technologically, and culturally conditioned interests. "Only a small portion of existing concrete reality is colored by our value-conditioned interest and it alone is significant to us," Weber wrote.[1] We decide what to study based on what matters to us; we cannot "discover what is meaningful to us by means of a 'presuppositionless' investigation of empirical data," and then begin doing research. No laws determine in advance what matters, or ought to matter, to a given group of people. These values and these interests operate in the social prior to the decision to do scientific work, which instantiates each time, therefore, the subjective conditions that make it worth doing for someone specific in a specific historico-cultural moment. The humanist's interest in a topic, rather than making it private and closed off to others, is precisely what "opens the possibility of shareable insights and of connection to shareable experiences." It is this possibility, alongside a connection to larger social issues, that sustains "the value of much historical and theoretical research in the humanities."[2]

The answers that researchers seek once they have determined a field to explore, on the other hand, must in principle be shareable and interpersonally explainable to all members of the human community. "Systematically correct scientific proof in the social sciences, if it is to achieve its purpose," Weber writes, "must be acknowledged as correct even by a Chinese—or—more precisely stated—it must continually *strive* to attain this goal."[3] As an extension of this (and minus the fantasy that the Chinese person is the be-all, end-all of how different someone can be from Max Weber), one might say something like this: Things that are "objective" or "true" are in principle shareable and teachable, and produced by methods that are shareable and teachable, to any other person in the social, in a reasonable amount of time; and that these things are subject to revision on the basis of future evidence, dialogue, and developments in method. That's "objectivity." Part of what this means is that things that are objectively determined to be true are *open* and holdable *in common*, and also changeable in common, even with effort, across the kinds of barriers of culture and language that separate us from one another. It also means that the objective and the true are fundamentally *interpersonal* (and hence, ha ha, subjective to some degree): they are so because the condition for truth is its shareability. I mean that something is "true" and the product of "reason" if and only if both the thing and the method used to determine its truthfulness are shared and dialogic.[4] So you could explain something to me, and have me come to believe it, but over the course of that explanation and understanding, I would be able to explain the same thing back to you in a new way and have *you* come to believe it. Neither of us would end up where we started. We forge the true together. And to do so, to participate in this intertwined social process, we must of course imagine each other and make efforts, as both speakers and listeners, to understand what Weber called the "rationality" of the other, which requires some sense of one's own rationality—some sense of how its procedures and its expression in language will strike another person and be hearable and learnable by them.[5]

In this way, we have a model for how objective knowledge, truth, can emerge from, and be the final goal of, a process that begins with a subjective decision to address a topic, and whose research may well be influenced by that subjectivity along the way. Even if, for instance, you tell me about how you feel about something that has historically happened only once, and only to you—so I have no comparable experiential basis upon which to evaluate your telling—nonetheless you can, using a variety of processes that I can share (including the things we call "description," "evaluation," "logical inference," and "symbolic interpretation"), bring me to a place where I understand what you have experienced and recognize it as objectively true, and, what's more—even though this might be difficult—can bring to your understanding of that event some new perspective or knowledge that will alter your perspective on the nature of your own experience, and therefore alter its truth. And then you can reply to me and alter once again both our perspectives, or generate alternative and potentially undecidable ways of thinking about the event that we recognize, together, to have a degree of potential legitimacy that would have to be included in a full understanding of the truth of the event.

That's reason—or at least a "weak and fallibilistic but non-defeatist conception of reason."[6] For obvious reasons, any such reason, by virtue of being bound to this goal of producing interpersonal objectivity or truth, will be profoundly interested in (1) its own rationality, because understanding oneself is a condition for understanding (and communicating with) the other; and (2) the rationality of others, because understanding others is a condition for understanding (and communicating with) oneself. These others do not have to be just our contemporaries, and not even be people at all: they can be past people, or the records of past people, records of behavior and art and literature and mythological systems and actions and events and so on, all operating not only at the scale of the individual person, but at a myriad of scales above and below it. Reason, knowing that it begins in subjectivity, will test its insights against other forms of subjectivity, against other forms of knowing (living or dead, textual or spoken), to arrive at the most socially compelling version of interpersonal truth.

As will become clear in what follows, I do not believe that this form of reason in common necessarily involves the coparticipation of a set of free, voluntary, and fully rational individuals; this is not an idealized model of the nineteenth-century public sphere. My assumption is that the participants in reason come to that conversation in a wide range of differently embodied forms, and with a wide range of historical experiences, forms of knowledge, and experiences of power and powerlessness, oppression and dominance, ability and disability. Reason as I understand it does not require its participants to shed their identities, become purely "rational" and "unemotional" (as if!), or to abandon their bodies at the door. The participants in *any* conversation will necessarily be different, which does not mean that they cannot be treated equally. The demand of (this version of) reason is that the knowledge and experiences produced by different forms of being-in-the-world can nonetheless be held in common if the participants in the conversation can manage to attend to one another and be open to the possibility of the revision of their "own" knowledge or feelings by others. That adopting this form of generosity and openness, that being vulnerable enough to abandon a belief or admit a mistake, require a certain strength and stability—and that participants in the common will often enter that common with very different levels or forms of access to that strength and stability, thanks to the social conditions that have shaped them—may well mean that some participants in the conversation have an epistemological obligation to work to create that safety and stability for their interlocutors, or else to work harder to dismantle and destabilize the forms of strength and stability that make their own views possible. Whatever reason is in what follows, then, it is a fully anthropological and historical form, embedded in human communities that have *never failed* to know inequality, that have *never failed* to exclude from the world of reason certain kinds of views or people, and that have nonetheless also sometimes succeeded in altering the sphere of reason and the shape of the common in ways that do create the kinds of change that I am describing here.[7]

I would like to suggest to you that this definition of humanist reason-in-action, despite whatever conscious reservations you have about the idea of claiming to say "true" things when you speak or write as a scholar, or any anxiety you have about whether humanist scholarship can be "objective," more or less describes the belief expressed by your work. You think that some things are true; you think that knowing is inevitably structured by forms of power and violence. Nonetheless, you try to say things that are both true and not structured by those things; and sometimes you succeed because other people come to believe that what you have said is true as well. This work is dialogic and interpersonal; it does not take place in your mind alone, but rather within a context of *"intersubjectively shared acts and contexts of meaning."*[8] Saying so openly allows us to get past a major trap of our common-sense thinking about "true" and "objective" (as well as "false" and "subjective," for that matter)—namely, the tendency (1) to believe that the sciences are in fact "true" and "objective" in ways that the humanities are not, a belief widely held and expressed by nonhumanists but in fact not very often by natural scientists; and (2) to respond to the projection of a positivist and stupid notion of scientific reason by rejecting the notion of reason altogether, saying, as we often do, that there is no such thing as truth because all truth amounts to an expression of power, and therefore we as humanists reject the idea of truth-seeking entirely. This seems to me to cede the ground of truth far too easily to one particular ideology of it—and to be an especially bad idea because in fact, most of us do believe that, if we are not saying true things with 100 percent certainty, then, if nothing else, we are at least trying to. If I say that the poetry of Paul Celan means this or that, has this or that effect, reflects this or that thing about the cultural context in which it emerged, or teaches this or that lesson about grieving, I am hoping in each case to make a claim that could be held to be true by others, and aiming to support that claim with methods that can be and are held by others, or, if they are new, that can be explained to others and then held and used by them in ways that will in turn change what I know. This is the humanist theory of truth. We ought to lay claim to it, and recognize and write its long and complex history, which is part of the general history of truth, full stop.

Having said all this, I wish now to lay out the basic principles of the practice of that reason. These are epistemological beliefs that govern contemporary humanist scholarship, derived not from first principles, but from the history of humanist truth-seeking and from the lessons that that seeking has learned from its engagement with the humanist evidence that it has encountered, shaped, and sometimes invented wholesale.

2. THE ARTICLES

ARTICLE 1

All Human Activity Is Context-Embedded, But Not Context-Determined.
This is true at multiple scales. Any historical object or moment, any
social act or feeling, takes place within a series of interlocking contexts, from the immediate and intrapersonal to the transhistorical
and quasi-universal. We are all embodied in our own particular ways,
at the scale of the individual; we are also embodied at larger scales,
including scales of social groupings or populations, and again at
the scale of the species in all its historically specific evolutionary
change, and again at the scale of the universe, whose direction of
time and laws of entropy require living things to organize energy in
order to endure.[9]

Contexts have no total explanatory or causal power. Although
much humanist scholarship aims to demonstrate the embeddedness
of an object in one or more contexts, it also frequently explores the
degree to which that object escapes or differentiates itself from what
one might think of as a pure contextual determinism, from being
merely an epiphenomenon, a supplement, or a superstructure for
some other, actually important system or sequence of events. Because
this escape or differentiation can acquire its significance only against
that background of deterministic normality, humanist scholarship
will necessarily generate (or simply assume) in its intial stages a sense
of determinist, contextual enclosure—or reproduce some normative,
acceptable version of that contextualization—before exploring the
degrees of latitude that such an enclosure affords (or those explored
or expressed by a given object, process, or event). The freedom of the
humanist object or event thus has no meaning without context; freedom itself, however one defines it, will depend on a sense of the affordances of a given socio-historical sphere. Such a theory of a given
sphere can then be explicitly or implicitly contextualized, placed
within a larger context of contexts, which would constitute a general
theory of history against which the possibilities of a given moment
or situation might be measured. One of the main tasks of humanist
reason is to explore the tension between freedom and context, and

thus to understand, as it rubs these patterns together at different scales of experience and being, the full, rich nature of human social experience.

One strong strain of humanist anticontextualism tends to emphasize the object's absolute capacity to transcend its context—whether, for instance, as a matter of total aesthetic relevance, as with the Romantic ideal of the transcendental artwork, or as a matter of radical historical possibility, as with Badiou's theory of the event. Both of these projects, which borrow fully from the historical metadiscourse of humanist reason, nonetheless fall within the practice of humanist reason as I am describing it here. That's because the claims they make are practically and philosophically impossible without recourse to context, since any claim for the radical capacity of a given work or art or event to breach its historical moment requires, quite simply, a strong theory of the set of possibilities of that historical moment. Practically, this means that the meaning of radical freedom cannot be gotten at, cannot be described within the history of humanist practice, without some historical description of the context from which it emerges. Radical freedom is thus itself contextualized by a strong theory of historical context, for which it serves (in someone like Badiou) as a total ontological limit. But the idea of radical possibility does not require the kind of quasi-ontological foundation that Badiou gives it.

If I believe, as humanists do, that all historical moments contain the possibility of being "surprised" by some occurrence, all I have to do in order to move that surprise "inside" the historical context is to make a general claim about the nature of human and social history: namely, that it constitutes a system so rich and complex, whose causal structures are themselves subject to such complex and figural modes of transformation, that it will almost certainly *always* include the possibility of genuine surprise.[10] The surprise, the possibility of some event or activity that has not been anticipated in advance by the social normativity into which it emerges, is baked into the nature of the human experience of the historical; it is a matter of the actually existing context of human life. The evidence for such a claim includes all of actual human history until now, which is full of surprises. (But also full of essentially predictable activity; the evidence suggests again and again that "surprise" relates to "context"; the relation between the two fields is socially determined within a larger "context," which would itself be subject to all kinds of "surprise.")

Here we see once again how the desire to resist a strong positivist claim about the nature of history—that everything is predictable if we just know enough, or that full social control can be achieved if we just have the right institutional and epistemological levers—leads a certain strain of humanist thought into an idealized theorization of freedom. As I've been suggesting, such a solution to the determinism problem cedes the name of reason too much to the positivist caricature. By responding to positivism in ethical terms, it essentially reifies the humanities/science distinction as one between ethics and reason rather than contesting the terms of rationality itself.

Against, then, a metadiscourse that insists on sharp distinctions between historical determination, on the one hand, and absolute freedom, on the other, humanist reason in practice mediates consistently between these two poles. At its least interesting, this mediating has the unconscious effect of producing facile criticism of other people's work—the kind of easy jab you see at Q&As for not emphasizing either the determining factors or the liberated ones in the analysis of a given situation. At its best—which is most of the time—this approach to an object, whether it seeks to interpret or explain it, will adopt a rich understanding of the sociohistorical situation and its various limits and affordances at multiple interpenetrating scales, each of which can be itself contextualized in relation to the others, and which accordingly can be the subject of further macro- or micro-contextualization. Understanding one's own position in relation to this problem, and grasping the ways in which a specific approach (especially when conventional, according to disciplinary norms) will affect one's sense of the meaning of an action/object or the possibilities of a situation, constitute a central feature of the self-reflexivity of humanist reason, which is why humanist scholarship so often—and especially in introductions—meditates openly on such questions.

That such meditation can never cease—that there can be no definitive resolution of the relation between context and action (a totally determined context would have no action at all)—is not, humanist reason believes, a function of our contemporary lack of knowledge, and therefore a problem to be resolved by some future predictive system of history (the fantasy of Asimov's *Foundation* series), but rather a function of the contextual embeddedness of that relation itself, the degree to which the very relation between action and context depends on a series of socio-historical and environmental forces, operating at scales from the viral to the individual to the planetary, that condition it and create, for any given moment, the conditions for understanding and explaining it.[11] Again, and to be plain about it: humanist reason can believe this not on the grounds that it would be "bad" or "unfree" for anyone not to, but because the analysis of the existing historical evidence suggests that to believe otherwise would be unreasonable, and because it is epistemologically "productive to wonder at the realization of what seemed virtually impossible at the time and cannot be reduced, even in retrospect, to the conditions that prepared it."[12]

This theory of the relation between context and action manifests itself in one largely unconscious but important consideration for humanist reason: the role played by historical events that did not take place. This consideration can be expressed as a strong ontological claim—something like "the nature of a historical moment includes its non-actualized possibilities"—but it can also be thought of as an epistemological principle: *understanding social activity requires a complex understanding of nonactualized possibility in it.* From this perspective, one can conclude that any historical moment (and any historical context) necessarily include as part of their momentaneity not only the explicitly articulated and lived degrees of freedom that were actually expressed by the people living at that time, but also the various degrees of affordance or possibility that were themselves never used at all, that never took place or came true. The actual historical future of any given context is not, then, its only determining factor. A full understanding of history must include the various what-ifs and if-onlys that never occurred, whose possibility actively orients our understanding of what did in fact take place at all.

Such a claim applies both to historical events and to the entire world of made objects and aesthetic activities. Any object means what it does (and acts in the social in the way it does) as a result not only of the entire world of actually existing objects that surround it and determine it in its material immediacy, but also in relation to all the objects that could exist, or could have existed, in that same context, and remained unwritten, unpainted, or unmade. A reading of Virginia Woolf's *Jacob's Room* makes sense only against an extrapolated imaginary of what it would have been like had she written a third novel that was formally identical to *The Voyage Out;* an understanding of the historical impact of the Mughal Empire on the Indian subcontinent can be arrived at only via some sense of what might have happened had Babur not managed to defeat Ibrahim Lodi in 1526, and the empire never consolidated itself at all.

This extension of epistemological concern to the realm of the nonactual (but nonetheless historically potentially present) does not appear as a single unstriated or unending field of possibility. "What if an asteroid had exploded the moon?" is an interesting question for historians of the solar system, but not for scholars working on the history of the *ancien régime*. In other words, the set of unchosen possibilities or untaken paths that determine the full potential of a given historical situation—that are relevant epistemologically to our understanding or explanation of it—is itself contextual. The limits of that contextualization can be discovered, or put into place, only by ongoing, self-reflexive acts of humanist reason, which in so doing generate en passant the conditions of their own legitimacy, as well as the subtending theoretical grounds of their reasoning work.

A final consequence of the general belief that all human social activity is context-embedded involves the production of knowledge itself. The feminist critique of Cartesian dualism attacked the claims that (1) the mind could act separately from its embodiment, and (2) that therefore only mind-based knowledge, freed from the trappings of its social and environmental conditions, could be truly universal. No—in fact, as any number of critics showed, mind never separates from body; and the putative universalism of the disembodied mind-concept usually turns out to be a screen for the blank and erased body (neutral, white, male) that organizes the system of knowledge from which it disapparates.

All knowledge is embodied. The claim—which amounts to a step forward in the recognition of context-embeddedness—can lead, in some hands, to purified relativism: if all knowledge-production is context- or body-bound, then no knowledge can be truly common, since it will forever be tied to the conditions of its own making. But the feminist critique, with its emphasis on embodiment, performativity, and action, did not intend to give up on the possibility of knowledge. We know that that's true because the feminists of that generation in fact believed, and knew, lots of things, and attempted again and again to say things that were true. The argument was not "All knowledge is embodied; therefore, no such things as knowledge or reason exist," but rather, " Against the claim that real knowledge emerges exclusively from disembodied minds, we assert that knowledge that emerges from bodies (and particular places, times, feelings, and other forms of subjective experience) not only *can* constitute knowledge shared in common, not only *can* be the subject of shared reasoning, but that indeed it *should*, and that any system of knowledge that does not include it amounts to a bare reproduction of patriarchal normativity." The *can* portion of this set of claims is definitively proved by the historical evidence of the last decades of humanist knowledge-production. That humanist reasoners have not fully grappled with its implications, that they remain to some extent intimidated by the fantasy of mastery implied in the theory of disembodied knowing, and that they so often reproduce it in their work and their classrooms, result both from the continued general dominance of the scientific-Cartesian imaginary and from the pressures of a certain strongly relativist humanist metadiscourse, which misrepresents, for all the reasons I've speculated on so far, the actual activity of humanist work.

ARTICLE 2

Human Life Does Not Follow Disciplinary Boundaries; Neither Does Scholarship.   The evidence for: there is absolutely no way to either teach or write in the humanities today without drawing from a variety of institutionalized disciplines: minimally anthropology, literary criticism, art history, linguistics, political, social, and economic history, history of science, philosophy, sociology, and psychology, not to mention knowledge developed in those fields primarily organized around topics—namely, ethnic studies, women's, gender, or sexuality studies, and area studies programs of various kinds, or the vast conceptual fields organized before the modern era, for which other terms (like "natural philosophy," "rhetoric," or non-European concepts like *wenxue*) are necessary. To be a serious scholar in any of these fields requires some knowledge of all of them. To teach a class in any of these fields requires, likewise, some occasional reference to the other disciplines, if not actual reading material from them.

Why, if this is so, do humanists in teaching and research institutions so consistently organize themselves into disciplines? Any response to this question would have to account for the reward structures produced for both individuals and the disciplines with which they identify by their bureaucratic systematization. This systematization provides, among other things, for the justification of tenure lines, the creation of disciplinary organizations like the MLA or the AHA, journals, conferences, and so on—the entire institutional apparatus of the disciplines, whose norms create realms of protection around specific topics or methods by guaranteeing that judgment about scholarly validity comes only from a group of self-chosen insiders, who can among other things be counted on to have the interests of the discipline at heart. At its worst, this produces the kind of policing behavior in which conservative scholars tell innovative ones that what they are doing "is not real history" (or whatever)—a reaction feminist scholars or ones focused on oppressed populations know all too well. At its best, such a procedure guarantees a certain disciplinary space of safety and freedom, a space whose protection can shepherd entire new fields into being (think in this context of the important roles played by programs, and then departments, of women's or gender studies, Latina/o/x studies, African American studies, Native American studies, Asian American studies, science studies, and so on).

The justification for humanist disciplinarity is, then, almost entirely institutional: we have disciplines to protect and reify practices of humanist reason, to create institutional space for the necessary work of humanist thought, and to produce, within the institution, the room for a variety of methodological approaches to the basic questions of human social life. In this way, we might think of disciplines as a kind of ecological necessity—as spaces designed to create epistemological biomes in which different kinds of thinking can flourish and compete, wane and grow.

Epistemologically, the danger is that the biomes become too separate, that the methods that succeed in one biome do not get countered or challenged by the evidence or methods developed in another. When that happens, the residents of one biome come to believe that they "know" what their topic is, and that only knowledge produced within the framework of their discipline can legitimately challenge it. But who among literary scholars believes that historians have an epistemological monopoly on the idea or practice of historical scholarship, or that sociologists have a monopoly on concepts that explain social life? And if literary scholars believe that, then they must also believe that they themselves have no monopoly on understanding or explaining literature; that their training in literature, though it reveals a great deal, may also obscure or ignore other ways of thinking; and therefore that the historians and sociologists may well have insights that could teach the literary folks a thing or two. Even if saying so makes you (my literary reader) feel a bit anxious, I want to suggest to you that the entire field of literary scholarship (you included) already believes this since its methodological history includes borrowing from all the other humanistic fields, including of course history and sociology, which have helped literary scholars develop better theories of their own methods and critical work.

At its simplest, the epistemological justification for interdisciplinarity is this: human life maintains no strict separations among the fields of activity whose differences define the humanist disciplines. Art does not exist in a realm wholly separate from that of literature, or of philosophy, nor does the social realm distinguish itself absolutely from the anthropological or psychological one; and none of the fields in the first group operate outside of the procedures studied by the disciplines in the second ones, which are constituted in turn by the very practices that define the ones in the first group. At some level, of course, the fields can remain separate, just as one can think of a history of painting that operates to some extent independently from the history of sculpture. But that "to some extent" is always only partial because the general social field does not know strong ontological divisions among its categories. Everything interacts. We know this about the social because we can, using the tools of humanist reason, prove it.

It would be a mistake to imagine that seeing things this way requires deriving the epistemology of humanist reason once again from the nature of its object: because human life does not and cannot separate these fields, therefore humanist reason, which studies human life, does not and cannot separate these fields either. One can just as easily derive the object from the method: humanist reason is a way of thinking that uses a variety of epistemological and evidentiary practices to see connections across existing social boundaries; in this way, it produces a model of the social as interconnected. There is no primacy here. But the model of the social as interconnected is reasonable, in the sense that it can be the product of shared methods and shared conclusions, all of which are self-reflexively modifiable in common. It is also realistic, not insofar as it responds to something that is actually or really there (beyond some human capacity to interact with or constitute it), but because it provides a potential ground for pragmatic decisions about how to interact with the social in ways that can be socially (and personally and politically) effective.

ARTICLE 3

All Social Processes and Artifacts Result from Combinations of Primary and Secondary Causes and Contain Primary and Secondary Information. The primary/secondary distinction dates back at least to Aristotle, who distinguishes between intentional and unintentional aspects of social artifacts. A marble statue has a shape and a weight; so does a piece of marble placed on a scale at the market. In the first case, the shape is primary, the weight secondary; in the second, it's the other way around. No one cares what the marble on the scale looks like, so long as it weighs 100 drachmae, and no one cares what the marble statue weighs, so long as it looks good.

The humanist interpretation of culture recognizes the primary/secondary, intentional/unintentional division at every level of the social, seeing it as an effect of the organization of human systems and the degree to which objects and practices operate within limited fields of active, conscious awareness. This is as true for artifacts—think of the way the shards of an Etruscan vase might teach us, by virtue of their chemical composition, about the kinds of ceramic and fire-making technologies the Etruscans possessed—as it is for processes. The hiring practices of a large corporation may not *intentionally* enact structural racism while nonetheless very much doing so. The act of cutting in line may express and participate in either the sustaining or the violation of a cultural norm without, for all that, being intention-ally directed toward that sustenance or violation. A full understand-ing of any of these objects requires attending to the many primary and secondary forces embedded and reified in them, and requires grasping the specific relations among those forces. Something like the critique of structural sexism or racism depends, for instance, almost entirely on this kind of thinking: against a purely intentional-ist theory of human activity, such a critique aims to reveal racism or sexism as a secondary effect of social processes that may well seem (or be) intentionally nonsexist or nonracist, and in so doing, make the social field as a whole responsible for recognizing those effects. Indeed one might say that systems of oppression depend in general both on the unconscious normalization of primary processes that have pernicious secondary effects (this is, in effect, ideology) and on the deliberate masking of pernicious effects as secondary (and there-fore uncontrollable) consequences of perfectly reasonable primary goals (as in, for instance, the development of seemingly neutral rules for the provision of social services whose ultimate consequences are to deny those services to members of certain groups, a practice known in the United States as "redlining").

Another place to witness the active use of the primary/second-ary distinction comes in the interpretive procedure known as "close reading." In contrast to the hermeneutics associated with the inter-pretation of holy texts, in which the effort is to radically determine the primary intention of the text—to create through the work of reading an object for which there is, in effect, no secondary informa-tion at all, but only primary or true meaning on the one hand, and illegitimate or blasphemous meaning on the other—secular herme-neutics almost always moves beyond the primary or intentional level of the source text in order to determine what the reading effort con-ceives of as its "full" semiotic field of production. I am not sure what

Cleanth Brooks thought John Keats thought of the urn poem, but the reading Brooks performs in no way requires, for its intelligibility, the idea that Keats intended everything Brooks sees; what's more, such a demand would be effectively impossible since Keats could not know everything Brooks knows, including, for instance, the history of poetry after Keats. The New Critical emphasis on the work of the "text" rather than on the author is a kind of theoretical expression of this mode of reasoning; the meaning and social force of a textual object do not depend on the intentions in it, but rather on the total activity produced by the interactions between its various processes of possible meaning—figural, literal, symbolic, structural, patterned, aural, visual, narrative, grammatical, and so on—none of which need be under the full intentional control of an original author. The same basic principles govern the humanist interpretations of social processes and historical events.

Any number of theoretical models exist to subtend the basic belief in the epistemological distinction between intentional and unintentional cultural and historical activity. These include the various theories of ideology, which explain the various large-scale mediatic (fake news), architectural (the classroom), interpersonal (the Althusserian appeal), professional (the vocation), or institutional nongovernmental (the church) or governmental (the law) processes that modify what one might think of as the very structure of intention itself, revealing it, in some cases, to be essentially secondary and unintentional in the Aristotelian sense. This goes as well for psychological theories of the unconscious, which describe a level we conceive as being "below" the self, and for sociological or anthropological theories of culture, which describe a level we conceive as being "above" the self. They also go, though more tendentiously, for claims one might make about evolutionary or ecological processes, both those that drive the specific development of the human species and those operating "below" (in the realm of viruses and the like) and "above" (in the various Ecocenes) the specific scales of human life and human culture. All of these amount to forms of secondary, unintentional activity that can and must be included in any understanding or interpretation of human social life, whether that interpretation be focused on matters historical, aesthetic, sociological, or philosophical, all of which must be understood contextually in terms of the actually existing sense that the human actors under consideration have of their own intentional motivations, without which the secondary levels would have nothing to act on, and therefore no significance.

In each of these theories of secondary activity, the very distinctiveness of the primary-secondary division is itself at stake, either in the mode of total confusion, as in the psychoanalytic reading of a behavior that feels in every way intentional but is also, at some other level, the unstoppable repetition of an earlier trauma, or in the mode of radical reversal, as when one or another theorist of ideology comes to argue that we do not so much perform individuality as individuality performs us—that in effect our sense of intentionality is in fact the secondary product of a system designed to produce efficient social subjects. (This is essentially the plot of *The Matrix*.) Every investigation of these kinds of distinctions thus contributes to a broader history of the primary-secondary relation, as well as to an extensive humanist metadiscourse on the subject. In keeping with the general practices of humanist self-reflexivity, the theories born of that metadiscourse will inevitably be measured against a variety of actually existing instances, whose understanding will be modified by that theory even as they also potentially modify the theory in turn.

The complexity of this humanist metadiscourse is not socially unique. Humanist reasoners are not the only people to recognize the primary/secondary distinction even if, like everyone else, we live most of our lives imagining that what we are doing is essentially intentional, while other people are motivated by ideology, or their controlling father, or whatever else. The distinction between primary and secondary is instead adjudicated on a quotidian basis at nearly every level of culture, including perhaps most obviously that of the idea of social control, whether such control is a matter of "the government telling you what to do"; some theory of historical cyclicality or the ages of humankind; kismet, fate, karma, or some other quasi-theological process; or simply some idea of "personality" as a determining factor in an individual person's choices at any given juncture. Even a word like "coincidence" exists in part as a function of the primary/secondary distinction: its social purpose is to assert that some event does not in fact have some more fundamental and primary "intention" behind it, but rather is the product—like the weight of the marble in the statue—of an essentially unintentional historical process, to which no significant hermeneutic or social attention need be paid. (One might think of paranoia, in this context, as an epistemological mode that aims to collapse all meaning into primary intentionality; you think that X is meaningless, but if you understand the true nature of reality, you will discover that X is full of secret meaning! Also: everything is X!!!)

The primary/secondary distinction as made in humanist reason corresponds, then, with a more general process of the organization of social life, in which knowing what is primary and what is secondary helps one figure out what to do and how to get by, and how to interpret objects, sentences, actions, and so on. The operations of primary and secondary meaning depend on an accurate apprehension of the context of the event, social process, or object under consideration. Knowing whether the piece of marble was made to serve in a temple or at the market square, having some broader sense of the general sphere of cultural production, the relative cost of marble and the labor to carve it, the social function and shape of other statues or weights, and so on—all of these are critical to a general projection onto the object of its primary and secondary features, not only for the cultural historian of the marble's future, but also for the actually existing visitor to the market where it is being used. Within certain specialized social realms, like that of the aesthetic, we may also confront the deliberate confusion of primary and secondary meaning, the using of this distinction in aesthetic production, and therefore the motivation of that feature of sociocultural activity in the work of art—as might happen if, for instance, someone made a statue of Margaret Thatcher out of material that weighed, once sculpted, exactly the same as Margaret Thatcher did.

Such work serves to remind us that all the cultural processes that humanist reason uses are themselves potential subjects of both primary and secondary, intentional and unintentional, and cultural practice, and that all these processes belong, therefore, differentially to primary and secondary levels of the cultural context under examination. This is as true for the marble statue of Thatcher as it is of the sly politesse of those colonial subjects described by Homi

Bhabha, whose civility functioned as primary, and intentional, for one audience, and as unintentional—here in the sense of forced or demanded—for another, even if that second audience was sometimes only the self.

ARTICLE 4

Human Social Life Is Not Flat; Scales Are Complex, Overlapping, and Porous.   The rise to prominence of computational analysis in literary studies in the last two decades, often under the general heading of digital humanities, has produced an extensive humanist metadiscourse around the idea of scale, as a discipline associated most prominently with the epistemo-ethically conceived practice of close reading has attempted to fight off a challenge posed to that practice on an epistemological level by the large-scale computational analysis of texts. Much of this debate, which begins around Franco Moretti's provocative coinage of the term "distant reading" in 2001, falls into patterns that resemble in every way the debates between the positivist and antipositivist humanists of the German *Methodenstreit*: on one side the protectors of sacred objects and ethical relationality to the other, defenders of the unique and the free, and on the other the imposers of hierarchy and subordination, the erasers of human difference, the totalizers and dominators. Alongside these essentially ethical claims come a series of more explicitly epistemological ones, which amount to the computational side asserting, on the basis of its scholarly research, that the work it does tells us something interesting about literature, and the anticomputational side asserting, in response, that such analysis only confirms, albeit in a different language, stuff that everyone already knows.

As Ted Underwood has argued, the specific use of computational methods or statistical analysis seems less characteristic of these recent critical shifts than a more general move toward large-scale, syncretic approaches, one frequently accompanied by critiques of the historical dominance of close reading and of the effects of close reading on the kinds of questions one could possibly ask about literature.[13] An epistemological defense of that set of ways of thinking would not have to defend (or even mention) computation at all, but rather could focus on the historical tradition of work that would include the midcentury structuralism of either the French (Claude Lévi-Strauss) or American (Talcott Parsons) type, or the kinds of thinking about literature done by Northrop Frye or Erich Auerbach, or indeed anyone who has ever made claims about the general history of the novel, or again the *longue durée* historicism of the Annales school, and so on. But even such a defense would have to contend with the fact that many of the forms of analysis one thinks of as involving heavy emphasis on uniqueness or particularity—close or psychoanalytic or deconstructive reading in literary studies, microhistory or microsociology, the ethnography or the case study—do not simply abandon the larger scale in favor of a kind of raw description, but rather arrive at exceedingly large-scale claims through what one might think of as, recalling Kant, a form of reflecting judgment that moves from the case to the general lesson, the single poem to the philosophical insight, the cheese and the worm to the entire life-world of early modern Italy, all of these local variations on the great adventure that leads from the particular to the universal. What we appear to be dealing with, then, is not a battle between one side that favors large-scale analysis and another that doesn't, but rather a battle between two (or more) methods that balance the relations among evidence, generalization, particularization, and exemplification in different ways. A full description of close reading or structuralism as a method would have to begin with serious observation of the patterns and structures of the active work of truth-production in a representative sample of the evidence (scholarship widely recognized to be doing close reading, for instance) in order to begin to make general claims about the kinds of scalar relationships that such a practice typically uses, and the patterns that govern its holding steady of certain categories at certain scales and not others.

What follows thus develops a theory of humanist scale designed to escape the caricatures of the idiography/nomothetism division on which so much humanist metadiscourse has rested since the *Methodenstreit*. To do so, I focus on a series of arguments about scale that take place in the discipline of human geography, a sociological field where the conversation about scale has been going on for several decades, and in which it has achieved something of a full poststructuralist (or even post-poststructuralist) expression. That this expression resolves none of the fundamental philosophical problems we have seen in our analysis of Kant—that it in fact mostly reproduces them, as it drives asymptotically to nominalism—suggests how much the epistemological metadiscourse of the humanities has to gain by thinking its way out of the Windelbandian inheritance, away from some of the forms of casual poststructuralism that subtend it in contemporary academic life. The exposition of those forms, as well as the tracking of a path forward, require a level of attention and citation that mean that the next pages resemble—more than those of the other articles—the style (and length) of a more traditional and less encomial piece of scholarship.

* * *

A beginner's discussion of scale in human geography launches us immediately into a domain of interest, and trouble. I quote from an entry on "scale" written by D. R. Montello in the 2001 *International Encyclopedia of the Social and Behavioral Sciences*. In a lucid exposition, the entry differentiates between "analytic" scale, the scale at which something might be described, and "phenomenon" scale, which refers "to the size at which human or physical earth structures or processes exist, regardless of how they are studied or represented." "Numerous concepts in geography," reads the text, "reflect the idea that phenomena are scale-dependent or are described in part by their scale."[14]

Although phenomenon scale is from this point of view a property of an object, although it is independent—insofar as anything can be—from the scholar who describes it, and thus exists "regardless of how" the object is "studied or represented," Montello nonetheless notes that it is widely agreed that "the scale of analysis must match the actual scale of the phenomenon." Scale in this way is a property of an object that produces an epistemological demand on the observer; good observation will entail observing scale and then adjusting one's observational tools to match the scale at which the object "takes place." "Identifying the correct scale of phenomena is" thus, Montello writes, "a central problem for geographers."

The delightful qualities of this last sentence stem from the combination of its nearly obvious correctness and how deeply it puts the reader epistemologically in the shit. If you think that objects *exist* at a certain scale, and you believe that your heuristic tools must be appropriate to that scale, then it makes a whole lot of sense to start by figuring out at what scale something actually *takes place*. But you can't figure out at what scale it takes place unless you are using some kind of tool . . . which ought to be appropriate to the scale, which you don't know.

Of course, it will turn out, first, that there can be plenty of argument about the actual scale of a geographical object or process (and thus the methods appropriate to it); and second, that most objects—the family, for instance—that might be said to exist and to operate at certain scales of social or spatiotemporal activity, that in fact might be scales of their own, turn out to be analyzable at an epistemologically gregarious variety of smaller and larger scales (the individual person; the neighborhood). This would seem, then, to suggest that some if not all phenomena operate at more than one scale at the same time, at which point "identifying the correct scale of phenomena" becomes a pretty tricky problem. All this happens well before you stumble across the tried-and-true Kantian objection that we cannot know the phenomena prior to the heuristic in any case. At that point, we might as well conclude that the objects of our analysis are as much the products of our methods as the putative sources of them.

This kind of metareflection on the processes of cognition forms part of the self-reflexive epistemological toolkit of humanist reason today. How do you know that some aspect of your observation is not influencing what you observe? The problem is intractable at every level, although it seems easier at the individual level than at the cultural one;[15] at the far end, the influences of society or the observer's position within it, its era and its relation to other eras, and the capacities and predilections of its species-type bind the observing-machine (human or otherwise) to its various observations—a binding whose first-order good is to decide (or rather to make it seem to be decided in advance) what it means for something to be deemed observable at all. In short, people fit objects in the world to the shape of the tools in their toolbox.

None of this means that the objects of the humanities or the social sciences are just figments of their methods, mere projections of the subjective position of their observers. But it does mean that no heuristic concept (or the method to which it is attached) can achieve the seemingly full-blown ontological separation from its objects that counts as one of the major triumphs of the natural scientific process. Wrongly! Humanists cede the ground too easily, as for example when they refer to race as a "social fact" in order to emphasize its material and historical force, despite the fact that it has no genetic basis. Implicitly, then, the genetic fact is simply a real fact, a factual fact, a fact whose facticity need not be managed with an adjective. To speak this way is to promulgate a theory of facticity that significantly disadvantages the claim of the humanities to relevance. Perfectly understandable, in these scientific times, but: not true.

The inability to separate the heuristic from its object may well feel—especially when one imagines those epistemologically satisfied scientists over there in the fancy new campus building—like a lack, or a loss. It isn't, really, if you consider that we never had the certainty in the first place. The feeling of nostalgia or loss for something that one has never had, a kind of psychic retrojection that organizes both the wound and its potential healing, is for me one of the major lived forms of the experience of Lacanian lack. That same pivot, in which something imagined or thrown forward, *vorgestellt*, standing in front of us as a possible solution to our ills, invents an original plenitude, "*nachgestellt*," set behind us, in the putatively lost or abandoned past, is one of the major mechanisms behind tragic theories of modernity or humanity more broadly; it is the droning echo of the third chapter of Genesis (which is itself an echo of an earlier drone). The fact is that concepts operate always *inside* the conversation that they are also *about*; objects always are *about* the conversation that they appear to be *inside*. Humanist reason can have no metaphysics of method.

Though we all "know" this, concepts will tend with time (as anyone who has used one knows) to become metaphysical, hardening their objects into ideas that, like Platonic forms, seem prior to the things they describe. This idealizing or generalizing detachment from an original set of generating objects is in fact what we mean by the concept of "concept" in the first place; "concept" is an ingathering (from *con-*, together, and *-capere*, to take) that is also a kind of withdrawal from the material with which it begins.

So also with scale, a concept whose splitting into the categories of "phenomenon" and "analysis" attempts to manage *internally*, inside the concept itself, the distance between the thing and its conceptualization by attributing to both concept and thing the property of having a scale. Scale in its practice in humanist reason is thus both a concept and a metaconcept, insofar as it represents to us not only a theory of objects and a theory analyses, but an argument for the relation *between* objects and analyses, grounded in the claim that they both "have" scale. To conceptualize via scale is thus to embark on a kind of interpretive work that begins from the idea that "the scale of analysis must"—or more minimally, that it *can*—"match the actual scale of the phenomenon."

Is the scale in the object or in the analysis? What kinds of ontological claims does the assertion that things happen "at" a scale make about the nature of things? A 1992 essay by Neil Smith, a near-classic in the field, presents a "schematic and exploratory" discussion of a sequence of scales—body, home, community, urban, region, nation, and global—that describes the ways scale produces and is produced by social effects.[16] Scale "*contains* social activity," Smith writes, "and at the same time provides an already partitioned geography within which social activity *takes* place."[17] Scale does not rise above the social activity that it produces; it is rather a ground for social activity, an active reflector of and site for contestation over social power and social control. A given social scale—that of the body, the family, or the city—is thus the temporarily fixed *expression* of political and social work, as well as the frame into which social and political work will tend to flow.

Smith's decision to see scale as an operative force in the production of social space—to recognize, that is, a concept like the nation as having scalar properties similar to those of, say, the body or the globe—resolves the ontology/method question by grounding the method firmly in the phenomenon. For Smith, "scale" describes the ways in

which social force (personal or impersonal, from above or below) organizes social space into "nested" units that contain and manage social
activity in both institutional terms (as when a city government reports
to a regional government) and cognitive ones.[18] Actors can combat the
ideological fixities of scale by "scale jumping," Smith argues, which
alters their appeals or frames of action to reframe disputes or rescale
spatial concepts that govern common sense.

Smith's essay was careful, already in 1992, not to reify scales, not to
turn them into fixed or transhisorical features of human social life.
"The point is precisely not," Smith writes, "to 'freeze' a set of scales as
building blocks of a spatialized politics, but to understand the social
means and political purposes through and for which such freezing of
scales is nonetheless accomplished—albeit fleetingly" (66). No scale,
therefore, is a mandatory expression of human social life; nor is any
single scale, or system of scales, socially permanent or immutable.
Scale is instead "actively produced" in the social (67), and, as the idea
of jumping scales suggests, movement between scales tends to simply involve local increases in the *degree* of friction between two recognized social orders, and not a significant shift in *kind* between two
ontologically incompatible worlds. In this sense, scale bears little
philosophical resemblance, despite the language of "nesting" and
even "hierarchy," to the fixed and ontologically separate concentric
circles of the Ptolemaic universe.

At least theoretically. Practically, however, it turns out that the use
of scalar analysis as a method in geography will tend, just as the social
does, to reify and fix social reality at a variety of normalized scales,
thus reproducing the problem of scalar ideologies of control at the
level of critical method itself. If, for instance, you describe the action
of a community organization as a function of its integration into a
higher system of boroughs or neighborhoods, you will potentially
naturalize the former as the ontological or political subsidiary of the
latter, as an epiphenomenon rather than a lever of genuine political
force. As a result, a system of scalar analysis designed to emphasize
the articulation and frangibility of the social can rapidly take on a
functionalist, deterministic mien, as its categories of analysis harden
into their Platonic near-equivalents and its hierarchies freeze into
images of the way things must always be.

In response to this inevitable process, in which the invention of a powerful new tool of analysis is followed by a subsequent awareness of its normalizing reification, the last several decades have seen a variety of attempts to adjust the terminologies associated with scale, to remake it, or, more recently, to get rid of the concept entirely. These critiques have tended to accuse Smith of having failed, despite his caveats, to fully extricate his work from the problems of conceptual reification. Adam Moore, for instance, writes that "scales in Smith's theoretical framework continue to be treated as discrete, hierarchically spatial levels—concrete 'platforms' of space around which daily life and political action are organized—and these very material and real scales serve as the central 'metric of geographical differentiation.' "[19] When "material and real" scales become abstracted into an "analytic framework," Moore argues, they cease to describe the real, and instead begin to "exist apart from" the processes they actually attempt to describe.

Critiques like Moore's proceed along a number of connected lines. Beginning often with Smith, they move quickly to address a number of bad habits in the widespread use of scale by geographers. Some writers, they show, collapse all scales into local-global binaries; others, including Smith, tend to imagine scales at "higher" levels (the global, for instance) as *causes* of activity at the "lower" ones (e.g., globalization makes a local grocery store close, but the store closing does not make globalization); still others make scale too abstract, theoretical, or reified to account for real-world political engagement and activity. By the early 2000s, some critics begin (like Moore) to reject the idea that scales are necessarily (or ever) hierarchical or nested; others argue that scale needs to reach beyond the political and economic to ecological or affective regimes. Others, drawing on the work of Manuel Castells or Bruno Latour, present alternatives involving "flow" or "network" models that emphasize travel across and over the entities formerly known as scales—reduced, in such conceptions, to speed bumps in a generally fluid and frictionless social sphere.

Seen from the outside, these critiques respond to intellectual shifts larger than the discipline of geography alone. They belong to the longstanding metadiscursive tradition of Windelbandian idiographism, with all its suspicion of positivism and subordination in

science. More immediately, they correspond to the broader integration of the poststructuralist critique of structuralism into the
humanities and social sciences, whose criticism of top-down, hierarchical thinking itself belongs to the longer idiographic tradition.[20]
And here, lest one miss the forest for the trees, it is important to recognize that the impact of poststructuralist thought depends, at this
late date, not on the influence of any single thinker or text, but rather
on the generalized acceptance (among a certain crowd, to be sure)
of a number of tropes of poststructuralist influence. Such figures
constitute the variety of subtheoretical or subconceptual habits and
preferences that alter the way scholars think, write, and talk about
their work. They operate in a number of linked critical modes, most
of which echo Windelbandian themes:

1. An intense distrust of typology and pattern analysis, especially in
   its synchronic, fixative varieties, which one sees in the preference
   (via Giddens in sociology, for example) for a term like "structuration" over "structure."

2. An emphasis on the irreducible, idiographic quality of the singular instance or example, perhaps best emblematized in literature
   by the continued dominance of close reading, but more generally
   in the preference for evidence drawn from lived experience, everyday life, anecdotes, or, at largest, a single "case."

3. A preference for plural concepts over singular ones, for the multi-
   plication of concepts across horizontal fields of differences, seen
   in the drive to theorize multiple modernisms or modernities, to
   posit transnationalisms, or the existence of many Asias, Africas,
   Americas, and so on. "There was not just one X; there were many
   Xs" is a thesis sentence that has launched thousands of humanist
   projects.

4. A distrust of "vertical" patterns of causality (and therefore of
   subordination), and an emphasis on the epistemological power
   of the "ground" or the "bottom-up," conceived as that which can
   uniquely escape the organizing logics of dominance, whether in
   language or in sociopolitical activity.

5. An investment in complexity over simplicity, especially forms of
   complexity that demonstrate difference inside fields of similarity,

and thus serve to destabilize normative categories of whatever kind. As a first sentence in a response to a talk at MLA or AHA, "I actually think it's more complicated than that," will produce instant nodding among the other people in the room, even though they do not yet know what kind of complexity you're about to talk about. The belief in complexity is visceral.

6. A strong preference for transactionality across what otherwise might be thought of as separate levels (vertical) or realms (horizontal) of the social field, visible for instance in the transnational turn in literary studies (for which "nation" serves as the derided, deconstructed term), or in queer theory ("gender," "sex," "male," "female," "normal," and so on).[21]

Together, these overlapping positions amount to a set of epistemological habits or preferences that dominate the contemporary meta-discourse of humanist reason. I'll call them, for short, by their modes of preference: (1) diachrony, (2) idiography, (3) plurality, (4) experience, (5) complexity, and (6) transactionality. These tropes appear both in what one might think of as the foreground of academic work that argues about scholarship, where they do explicit battle against the nomothetic, the totalizing, or the structural. But they also operate as a kind of background noise, serving as grounds for preference in book or conference titles, as patterns belonging to a general humanistic rhetoric of truth and seriousness; and most important, as unstated warrants for epistemological claims about the nature of valid concepts, or, for that matter, of reality.

It is both as background and as foreground that they sustain the critique of scale in geography. Look at the conclusion of a Richard Howitt essay on scale, where a general review of the history of the concept is coming down, in the final lines, to a series of explicit criticisms and prescriptions whose metaphorical and conceptual wardrobe I have placed in italics:

"Scale" is rendered most meaningful in its development as an *empirical generalization*—a concept made real by *building up* an understanding of complex and dynamic relationships and processes *in context*. As a theoretical abstraction the risk is that "scale" is reduced to a set of *meaningless labels* that say something about size and complexity, but which hide precisely the *terrain* with which critical geopolitics is most interested—the terrain of *real landscapes* in which spaces of engagement offer a *myriad* of transformational opportunities at a *myriad* of scales. What is paradoxical, perhaps, is not the nature of scale, but geographers' efforts to theorize scale in some way that *divorces itself from its geographical context*. If the role of our theory is to better equip us for *our situated engagement* in struggles for justice, sustainability, and transformation, then theory *divorced* from scaled landscapes of change is probably of limited value.[22]

Howitt's conclusion pulls together a number of themes developed earlier in his essay. To each theme, we may assign one (or more) of our poststructuralist tropes, noting how Howitt's interest in "building up"—the assumption that building up is epistemologically good, that it is the proper way to construct a concept—depends for its force on the presumptively good qualities of the idiographic and the experiential; seeing that the plurals in "landscapes" and the two "myriads" emphasize the internal multiplicity of experiential "terrain"; observing how a phrase like "meaningless labels" and the references to "divorce" (as against "engagement") give us a vision of abstraction as always potentially disconnected (high, loose, top-down, irresponsible) from its putative objects. These various critiques of the airiness of concepts and the seemingly paradoxical demand that stems from them appear *in nuce* in the conclusion's first sentence, where the catachresis "empirical generalization" stands in for an entire program of binding the concept fully to the ground that it conceptualizes—without losing the capacity to use concepts at all.

At some level, one wants to say, Howitt is just arguing, in a slightly more prescriptive tone than I have here, that methods cannot escape their objects. Any theory of something will inevitably have the touch of that something it theorizes about it; and the method will carry with it an implicit and shaping notion of the thing it interprets. This implies that all theories are "grounded" or "built up," so long as one conceives the level of the actual or the real as (conceptually) lower than that of abstractedness or thought.

But to say that the concepts *should not* leave their objects behind, that they *ought to* draw from and remain connected to the grounds that generate them (which Howitt is doing), is not exactly the same thing as saying that they *cannot* do so (which I am doing). From the point of view of the latter claim, it is possible to forget that one's concepts are shackled to the examples, but it is not possible to unshackle them in the first place. "Should" doesn't really come into it. And from this more neutral perspective, one might also observe, as we do with hammers and nails, that it is not clear that the examples can unshackle themselves from the concepts either. The interaction between object and method goes both ways; it's not (or not necessarily) just a question of the hammer's inevitable violation of the nail's integral quiddity, its abstraction of the nail's proper terrains of possibility, but also of the interpellative call that the nail makes, simultaneously with its appearance, to the hammer, of the ways in which that call just as surely violates the hammer's various other potential uses. Hammer and nail birth each other as much as chicken and egg; it's not clear why one should be "lower" than the other, or rather, why we should conceive them as such. The same goes for concepts and things, neither of which exist in the social lifeworld prior to a mindful distinction between them. There is no human thinking without concepts, and there never has been. There is no prehistorical moment (*pace* Rousseau) at which thought emerges into the human lifeworld from an outside, interrupting the peaceful ignorance of a pure and instinctual relation to nature.

That is not, however, what Howitt seems to believe. His critique of scale organizes itself around a binary logic in which one side of the term, the low or the grounded, the actual, is heavily privileged as a moral and political good. The flow of influence between object and method *should* go only one way. This privileging reframes, in a moment of profound irony, the entire conceptualization of scale itself in vertical terms. The way you know that scale is bad, that is, is because it hierarchizes something that should not be hierarchized. Why should that something not be hierarchized? Because it is *lower on a hierarchy*: a "ground," a "terrain," lower and therefore more epistemologically legitimate than higher things. "Ground" is *already and in advance* a member of a scalar hierarchy whose privileged term is not *high* but *low*.

It seems to me that it is precisely here, in places like these lines from Howitt, that one sees humanist metadiscourse failing to reckon with its actually existing practice.

The critique of scale Howitt develops thus aims to reframe or retheorize the term, to resolve its conceptual reification, by returning it to a "real" the geographer takes as ontologically primary, as itself an as-yet-unreified domain of thought, of lived experience, of multiplicity, and of historical change. We see something of the same value system in another major critique of geographic scale, in which Sallie A. Marston, John Paul Jones III, and Keith Woodward propose doing away with the concept entirely. Against attempts to reimagine scale as horizontal, or models that replace scale with flow, they argue for a "flat ontology" oriented toward "sites," which would account both for the "varying degrees of organization" of social space, as well as the "virtual" potentialities for change, "dynamic collections of potential force relations and movements."[23] Consider the following sentences:

> For one encounters these "structures" [that organize juridical life] not at some level once removed, "*up there*," in a vertical imaginary, but on *the ground*, in *practice*, the result of marking territories *horizontally* through boundaries and enclosures. (420, my emphases)

> In a flat (as opposed to horizontal) ontology, we discard the *centering essentialism* that infuses not only the *up-down vertical imaginary* but also the *radiating* (out from here) spatiality of horizontality (422, my emphases)

> A flat ontology must be rich to the extent that it is capable of accounting for socio-spatiality as it occurs throughout the Earth without requiring prior, *static conceptual categories*. (425, my emphases)

> Sites thus require a *rigorous particularism* with regard to how they assemble precisely because a given site is always an *emergent* property of is interacting human and non-human inhabitants. . . . That is, we can talk about the existence of a given site only insofar as we can follow *interactive practices* through their *localized connections*. (425; first, third, and fourth emphases mine)

When it comes right *down* to it, a flat ontology helps theorists
"keep in *touch* with the states of affairs [we purport] to describe"
(Schatzki 2002, xix). And if . . . we lose the beauty of the "whole
thing" when we downcast our eyes to the *"dirt and rocks,"* at
least we have the *place*—the only place—where social things
happen, things that are *contingent, fragmented and changeable*.
(427, my emphases)

Against the various errors of scale, flat ontologies of sites stay
in "touch" with the "ground" where "social things happen," where
pluralities of "practices" and "connections" operate locally and
transactionally. Against the temporal fixity of the scalar view, sites
are dynamic, diachronically changing, "emergent" and dispersed,
uncentralizable. Such sites require "a rigorous particularism" that
reflects their own relentless particularity, their singular internal
multiplicity, the complexity of their forms of connection and self-
connection, and social being; they orient us toward (warm, human,
lived) place, away from space, away from modes of thought whose
bird's-eye views fix and frame human activity, rendering moot the
possibility of historical change. Considering social activity in terms
of flat ontology restores our recognition of the "contingent, fragmented and changeable" nature of human life, and thus opens up
the possibility of a future we humans might decide to make unlike
the present.

I will have to more to say about this engagement with history in a
moment. But for now let me lay some cards more plainly on the table:
these critiques of scalar models don't make sense without their own
scalar metaphors, without, either, their own bird's-eye views of their
disciplines or of the workings of the social. Howitt and Marston et
al. borrow from a vertical, ground-up language to argue against bad
(or, in the latter case, *any*) use of scale. This happens because their
arguments are at least partially structured by a scalar conception of
the relation between concretion and abstraction, in which the first
is lower, smaller, and epistemologically central, and the second is
higher, larger, and epistemologically secondary. This vertically organized opposition is most insistently organized around metaphors
of ground (down, terrain, landscape, "dirt and rocks"), from which

theory may be only provisionally built "up" (Howitt), or may not be built up at all (Marston et al.). In this way both essays regularly describe scale as a verticalizing gesture that does injustice to the phenomenon under analysis. The latter's quiddity is taken to be located firmly in the lived, dynamic stuff of its active emergence in time. And this stuff cannot be understood unless it is mapped within a larger hierarchical and vertical structure that organizes the very structure that describes and conceives it.

Already in Montello's encyclopedia entry we saw the way that the attribution of "scale" to both the analysis and the phenomenon mediated, or leaped over, the ontological gap separating the idea from the thing. We encounter that same problem with Howitt and Marston et al., where the problem of scale's distance from the ground it putatively describes is resolved by describing the conceptual sphere in scalar terms, terms that then justify jettisoning scale in favor of flatter approaches. The tendency of scale to sneak in through the conceptual back door is, as I suggested earlier, the result of the larger attempt to resolve the epistemological distance between the object and the method, while protecting the object from methodological interference. That such an attempt produces a kind of metaphorical approximation between scale (or flatness) in the real world and scale (or flatness) in the conceptual-methodological one is of no real consequence—approximation and metaphorization happen in all homologies, so no one should feel too bad about it. What's worth noting however is that from the beginning, scale names a kind of solution to the problem of the object and the method, the observer and the observed, which has haunted humanist reason since Kant.

For Marston et al., the fact that the "macro-micro distinction in social analysis . . . enter[s] into the terrain of scale theorizing," or that "the theoretical delineations between abstract/concrete and theoretical/empirical are often aligned with the global-local binary" (421)—that, in other words, there is an unhealthy traffic between methodological and analytic scale—is yet another reason to abandon the concept entirely. I'm suggesting that any such attempt is doomed to failure, and, moreover, that the attempt to do so reproduces a Cartesian epistemological fantasy (with the right politics, this time) that Marston and other humanist scholars have elsewhere explicitly rejected. For evidence, we have the wild unself-consciousness of Marston et al.'s own work, whose proposal for a conceptually flat ontology generates much of its epistemological justification from the idea that social reality *is in fact ontologically flat*, and thus just as much as any unsubtle theorization of phenomenon scale begins with the notion that the nature of reality should interfere with the production of concepts about it. You're not supposed to begin your flat-ontological analysis with any "static conceptual categories," except, of course, for the concept of flatness and of a noncentering horizontality that reflects what life among the "dirt and rocks" is actually like. It seems awfully unlikely that the flat ontological approach would not, like scale, produce an unwelcome interference between object and method.

This unlikeliness owes itself not to this particular case, but to the general field of method, as I have been saying all along. Though in the case of scale or flat ontology the interference seems especially obvious since the gap between the methodological appearance of the concept and its phenomenal one must emerge from within a single word ("flat" or "scale"), the general problem of the interaction between analysis and phenomenon appears to us from the very beginnings of epistemology, as well as from the very beginning that is Montello's encyclopedia entry.

If all the examples so far seem to be worrying about the same problem, it is because, I am suggesting, first, that they *are* in fact worrying about the same problem, and, second, that such a problem is well worth worrying about. It goes to the very heart of a number of linked relations central to the problem of knowledge: method and object, concretion and abstraction, and (more broadly, if one can say so without calling the ghosts of scale down upon us) reality and perception, life and thought.

We get some sense of the way these problems have been historicized—understood, that is, as epistemological effects of human historical activity—in remarks that Edmund Husserl once made on the impact of the Galilean philosophical inheritance. Husserl contrasted that mathematizing legacy to the nonidealized ways in which we actually live in and experience the world:

> Mathematics and mathematical science, as a garb of ideas, or the garb of symbols of the symbolic mathematical theories, encompasses everything which, for the scientists and the educated more generally, *represents* the lifeworld, *dresses it up* as "objectively actual and true" nature. It is through the *garb of ideas* that we take for true being what is actually a *method*—a method which is designed for the purpose of progressively improving, *in infinitum*, through "scientific" predictions, those rough predictions which are the only ones originally possible within the sphere of what is actually experienced and experienceable in the lifeworld.[24]

We take for true being what is actually a *method*: with these words, Husserl addresses the object-method problem to nothing less than the entire experience of life. He thus posits an initial, prescientific condition of inductive reasoning as the ground of ordinary epistemological practice—"All knowledge of laws could be knowledge only of predictions . . . which are verified in the manner of inductions"—which is then taken over by science and made into an infinite, idealized limit.[25] To the world of actual experience, he says, "belongs the form of space-time together with all the bodily shapes incorporated in it; it is in this world that we ourselves live, in accord with our bodily, personal way of being."[26]

Notice how closely these arguments, in which the lived, the body, stands as the ground of being, of knowledge, which science only potentially abstracts, idealizes, or "represents," align themselves with Howitt's and Marston et al.'s critiques of scale. Living is not a "method." Like Heidegger's Greek temple or Kant's work of art, it gives itself the law; it inhabits itself in an in-dwelling. And so whatever method we use to think of what living is, it will hardly be a "method" in the Cartesian sense. The method will owe—if we are interested in aligning our methods with our phenomena—something to the ontological nature of the phenomenon as we conceive it. In this way, the debates about scale, on every side, are also debates about the nature of human life itself, about the properties—temporal, spatial, social—and forms of organization and articulation—nested, net-worked, embedded, emergent—of the human lifeworld. "The scale of analysis must match the actual scale of the phenomenon." Yes, one sees how you would come to think so. And how, if you did, "identify-ing the correct scale of phenomena" would become "a central prob-lem" for the humanistic disciplines.

But what if you said instead something like, "The scale of analy-sis must understand and include the primary social scale of the phe-nomenon, while recognizing that this primary social scale does not, in fact, constitute the full reality of the phenomenon, and that doing justice to a phenomenon does not (and quite literally cannot) entail reproducing it at the epistemological level"? That's a mouthful, I know, but it corresponds to how humanist reason actually works.

Husserl's critique of mathematical science makes it clear that one humanist way to conceive of "bad" (scientific, dominating) episte-mology is as a specifically *historical* disaster. Prior to the Scientific Revolution, Husserl says, the analytic ideology of the everyday life-world essentially operated in accordance with that world's living actu-ality. Modern science presents itself as a realistic way of seeing things, disguising the fundamental truth that it is a "method" with only a restricted purchase on the variety of life. Human (or European) history after the Scientific Revolution thus amounts to a dislocation or dis-ruption in the phenomenon, a kind of excess or supplement that can and ought to be removed from consideration of the phenomenon's ontology. The old phenomena are still there, beneath the conceptual armature; only the Scientific Revolution has oriented us toward this new set of phenomena or caused us to reimagine the already-existing stuff as "scientific" phenomena. Such a theorization of the phenom-enon as *that which appears in the lifeworld prior to its conceptualization in modern science* amounts to a philosophy of history—an argument about the proper historical relationship between human activity and human being.[27] In it, the ontology of the lifeworld has been flat all along and is simply waiting to be revealed to us for a second time (a second time that would also be, of course, a first).[28]

But: how would you know? What possible ground could guaran-tee the ontology of the phenomenon long enough to generate an analytic method proper to it? This is more than just a claim about the cross-contamination of methods and objects. It is, rather, an observation that in all these cases, the entire structure of critique is sustained by the holding steady of figures that are not subject to the process of analysis applied to everything else. No matter how flat your ontology is, the frontier that it does not breach is that of flatness itself; it does not think the role flatness plays in expressing the distinction between concretion and abstraction that justifies it. So let me say it as plainly as I can: "flatness" is an abstraction. "Ground" is an abstraction; "terrain" is an abstraction; the body that science idealistically "dresses up" is an abstraction; "life" is an abstraction. The idea that somehow these things are certainly, ontologically concrete, that they constitute reality, the lifeworld, in any simple way, that they are "flat"—that they can serve as the unshakeable source of both *evidence* and *interpretation*, that, in short, they produce the final marriage of analysis and phenomenon—is an expression of an understanding of poststructuralism that does not go far enough. (In this way, it constitutes also, and ironically, simply a mirror image of Cartesian dominance.)

If every "concrete," phenomenal object can be recognized as an abstraction—which it can—then it is also true that every abstraction can also be understood, from another perspective, as a concretion. "Ground" concretizes concepts like space, landscape, or terrain; it phenomenalizes them by orienting them toward an inductively more physical regime (I am avoiding the term "level," though without much hope for my conceptual purity in the long run); "the body" concretizes (differently from "a body" or "bodies," let us note) a mixture of social activity, intellectual and emotional experience, and spatial force (among other things), binding them temporarily in an intuitionally sensible package. And life is, from a certain perspective, the concretion of one of many kinds of species-being (another major one of which is, of course, death). The process whereby concepts and abstractions pass into one another depends, it does not go without saying, not simply on "perspective," but on a process of orientation including embodied orientation, an orientation that is— if one proceeds through a certain analysis—emergent, discontinuous, dynamic, and so on. There is no thinking and no language, no human social life, no humanist reason or humanist scholarship, that does not rely on this concretion/abstraction dynamic.[29] Humanist epistemology ought to begin by seeing that dynamic not as a problem to be overcome, but as *already an overcoming*, already a solution to the challenge posed to us in our species-being by the dynamism and multiplicity that characterize our (experience of the) world.

It is not, therefore, a question of restoring to the discussion of scale a proper hierarchy—a hierarchy that would be proper to it, in which the presumptive opposition between the flat and the scalar, the ground of life and the abstraction of theory, would regain all its perpendicular glory. We do not have scales "after all." It is rather a matter of observing, and tracing, the fold that brings together, continuously and discontinuously, in precisely the moment of a disavowal, the flat and the scalar, the lived and the thought, the object and the method. Continuously and discontinuously: because in the very act of asserting a total ontological continuity among the human and nonhuman objects of the world, thought—scale—emerges as a discontinuity, a rupture, a potential violation of continuity precisely insofar as it becomes a resistance to it. Scale, like all thought, *discontinues*: it breaks away from, leaps above, escapes the field of the (putative) real, inserting into the field of play a concept that claims an impossible, unethical distance from its object. And at the same time, scale *continues*. Excluded from the field of an ethical relation to the object, it stands above it as the negative image of the dynamic, the lived, the emergent, and the engaged, which gambol in the gritty horizontal landscapes of the real. Scale—thought—assures by its exclusion the stability of the field about which it is forbidden to speak. And about which it speaks nonetheless, in a whisper that gives the ground its "first" pneumatic breath.

We tend to act as though we have given objects and methods that either matched them ontologically or did them an injustice. To imagine that injustice in scalar terms—to see the method as "above" the object—means disaggregating with too much sureness the phenomena from the analyses. (This is true whether one privileges the former or the latter; in this dimension of the problem, the avatars of scale and their enemies are on the same side.) I am simply saying: methods are also objects. And vice versa. There is no reason to imagine that the form of transactionality that assumes the object's phenomenal passivity and the method's abstract activity could not be subject to the same analysis performed here. The entire sense of the modes of relation between method and object—and the value judgments attached to them—would need to be retheorized in the general terms developed by any immanentist position, be it Spinoza's, Latour's, or something from the object-oriented ontologists. If the ontology is flat, more or less, it will have to be flat for everything. Including flatness, more or less.

I am not therefore concerned here with erasing every difference between what I have been calling the object or the phenomenon, and what we commonly think of as analysis or method. It is not a matter of confusing what happens when Samuel Johnson stubs his toe and what happens when someone refutes Bishop Berkeley. I am even less concerned with attributing to something like *method* all of the phenomenal quiddity or embodied effectiveness of an everyday social space like a classroom or a neighborhood such as would, for example, allow us to collapse method fully into its objects (even if such a homologous situation cannot be completely excluded for certain methods, in certain contexts—we can imagine some hypotheses that would allow us to refine the analogy). My hesitation concerns the purity, the rigor, and the indivisibility of the frontier that separates— already with respect to "life" itself, and along a horizontal axis— objects from methods; and as a consequence, especially, the purity, rigor, and indivisibility of the concept of *objectivity* that ensues.[30]

For this reason, the homology between methodological scale and spatial scale, which so seductively recalls the structure of analysis and phenomenon, is for me nothing like an inimical confusion, whose clarification would allow us finally to know the objects right. It is rather a call, an enticement to wonder at the intensity and reach of a number of other homologically related binaries, or continua, that organize the way we marshal humanist reason today. Which binaries? To start (more generally?), the distinction between quantity and quality, or the distinction between kind and degree, but also (and more specifically?) the difference between the *longue durée* and the everyday, in approaches to history, the difference between the irreducible density of language and the laws of genre, in approaches to literature, the difference between practice, praxis and theory, in

Marxism, or even the difference between the event and the performative convention, all of which may amount (more generally, once more?) to the difference between freedom and necessity.[31] Together these distinctions, whose family resemblance and power are not so much a product of heterosis as of incest, or so I am trying to suggest here, go to the very heart of the kinds of thinking that humanists do, and can do, today.[32]

Accounting for the active work of such binaries, rather than reifying them as the justifications for an impossible epistemology, would (among other things) save us some time. In a redescribed model of humanist reasoning about scale, there would be nothing inherently bad (politically or epistemologically) about larger scales, or good about smaller ones; rather humanist reasoners would pay careful attention to the transactions and jumps across and among scales, as well as to the ways in which nesting and verticality are disrupted in the social by the various forms of human activity.[33] They would also remember that all active scales of social life depend radically on their production and reproduction by human actors, whose daily acts of reification maintain (and change, over time) all the conceptual and institutional patterns that define the social as such, all of which may well be conceived in scalar terms as a primary function of social life. If we keep seeing scales in the social, that's because actors in the social use scalar logics to construct, maintain, and adjust their realities. When Rabindranath Tagore wrote *The Home and the World*, he was registering and using the scalar difference between "home" and "world," as units already in common practice in the daily social existence of the characters whose life he described, and, over the course of the novel, demonstrating quite clearly the ways in which those two scales interpenetrate and, in the long run, cannot be taken (or lived) as fully hierarachized and nested units of social experience. In the long run, any scholarly description and analysis of the social activity of scales would have to confront, self-reflexively, the history of scale-thinking in humanist reason more generally, and the scale-work of a given research project, in particular, without falling prey to the kind of virtuous denunciation of scales that inevitably produces conceptual hypocrisy in the scholarship. How could you understand Queen Victoria without understanding queens? How could you understand

Nervous Conditions without understanding the postcolonial novel? And how could you understand queens or postcolonial novels without understanding Queen Victoria, or *Nervous Conditions*?

ARTICLE 5

Historical Causality Includes Nondeterministic and Indirect Forces Operating at Multiple Scales.   A corollary of the humanist investment in multiscalar analysis (and the description of social processes at multiple, convoluted scales) comes down to a series of beliefs about the nature of historical causality. Against a positivist causal model that might imagine historical effects as resembling those of billiard balls on a pool table, humanist reason expresses the following forms of evidence-based resistance:

1. "Multiscalar causality" means that some causes are operating above, below, or to the side of the billiard balls; no series of actions on the given table/social field can be explained exclusively by causes emerging exclusively from that social field.

2. "Complex causality" involves forms of influence and causation that are not only direct and proximity-driven (as with the billiard balls), but also forms that act indirectly, through and across a variety of social mechanisms that may well cross or jump scales. For instance, the *Zeitgeist* or the "race system" might be a causal factor in a single interpersonal interaction, but so might "got up on the wrong side of the bed this morning." The links across or among such causal factors are not only physical, but also mental, linguistic, social, or psychological; semiotically, they can be symbolic or figural or affective, denotative, or connotative, referential and representational. (Think of how a poem works; see the poem as a synecdoche of the cultural process.) In other words, social causes and effects can "translate" across what we conventionally think of as ontologically distinct levels or spheres of the social. Such translations include the obviously symbolic and semiotic processes whereby an idea becomes language, becomes a law, becomes a judgment, becomes a feeling, becomes a socially prescribed norm, becomes an uncodified set of habits, becomes an argument. But it

also goes to processes that are not explicitly linguistic, as when a building creates (or is created by) an idea, or when a feeling comes from a taste (like a madeleine in tea), or taste is modified by feeling (a preference for dipping one's madeleines in beer).

3. Although all kinds of humanist work will, when confronted with this causal variety, attempt to differentiate between the various degrees of influence among causes, the sum of those degrees of influence does not necessarily add up to 100. Against, that is, quantitative explanatory models that attempt to determine what percentage of a phenomenon stems from certain causes (and indeed mathematically assumes that the total sum of causes adds up to 100 percent), humanist reason argues that, first, the quantification of that kind of influence risks fantasizing a level of precision that does not and cannot exist in the social; and, second, that the sum total of causes will, from this general perspective, often exceed or undercount the idea of a "total" causal inventory. If I ask, for instance, "Would World War I have happened had Gavrilo Princip not assassinated Archduke Franz Ferdinand and his wife, Sophie, on June 28, 1914?" people who know enough about the situation in Europe in 1914 might well respond, "Yes, it probably would have happened anyway. Not exactly in the same way, but probably in a similar way." Of course, we'll never know, but this not-knowing does not interfere with the basic supposition that causes and causality cannot be reduced to historical actuality, but must be considered in relation to various possible worlds that make up any given moment, process, or event. (When humanists perceive the total sum of causes to "add up" to more than 100 percent, they use the word "overdetermination"; events that occur despite what seems like—from a given explanatory perspective— "not enough causes" are, by extension, "underdetermined.")

4. The same holds true for humanist models of cultural influence; indeed, the entire humanist theory of social causality stems from the evidence left us by patterns of cultural influence and meaning that form the backbone of our work. Historical evidence shows that the same cause can have radically different effects in different populations, or even in the same person, at two different times, and that the same effect can stem from radically

different combinations of causes. Consider what we know of the psychology of crowds, and of the ways in which mass behaviors can emerge from a collection of individual motivations that in no way add up to the sum total of the behavior of 50,000 soccer fans, or of a mob.

It would be easy enough to sum this up by arguing that humanist causality draws heavily on chaos theory or descriptions of butterfly effects, so that it would turn out that the humanities were merely intuiting a series of causal mechanisms that have been definitively "proven" by scientific reason. The truer thing to say is that humanist reason modeled both these processes well before their scientific "discovery" in natural phenomena. The idea that regularized effects can emerge from seemingly disconnected phenomena is not new to humanist reason, nor is it new to people in general. Everyone living in the social world lives that situation every day, and any number of theories developed through the apparatuses of humanist reason attempt to explain it. (Consider, alongside the obvious theories of fate or ideology, specific instances like Adam Smith's invisible hand, Hobbes's leviathan, or Rousseau's social contract.)

As for the butterfly effect, as a model for physical processes, it amounts only to a theory of a complicated billiard ball table. As I understand it, the idea is that some butterfly flapping its wings somewhere will cause a series of linked physical events that will lead to a thunderstorm somewhere else very far away. The reliance of this narrative on some very obvious rhetorical strategies, most notably its ironic superposition of the small and the large, the minor and the sublime (but also its aestheticizing use of the flapping butterfly, as opposed to a clomping cockroach), ought not conceal the fact that the causal model it describes is completely banal: one physical thing touches another physical thing, which touches another thing, which touches another thing, and so on, until some balance is tipped on some scale and you get a big physical thing as a result. Straw, meet camel's back.

Humanist reason imagines instead that the flapping of a butterfly might, if registered phenomenologically by an observer, cause that person to write a series of influential poems (themselves altered in form and reception by a variety of complex cultural processes), which might then shape the cultural sphere such that butterflies acquired a level of social meaning over and above their role in a variety of natural activities (such as pollination), which might in turn, and for centuries hence, affect people who never read the poems or who live in a world in which the original poems have entirely disappeared. One day, one of those people might write a new poem that, echoing this social meaning, would be taught in the schools. And one day, a student who had failed a test on that very poem might come home and kick their dog. Did the butterfly cause the dog-kicking? Not really . . . but without it, would the student have kicked the dog? Maybe not. Humanist reason exists to explain and understand causal processes like this one, which ladder up and down scales and across a variety of actors and social forces, and to use such processes as possible evidentiary sources for larger-scale models and explanations of how the social works. Humanist reason believes, on the basis of plentiful evidence, that the social productivity or effect of any given object of culture can take place in a variety of registers, including physical contact, but also psychological, linguistic, and social processes, each of which requires a complex theory of possible modes of activity and influence.

This causal complexity means that for any given epistemological particular, the total sum of interesting or useful causal explanations almost always exceeds the scope of a particular piece of research. Years ago, a friend of mine, a quantitative political scientist, was in the habit of asking after every conference presentation he saw, "Is there another equally plausible explanation of the data you've shown us here?" For a humanist attempting to understand the meaning of an Anna Akhmatova poem or the Haitian revolution, the answer will necessarily be, "Of course there is!" The existence of multiple reasonable explanations for any object does not constitute an epistemological problem. It manifests rather the actual social complexity investigated by (and therefore partially produced by, and partially productive of) humanist research which, in being multiscalar and causally complex, socioculturally embedded and interdisciplinarily produced in the ways I have described here, will necessarily produce research paradigms that register those things. Humanist scholarship subjects existing and reified objects to new ideas and new methods; it also, using new perspectives, finds new objects or creates new objects of analysis that draw from or cross the boundaries of existing objects. In all these endeavors, much of the work of humanist reason is cumulative, tending to increase the richness of our understanding of the workings of culture, rather than attempting to simplify or reduce it. This is so even when it comes to the development of competing large-scale simplifications like structures, systems, or theories, which often serve a mainly heuristic function, existing to highlight features and patterns that emerge when one adopts a certain point of view toward a given object of study. Which of these simplifications will be explanatorily compatible, and which will not, can usuallynot be worked out in advance, but must be the subject of self-reflexive metadiscourse.

None of this means that humanist work makes no falsifiable claims; I am not saying that anything goes. It does mean that humanists ought to be (and usually are) especially careful to resist any epistemological claims to have discovered the single "level" or process at which things are "really" happening, and in relation to which all the other levels are merely epiphenomenal (as might happen, for instance, were a psychoanalytic reading of *A Raisin in the Sun* to suggest that its racial tensions were merely extrapolations of family drama, and therefore not relevant to the play's essential meaning).

Much humanist scholarship is therefore additive. In making richer and more complex the systematic, semantic, or causal qualities of some whole, it adduces to the sum total of evidence around that object a set of new considerations, and demands that they be included in any future understanding of the thing in question. Or, in a gesture of typical self-reflexivity, the humanist will demonstrate that the wholeness of a socially stabilized research object ("the *Bhagavad Gita*" or "the Han dynasty," for instance), can be undermined, made partial or extensible by approaching that object from another direction or with another set of causal priors in mind; this too is a kind of additive, recursive work, in which humanist knowledge shapes and reshapes what we might think of as the sum total of available understandings of the anthropological field, down to the very understanding of what forms of stability operate in it, or the nature of the field itself.

ARTICLE 6

Complex Social Systems Do Not Necessarily Follow Statistical or Linear Patterns; Outliers Often Have an Outsized Importance; the Historical Record Makes Epistemological Demands on Concept-Formation; Materiality Is the Limit to Idealism.   The theory of causal complexity affects humanist reason's relation to exceptions, outliers, and other exorbitant social processes or effects. Against a statistical model of social activity (or even of epistemological activity) that would emphasize the degree to which such processes constitute themselves and are made meaningful by the vast majority of behaviors devoted to reproducing their normativity, humanist reason emphasizes the degree to which the minor, the small, the overlooked, or the abjected must be accounted for in the description of social life.

This emphasis is commonly conflated, in humanist metadiscourse, with a certain left politics that seeks to recuperate or protect the minor from the various tyrannies of the majority and sees in the history of ideology and normativity the worst consequences of the basic human drives toward fear, violence, and self-protection. But the claim that outliers must be accounted for—or the stronger version of that claim, which is that the study of outliers best reveals the truth of a given system—does not require an ethical justification. It can be made on primarily epistemological grounds. The most basic insight of structuralism, that systems are composed of negative relations, means that no study of a system can rely (epistemologically) exclusively on the central or major or normal elements of that system because the normal, major, and central themselves rely on the systematic definition and reproduction of fields of abnormality, minority, and eccentricity. Insides and outsides mutually constitute themselves. Which means that no inside can be correctly understood without reference to its outside, and vice versa.

Beyond this structuralist claim, the epistemological emphasis on social and statistical outliers takes two other, related forms. The first rejects on principle any attempt to exclude, on whatever grounds, actually existing practices from a set of claims about the nature of a social field. One of my favorite versions of this kind of argument comes from Derrida's rejection, against Searle's theory of speech acts, of the idea that a serious study of the nature of language can begin by excluding all kinds of nonserious language (jokes, theatrical dialogue, and so forth). Derrida's argument boils down to this: no human language has ever not had jokes, quotations, and the like; no human society that we know of has ever lived without them. Therefore, any theory that purports to be a theory of language *must*, on epistemological grounds, include evidence from these types of language. A theory that does not would not be a theory of human language, but a theory of the language of some other set of beings which have never actually existed. As Derrida argues, this epistemological demand would remain legitimate even if the entirety of the cultural record included only one single instance of citation or one single joke—the very fact of its possibility, and the evidence of its possibility, requires that any theory of language *in general* should include it.[34]

This rule can be extended in any number of directions, most of which are fairly common-sensical, but all of which are nonetheless regularly violated by humanist scholars, and therefore in need of substantial self-reflexive work. You can't have a theory of the novel in general if you do not base your theory on the evidence of novels drawn from more than one language, one country, one time period. Note that this does not mean that a theory of novels must include all novels, or that a theory of revolutions must consider all revolutions; it demands rather that the evidence used with respect to a general claim be *representative* with respect to that generality. The humanities share this aspect of reason with the sciences and social sciences (you can't base your claims about viral behavior on the study of a single virus, etc.). Where they tend to differ has to do with the treatment of outliers more generally, as well as with the models of influence that allow causation or relevance to leap across scales or other fields of quantitative or conceptual stability.

For those reasons—and because we have a rich understanding of the negative structuration of the social field—you also can't have a (good) theory of the novel in general unless you include evidence from the novel's outside, whether that outside involves poetry or drama or prose fiction from other places and times. And you can't have a theory of the novel in general that does not include works that operate on the margins of novelness, which you might be tempted to exclude by declaring that Jean Toomer's *Cane*, for instance, is not "really" a novel. For the same reason, you can't have a theory of revolution that draws only on one revolution. You can't have a theory of biological sex that ignores that fact that a small percentage of human babies are born each year with sexually ambiguous genitalia or chromosomes; you cannot simply consign such people to the realm of the "exception" or the "abnormal" and then (as an extension or enforcement of this epistemological laziness) argue for the surgical correction of such bodies so that they conform with your theory.[35] And you cannot build an entire theory of political life around the idea of the single rational individual body when, for the entirety of human history, more than half the population of existing humans have had the capacity to carry for some time two individuals in one body, and have (which we know because we are all here) frequently exercised it.[36] In each case, humanist reason insists that the so-called exception must be included in the theorization of the whole, and does so in the full knowledge that the exclusion of those exceptions has so often been made in the name of the production of some form of dis-abling normativity and has so often coincided not with the ideal of democratic and common knowledge, but with the expression of self-regard and of normative power. In this way, the humanist critique of the racist, sexist, or otherwise unjust consequences of epistemological stupidity can stem both from a political distaste for those consequences, but also, and even primarily, from a rejection of the epistemological practices that produce them.

Let me extend my argument about outliers a bit further: in anthropological situations, the outlier or the exception has a relation to the center that is fundamentally *nonlinear*. Relative to its social frequency or normative importance, relative to the amount that it is discussed, noticed, or operationalized in the social, the outlier or the exception may in fact be, on statistical grounds, quite unimportant. But from the perspective of the construction of the social itself, humanist reason argues, this statistical or linear unimportance does not account for the potential structural, psychological, or social centrality of the outlier, which, like the scapegoat (or the shorn woman, or the Jew) may take on an outsized burden of cultural work.

One of the major functions of humanist scholarship involves identifying such outliers and exceptions and reintegrating them into a full and more coherent understanding of the work of social and historical life; indeed, it is the humanist study of such outliers that has given us the more general theory of the nonlinearity of the social that I am reproducing here.

These principles of historical realism and social nonlinearity can be organized into a succession of progressively more demanding assertions:

1. *The principle of evidentiary range:* Theories of X have to draw on evidence from a wide variety of socially recognized instances of X. Otherwise, they are theories of subsets of X (of the British novel, and not the novel in general, for instance).

2. *The principle of evidentiary inclusion:* No feature common to all X can be reasonably removed from the theory of X without producing only a theory of some non-X. Such exclusions are likely to mistakenly produce a "primary" version of X, against which the removed features will count as "secondary" or epiphenomenal.

3. *The principle of nonlinearity:* Not all of those instances of X need be treated equally; indeed, the treatment of all instances of X as the same X will likely miss out on the uneven social structuring of X, as well as the internal diversity of X as a category. Outliers and exceptions are likely to have a strongly nonlinear importance to the social reproduction of X.

4. *The principle of negative differentiation:* Theories of X need to account for a relevant subset of instances of non-X, near-X, or just-barely-X (outliers and near-misses), as well as theories and instances of normatively designated X; they also need to account for social objects that share significant features with X but are not generally recognized as X for whatever reason.

One simple and very beautiful expression of the second principle comes at the end of the introduction to Dipesh Chakrabarty's *Provincializing Europe*. One assumption running through modern European thought, Chakrabarty writes, "is that the human is ontologically singular, that gods and spirits are in the end 'social facts,' that the social somehow exists prior to them." Such an assumption permits one to imagine that gods and spirits are subsequent to the production of the social, that the social is something that throws up the idea of gods and spirits on occasion for particular reasons. But since, as Chakrabarty writes, "one empirically knows of no society in which humans have existed without gods and spirits accompanying them," any theory of the social that excludes those things has a great deal of explaining to do. He continues:

> Although the God of monotheism may have taken a few knocks . . . the gods and agents inhabiting practices of so-called "superstition" have never died anywhere. I take gods and spirits to be existentially coeval with the human, and think from the assumption that the question of being human involves the question of being with gods and spirits. . . . And this is one reason why I deliberately do not reproduce any sociology of religion in my analysis.[37]

This is an evidence-based argument: there has never been a society without spirits. Therefore, no concept of society should treat spirits as an optional or epiphenomenal factor in human social life; the evidence suggests, rather, that the ideas of the social, the human, and the spiritual or godly have historically been coconstitutive. This does not mean that it is not possible to study religion, but it does mean that treating religion as though it were somehow a "feature" of the social, rather than part of what organizes the social *as* the social in every human community that has ever existed, confuses the ontology of institutional topics with the actuality of human practice.

The Derridean version of the Chakrabarty rule (principle number 4) extends the general statement—that things that have never *not* happened need to be included in theories of the social structures that include them—to things that have only ever happened *once*. Together, these amount to a general principle of *historical realism*.[38]

We have already seen how a sense of historical realism must be influenced by something like historical unrealism (i.e., by the imaginative reconstruction of nonactual events, objects, and processes, all of which form the critical context for the understanding of historical actuality as such). More speculatively, we may wish to ask what role such historical unrealism plays in the full epistemological construction of concepts. Must a theory of X include instances of X that have *never actually happened* but could be imagined to happen? We can imagine, even if we have never lived in one, a United States in which white supremacy does not play a central role; does the possibility of such a society need to be included, as a potential capacity, in the more general understanding of the United States as a political entity? To what extent does the fact that some people have experienced smaller-scale social situations (friendships, classrooms, clubs, or groups of any type) that do not seem fundamentally organized by white supremacy need to be considered as a marker of such possibilities at the larger scale of society in general? (Have such smaller-scale situations ever actually existed? To what extent did their existence depend on the larger structures that surround them?) Against all these questions, does the Chakrabartian reminder—that one empirically knows of no American society in which humans have coexisted without white racism—require one to reject, on reasonable grounds, the inclusion of such a capacity in a full understanding of the United States?

Here, we confront the way that all humanist reason encounters, in its orientation toward its own present, the political valence of its work. It is easy to see how a certain kind of historical realism can lead to political cynicism: "We have never known a world without violence, so we might as well stop trying to make the world less violent." And at the same time, it is clear that historical realism can sometimes be very much on the side of an opening of the social toward a juster and more common life for all its human and nonhuman subjects, as when, for instance, Chakrabarty shows how a fully Europeanized secularism fails to account for the lives of billions of others and asks what kinds of ideas might perform a fuller accounting of the anthropological field. There are no easy answers here; no set of decontextualized epistemological practices guarantees the production of a good world or leads inexorably to a worse one. As a matter of historical realism, one may well see that things have often been bad, and are still very bad; and yet we can also see that things have gotten better, here and there. And it is easy enough to imagine, again as a matter of mere realism, how they might be better still.

Such questions are not, for humanist scholarship, merely epiphenomenal. They belong, rather, to the heart of the transition between the subjective interests that motivate the work of scholarship and the potential objectivity of its conclusions, since to know the anthropological lifeworld, to know the forces—human and nonhuman, momentary and transhistorical—that shape it, is always to open oneself to the objective return of one's work to its subjective and generating present, and thus to the possibility that not only oneself but others could be changed by this new knowledge, by the holding of this new knowledge in common.

To be absolutely clear: nothing about the character of this material reality (or indeed the vast multiplicity of material realities) implies that a full accounting of its character will lead, in the long positivist run, to the production of a complete or simple vision of a whole that would come to dominate it. In other words, the working of the social is not like the movement of the billiard balls on a table, but more complicated. The difference between the two is not a matter of simply increasing the number of factors to be calculated, or the amount of computing power at hand, until we master every element of the system and can reduce its operations to a set of general laws. The laws, the ideas or concepts, that we might bring to the analysis of the social—and which may well participate in the construction or consolidation of that social, both from a position "above" the social as well as "around" or "through" it—confront continually and *over a continuously changing temporality* the materialities that express, constitute, and alter it.[39] Here, humanist reason rejects—though it is, like scientific reason, continually tempted by—models of unitary determination that emerge from things like a vulgarized Hegelian idealism, in order to emphasize, as Aijaz Ahmad once put it, the *"tension . . .* between the problematic of a final determination," on the one hand, "and the utter historicity of multiple, interpenetrating determinations" that will finally resolve it (for a given moment) into something that none of the "historical agents who struggle over [its] outcome" will have exactly predicted, or wanted.[40]

ARTICLE 7

Fuzziness, Ambiguity, and Contradiction Are Socially Functional; Any Humanist Analysis That Treats Them Necessarily as Problems to Be Resolved Has Misunderstood Its Object. A person says "I love you" to another person. The second person says "I love you" back. If you push hard enough, you will find that what they mean is not exactly the same, not only because one said it first (and therefore may have meant something like "Please reassure me that you love me") and the other second ("Don't worry; I love you"; or possibly "I don't know why you need this reassurance, but here you go anyway"), but because at a more intense level of analysis, the very conceptions of "I" and "you" that characterize the thought of our two interlocutors borrow from, and express, large-scale differences in attitude toward the very nature of the self/other relation, whether these are the result of individual, psychological factors or larger, sociocultural ones. And forget about figuring out what either of them means by "love"!

The same sort of analysis can be applied to any conversation, to any social process. How do we ever really know, at a certain level of analysis, that we understand each other, or that we mean what we say? How can we ever know what it might mean to live justly or fairly, to have a good society, to be a good person, to be "fulfilled" or "happy" or "sad" or "embedded in a rich lifeworld of possibilities, one shared by all members of a community and supported by a democratic social welfare state"? What if it's just the Sapir-Whorf hypothesis all the way down, and no one ever actually understands anyone else?

This drive to specificity, and the problems created by our awareness of the deep historical and social uniqueness of any given element of the anthropological field, characterize a great deal of humanist thought. They do so usefully, much of the time, as they emphasize the ways in which contextualization shapes the meaning, import, and effects of any given social situation, process, or artwork. More self-reflexively, this more general interest in uniqueness helps humanists recognize the possible forms of contamination that will cross from their epistemological tools (concepts, words) to their epistemological subjects, or grasp the ways in which all knowledge developed from a subjective process (even when that process is reified and therefore made at least putatively objective by institutional structures or dis-ciplinary norms) will necessarily be mediated by that subjectivity, which determines not only the matter of *individual* bias but the larger forms of subjectivization that we might think of as institutional or ideological. We all think, we think, in terms determined by the parameters of our selves, of our languages, of our social formations, of our eras. And those forms of subjectification necessarily influence our conceptualization of the past: if you approach the psychological world of the Tang dynasty with Freudian analysis and no understand-ing of the concept of the Chinese heart-mind, *xin*, you will probably miss a few things about what was going on at the time.

At its worst, this approach to contextual specificity leads to a stultifying or self-righteous pseudonominalism that demands that everything be considered "on its own terms," even when such a thing would be, as I said at the beginning of the book, essentially impossible. To study the Tang lifeworld with concepts drawn exclu-sively from the Tang lifeworld can no longer be done. None of us are natives of the Tang. Beyond that, though all humanists believe that the study of the Tang lifeworld (or whatever) ought to include at least some awareness of the concepts native to it, our scholarship shows over and over that it can generate useful knowledge by bring-ing to bear social, cultural, and historical concepts that emerge from outside the native situation. The major epistemological problem is not that humanists bring concepts from outside to their objects, but rather that the selection of concepts has tended historically to cast a geographic shadow over humanist work: if only the privileged parts of the world can produce concepts or methods (for which the less-privileged parts will then only serve as test cases or illustrations), then we are almost certainly likely to be making epistemological mistakes. Similarly, if our "outside" concepts only come from the his-torical present and apply mainly to objects of the past, and never the other way around, well . . . some basic sense of epistemological mod-esty ought to warn us that we are probably doing something wrong. Social concepts don't wear out; their value is not finally determined by either their original context or some later one. Conceptual value always exists as a form of potential that can be activated by someone willing to do the work. Concepts developed in the classical Chinese analysis of poetry may tell us as much about William Blake as concepts developed in the analysis of William Blake tell us about classical Chinese poetry.

All this would be enough to make us suspicious of the ways in which an awareness of the uniqueness of historical situations (or the meanings of individual words) can lead to a stultified metadiscourse of humanist epistemology. But there is more to say. Because the real problem with this emphasis on specificity is that it ignores the fact that the specificity and uniqueness it observes *is itself a function of a particular scale of analysis*—namely, that of singularity-production— that cannot be extended into a general theory of the social unless it considers the work that the social does at other scales.

Remember the Chakrabarty test: If no one has ever known *exactly* what something means, if no one has ever taken something *fully on its own terms*, then you probably should not build your theory of reason around the demand that someone do so, despite the obvious comfort of appealing to a Kantian regulative ideal. Instead, you probably ought to account for the fact that despite the fact that this gap between what one person means or does and what another understands about it exists in every historical situation that has ever taken place, people seem to understand one another perfectly well often enough to make friendships work; to make institutions work; to make jokes, novels, and plays work; or to make, in general, the entire labor of the social so effective.

Come back to our couple. They say "I love you" to each other. Neither of them means exactly the same thing. But still: it works. Each of them feels satisfied by the dialogue; each of them feels addressed or responded to *enough*. The fact that they don't engage in a long metaconversation about exactly what they meant is not a relationship disaster or a sign of their lack of epistemological will; the lack of precision is a feature, not a bug, of the social situation they're in. They don't need, or want, to absolutely understand each other—at least not right then—because they're getting ready for work, or going to sleep, or watching a show. The fuzziness of their dialogue is, though probably unconscious, nonetheless essentially deliberate. Each of them gets what they want from the conversation. Its ambiguity is *socially functional*, at a certain scale. It *works*.[41]

The history of humanist scholarship demonstrates over and over the capacity of a wide variety of nonprecise, nondetermined, and nondeterminable social forms to function in just these ways. Most human verbal and visual signification depends on such mechanisms—the entire world of tropes and figures, jokes and plays on words, symbols and emblems, intertextuality and reference of all types, all of which have never *not* existed in the social in one way or another. The same goes for the entire world of personal identity and identification, not only in socially intense and even dramatic situations like racial or gendered passing, but in all of the small and ordinary ways in which individuals and institutions mobilize, consciously and unconsciously, ambiguity, fuzziness, or apparent contradiction in the service of their social selves.

One human response to all this ambiguity has been historically consistent: to attempt to pin it down, define it once and for all, to fix and determine not just meaning, but social position, the nature of God, the limits of the law, the forms of legitimate kinship, or the procedures for the distribution of welfare benefits. These attempts to reduce or confine ambiguity, to resolve mystery or contradiction, whose histories organize the strain of iconoclasm that extends from religious life to the fashion system, can be socially useful (it's good to have some basic agreement about the laws of the road), as well as socially destructive (when they justify, as they so often do, forms of institutional violence or, say, religious warfare). But none of these practices or arguments, these drives to fix absolutely and for all time, has ever finished the job, has ever resolved social ambiguity entirely. Ambiguity lives on. Which suggests rather strongly that the *nature of social life is functionally ambiguous at certain scales*, and that it will probably always be so.

The obvious target of my critique is any positivistic epistemological system that would attempt to define absolutely a series of social relations or processes, whether these be interpersonal or semiotic, or that would spend a great deal of time refining its descriptive terminology to an exactitude that would attempt, finally, to reduce the social to a set of determined and determining terms. But the acceptance of ambiguity as a form of socially functional activity also exposes weaknesses in two strains of humanist scholarship.

The first overfetishizes ambiguity. Finding socially functional instances of ambiguity that support the powerful at the expense of the weak, such scholarship confuses the political outcome of that process with the nature of ambiguity itself, and falls into the utopian trap of imagining that we need to build a world in which everything says what it is and is clear about what it means, a world without ideology or unconscious coercion of any kind, a world in which everyone uses the right words at the right time, all the time. In so doing, it aligns itself, like all utopianism, with a vision of the end of history.

The second strain takes its discovery of these forms of ambiguity as the revelation of a great secret about the nature of all power—that it has at its heart a contradiction, a fuzziness, or an aporia that constitutes itself in the form of a fundamental emptiness. As a counterpoint to a common-sensical, pre-Foucauldian idea of the workings of power, and as a balloon-puncturing gesture against certain too-optimistic visions of the nature of human existence, such a position can come in handy. But making ambiguity a secret, projecting onto it a kind of dark and terrifying valorization, ignores the ways in which ambiguity, by virtue of its constitutive action in every dimension and at every scale of the social, does not so much constitute a secret—how can it be secret if everyone uses it all the time, daily?—as a matter of living practice, one that can have a wide variety of consequences, including the consequence of undermining or even transforming not only the structures of social power, but its very nature. If we imagine this ambiguity or aporia as a functional aspect of the conceptual management and daily navigation of the social world—if we see ambiguity (or paradox, or contradiction) as a positive social form rather than as the negation of the social itself—then we let go of the quasi-theological fetishization of the revelation of contradictions. In so doing we also forgo the rhetorical Romanticism of much humanist scholarship, which depends for its force on our tragic recognition or anticipation of a world in which all our values, all our social systems and hopes and plans and stupid organizing and shoring up of life against its various tragedies, all our ridiculous effort at being kind or decent where we can, mean nothing after all.

To frame this argument now as a project: What happens if instead of taking the aporia at the heart of the justice-law nexus as a kind of conceptual failure in the nature of humanity itself, as a tragic reminder of the impossibility of the full achievement of justice—or if, instead of treating the impossible horizon of a total hospitality as a constitutive absence in the actual performance of any genuinely functional hospitality—one recognizes that these gaps or failures, these aporia, are generated by the social in order to manage the distance between the equally social work of imaginary ideals and living practice? What if, that is, we treat the social as though it were *putting into play* the very concepts that we believe we reveal within it? And what if, in that case, the deconstructive act of seeing and naming this kind of social work were not a matter of unmasking a crisis, but rather of discovering a living, manipulable process? What if, that is, the ambiguity inherent in all social processes, the forms of contradiction, paradox, and eccentricity that so consistently form the topic of deconstructive revelation, were in fact inside the social after all, not as blind spots but as forms of actually existing utility? In such a case, these aporia, and the work they do for us in helping make possible a distinction between justice and law—and hence in producing, for instance, a demand on the law, an insistence that the law be held to account in relation to some other concept that lies both within and without it, would be understood as the institutional structures whereby social actors of all kinds attempt to manage the gap between the utopia of their imaginations and the strictures of their actual lives.

ARTICLE 8

The Imagination Is an Epistemologically Necessary Response to the Actuality of Humanist Evidence. The ideology of understanding and empathetic identification that defined certain justifications of humanist reason during the German *Methodenstreit*, which appears most notably in Wilhelm Dilthey's emphasis on *Verstand* as a key element of humanist practice, points us to the long-standing association of *imagination* with humanist reason. Experiment, on the other hand, belongs as an epistemological term to the natural and quantitative social sciences; it describes the capacity to radically control the conditions of the epistemological field of observation, such that the processes under investigation can be reliably repeated. No such capacity characterizes humanist work. The contextual complexity and semiotic/social richness of our evidence simply do not allow for it.

At its worst, and in ways we all know, this distinction justifies claims that humanistic knowledge is, unlike scientific knowledge, fundamentally uncertain—that it is a matter of the scholar's "telling stories" or "making things up," that it relies heavily on the rhetorical power of its presentation or the charismatic force of institutions and people. Humanists have often responded to this caricature by defensively pointing out that the sciences too benefit from institutional and personal rhetoric, that they too are social procedures (a fact clearly proven by ethnographies of scientific laboratories), that they too are "biased." All this is true enough, at some level, but it does not adequately reckon with the epistemological legitimacy of humanist practice, since rather than make explicit the reasons why such practices are epistemologically necessary, and therefore reasonable, they seek to bring the sciences down to the level of the humanities. My goal here is not to perform the same procedure in reverse, to elevate humanist practice to the caricatured certainty of scientific rationality, but to produce a clearer picture of the legitimacy of humanist work. That the "two cultures" of modern reason come, after this legitimization, to resemble one another and to overlap in a number of ways does not motivate the approach, though it is a consequence of it.

So, the imagination. I have already argued that historical reason must consider counterfactuals and nonactualities, and that it must do so within a disciplinarily specific and epistemologically articulated field of relevance and plausibility. No anthropological analysis of a cultural object, no sociological description of a social process, no close reading of a work of art, no description of a historical event, is possible without it. In this way, we might say, humanist reason *requires* that we "make things up." Making things up is central to any kind of knowing that considers the complete nature of the contextually bound evidence it processes.

Because whatever context humanists study will be lost or distanced from them in some crucial respects, and because humanists recognize that the full understanding of any given social situation or object requires, ideally, drawing on as many kinds of possible relation to it, humanist reason depends on the imagination in another important way. Humanists *must*, as a matter of epistemological practice, imagine what it might have been like to "be there," whether that being there involves participation in a social process or event, the experience of a maker or producer of some cultural artifact, the experience of a member of a culture encountering that process or artifact in situ. Of course such imagination will necessarily be speculative; of course it will get things wrong; of course it will run the risk, always, of failing to account for the ways in which its own historical situation distorts its imaginative capacity. But humanist reason will always attempt nonetheless to reconstruct that primary embodied experience of the social, and it will do so on the basis of plentiful evidence—historical documents, theories of human behavior or the psychology of crowds, an informed understanding of the patterns of institutional development, and so on. This imaginative work, which can extend to the effort to sustain a full empathetic awareness of the consciousness of a single individual, is bound by disciplinary practices and codifications of legitimacy. It constitutes a critical element of most humanist epistemological practice.

As for the criticism that humanists are just telling stories, this practice too can be understood as a necessary outgrowth of the epistemological necessity created by humanist objects, which are necessarily *bound in time*. This does not prevent humanists from developing synchronic models of diachronic processes, nor does it keep them from using transhistorical categories that necessarily organize a wide variety of data points into a single, stable structure (concepts like "the novel," "the working class," or "feudalism" do this kind of work), even if the general humanist suspicion of subordinating hierarchism necessarily will thereaftertend to reduce and specify them. But this synchronic structuration operates always within the framework of the actual existence of human communities, with all their embeddedness in sociohistorical and environmental processes, the most fundamental and universal of which is the forward direction of time. That does not mean that human societies have not developed alternative conceptualizations of their relations to historical time—cyclical, millennialist, or stage-oriented—or that the phenomenological experience of time works in this way, but it does mean that for modern, secular humanist reasoners, these social formations are themselves operating in a continuous temporal continuum that is shared and transhistorical.

That is why so much humanist scholarship aims either to establish delimiting structures (e.g., the nineteenth century, the modern period) or to destabilize them. This back-and-forth does not signify uncertainty or wrongness. It stems from the ongoing social life of the various pressures of humanist knowledge-production, which operate always in a context determined by what most people believe about X. In a world where people believe that X is stable, humanists will work to demonstrate its instability; in a world where people think that X is unstable, humanists will work to demonstrate its stability. This thermostatic role, which is partially determined by the subjective conditions of the production of knowledge, is one of the main functions of humanist work.

The scholarly value of a social object will not be, therefore, limited to its immediate present or to the socially or individually conscious apperception of its worth. It will be contextually bound across multiple temporal scales, moving forward and backward. This boundedness is in many cases nonlinear: the force of an object does not diminish incrementally as one moves further, temporally or spatially, from its origin; neither do its explanatory contexts grow in relevance as they approach the "natural" scale of the phenomenon. Rather, any object or movement may reemerge, become newly relevant, for reasons that belong to the context of some historical future that fastens onto it. Likewise it may turn out that the causal structures that feel most explanatorily relevant for a given object may stem from scales operating far from it, temporally or geographically; it may be that the best contemporary understanding of a given object comes from methods developed long after, or long before, that object's emergence into culture, or that new tools will make visible or relevant a process that was neither visible nor relevant to the people who lived in or around it, who may not have experienced that process in a primary sense at all. That various elements of the social lifeworld that humanists study model for us this very set of interactions across space and time—that people still believe in religious ideas developed by nomadic Jews, that our hour has sixty minutes because of Babylonian mathematics, that a classical work of art can be remade and renewed in the present by a work that cites or modifies it—each of these examples illustrates the ways in which humanist reason develops out of the evidence that the history of the planet and the universe have placed before it.

ARTICLE 9

Humanist Scholarship Creates Social Value. Humanists Value Scholarship That Increases Richness, Makes the Secondary Primary, and Creates Transportable Concepts.   Consider two kinds of scientific value: the first, the value that science produces for society at large in the form of various truth-claims (about how to measure and think about force) that lead to social practices (the building of bridges or airplanes) that benefit nonscientists and scientists alike. Let's call this "social" value. Then consider a second, more restricted form of value: the value that scientists accord to the work of other scientists by virtue of its being *scientifically* useful—by virtue, that is, of its capacity to extend and engage the work of science more generally, to contribute to the epistemological and disciplinary development of a field. Call this "epistemological" value.

The standard claims are that the humanities produce little to no social value at all (a position common to enemies of the humanities everywhere), and that, where they do, it is by virtue of an increase in the value of the individuals formed by a humanistic education (a position fairly common among humanists themselves).[42] But this thinking ignores all the ways in which humanist scholarship shapes the world by altering its sense of the past, of the functioning of social processes, of the operation of social categories, of the structures and patterns that organize aesthetic culture, and so on. The idea of social democracy is a humanist idea. It has effects. The idea of environmentalism is a humanist idea. It has effects. The idea of the modern prison system, and the idea of prison reform, are humanist ideas. They have effects. And so on. The tendency of the most effective forms of humanist work to expand and to belong to everyone, so that their results no longer count as a matter of humanist work,

partially explains why people imagine that the humanities do not create social value. The reality is that humanist social value at its most
valuable belongs to everyone, including scientists and social scientists (who then do research on things like democracy or the environment), which is why it seems not to exist at all.

The social effectiveness of humanist work in such realms as the
law, social formations, self-conceptualization, institution-building,
or aesthetic production are counterparts to those provided by scientific or technological advances. This capacity to be effective is
a measure of scholarship's *realism*. What I mean is that the fact of
effectiveness in the world tells us something about the world; being
effective responds to and addresses something in the world. This is as
true for the various equations and principles governing the construction of an effective bridge—effective because it crosses the ravine,
because it does not fall down when walked upon, and realistic, therefore, in its capacity to engage with and address reality (whether this
reality exists specifically in the terms that humans give to it ["gravity,"
"mass"] matters not)—as it is for the various principles and evidentiary procedures governing a set of claims about the effects of colo-
nialism upon the psychic makeup of the colonized. If these latter are
effective, if they make a difference in the world, it is because like the
bridge they respond to, and address, the social reality in which they
act and from which they emerge. Claims do not have to be true to
be effective; but anything that is effective in the world is realistic in
this sense, and its effectiveness can be explored in order to understand the nature of the reality that it successfully addresses. (Imagine a study that asks: Why are the lies told by narcissists so effective?
What kind of reality do they address, and what in them—clearly not
the truth-claims—addresses that reality?)

So much for social value.

The epistemological value of humanist scholarship—the forces
that make humanists value a particular piece of scholarship and
hence use it, cite it, respond to it, extend it, and so on—stems largely
from three linked factors:

1. Valuable humanist work increases the richness of our understanding of a social process, historical event, or cultural artifact. There

is value, that is, in adding to the total store of knowledge about something, even if that increase does little other work—does not make new things possible, does not intervene in some important debate, does not substantially alter our understanding of the past. Because humanist objects remain relevant over time and can be seen in new ways as their own historical contexts change—think of the way that our understanding of mid-twentieth-century fascism has been altered by the recent rise in nationalism and anti-Semitism—increases in richness are always possible. And because humanist scholarship does not and cannot maintain a strict boundary between the objects it studies and the present in which they are studied—because humanist scholarship is subjective in origin and epistemologically relational—this increase in richness will not just be an increase in richness of the *object* of knowledge, but also always a potential increase in richness of our understanding of the motivating *subject* that creates it (i.e., both ourselves and our methods).

2. Valuable humanist work makes *secondary* social formations, effects, and activities visible, and thus potentially moveable into the realm of *primary* social life. This is true at a wide variety of scales, from studies that show how common reading practices shape communities of readers to ones that address the scope and effects on human subjectivity of vast geological forces like ice ages or contemporary climate change. It is also true for studies that look at individual people from a social or psychological perspective, as well as studies that examine the formation of ideological norms, of sociocultural discourses, of intellectual movements, shifts in labor markets, impacts created by shifts in legal or social practices, new media technologies or structures of feeling.

In practice, making secondary aspects of culture primary can take a number of forms, ranging from the symptomatic or unmasking model typical of the hermeneutics of suspicion to the seemingly atheoretical and descriptive emphases in the sociology of Erving Goffman or Harold Garfinkel, recently taken up in literary studies as a counter-model to symptomatic reading. Both sides of the so-called reading wars can be thought of as emphasizing, from this perspective, two different kinds of secondary

formation—the first a subterranean secondariness whose organizing force goes unnoticed precisely because it is so deep; the
second a surface secondariness that goes unnoticed precisely
because it is so plainly there, because its evidence is so much in
front of us that it appears completely unremarkable. In this way,
"surface" and "depth" (as well as "closeness" and "distance," for
that matter) reveal themselves most clearly as terms not in relation to one another, but in relation to their truest opposite: the
normal or *average* point of view, which is neither close nor far
away, which has neither umbral depth nor matte superflatness,
the undermining and complexifying of whose primary and completely "obvious" there-ness constitutes the true object of much
humanist epistemological work.[43]

That such work calls to and claims, in the end, a certain social
value, is one of its most prominent rhetorical demands. Many
close readings in literature, many case studies in sociology or
ethnography, and many historical arguments sustained by archival research, make claims about their value on the basis of their
capacity to clarify and reveal the mechanisms that have shaped
human experience (epistemological value); and then make claims
about the ways in which these clarifications and revelations might
help us understand our contemporary moment or give us some
more *primary* purchase on some previously *secondary* force that
has determined the workings of our lives (social value). That the
ordering of these claims proceeds almost always from epistemological to social suggests something of the necessary armature of
humanist rhetoric, as well as something of the deeper social forces
governing the transition from subjective to objective knowledge,
as we understand those terms today.

3. Humanist scholarship produces value when evidence that has
been generalized into a conceptual formation becomes relevant
to cases beyond the particular ones used in the generation of that
concept. This happens when, for instance, the study of a particular food riot teaches us something about riots in general, or about
the history of a time period in general; or when the study of the
workings of the racial imaginary in a certain set of texts or novels
teaches us something about the racial imaginary in general, or in

the nineteenth century, or in novels in general, or in the northern United States. The most valued humanist work almost inevitably generates "strong theory"—a theory, that is, that acquires a large-scale comparative force insofar as it applies not only to the original evidentiary conditions of its making, but also to a much wider variety of conditions: a theory of performative gender, for instance, that is useful for thinking not only about gender today, but also about gender at any historical moment in any historical place.

Humanists tend to value strong theories over weak ones, even when they say they don't (even the idea of strong versus weak theory is a strong theory; claims that we should do more weak theory are themselves strong by virtue of their interest in their own transportability). But theories can be too strong; these create less epistemological value than strong but flexible ones. Work that simply reproduces a strong theory verbatim in relation to some new evidence ("the study of this poem once again proves that Lacan's analysis of the relation between the Real and the Symbolic is correct"), does not follow the idiographic injunction to allow the object to have its say, and also tends, as a result, to be less valuable to humanists than work that allows the object-theory relation to go both ways.

Together, these forms of social and epistemological value make up much of the ways in which humanists value their work. But a number of other factors also interfere in the production of humanist value, many of which take place at the level of form. I love work sometimes for the quality of its sentences. I also love those moments when the author does something clever with the evidence, makes some surprising intellectual move that I had not seen coming, or connects, like a lightning bolt, two ideas that I had not imagined together. I love them for the same reason that I love seeing someone score an amazing goal or play, extraordinarily, a piece of music: for the thrill of seeing someone do something so well that I feel my own humanity extended and honored by its accomplishment. The awareness and recognition of these forms of value are of a piece with the humanist recognition that form matters—that intellectual work, even when it can be paraphrased, nonetheless happens in a crucible, in which the expression of the idea, not just the idea itself, is what sets the mind on fire.

The humanities are nothing without this recognition, and they are nothing without a strong and conscious awareness of the value of its practice—not only for humanists but for humans in general.

3. AN OPEN FUTURE

For a rethought and redescribed humanist reason, nothing is inherently sacred. Nothing is inherently singular. Everything from the speck of dust to the body of a loved one is defined by a malleable, socially manipulable and socially determined *Affektionspreis*. Sacredness and singularity are forms of social value produced by human activity, including the action of simply paying attention to something, of caring enough about it to recognize its uniqueness or its beauty. That such sacredness and singularity have been reified in social institutions (such as museums) is not in and of itself epistemologically bad, though the partial distribution of those reifications can be, as any analysis of the differential distribution of objects in the "art museum" and the "anthropological museum" will suggest. But the reifications of singularity in objects do not prove that singularity only exists there; they prove only that the social organizes itself around the uneven distribution of singularity and organizes its concepts around just such a distribution, even when those concepts no longer adequately describe the actual distribution of various socially determined *Affektionspreise*, or even when in fact they never did. Singularity is the product of a relation; it is determined by personal and institutional action, not by the ontology of any object as such—even if that object is, as it is in Kant, a unique historical event or a rational human being.[44]

One major social site for the reification of singularity has been, as I have been suggesting in this book, the metadiscourse on humanist reason, which has derived from the reification of singularity in aesthetic objects and in human history the ethico-epistemological justifications that have helped humanists for over a century understand and explain what they do. I have been arguing that this explanation is wrong. Remember Chakrabarty: if the humanities have never actually worked the way this metadiscourse claims they do, then neo-Kantian descriptions of the human sciences *do not actually describe the human sciences, but some other thing that has never existed.* My first claim, therefore, is that we ought to stop deriving ethical principles or justifications for the humanities from bad descriptions of what they do. My second argument is that we ought to try to describe the actual work of humanist reason and derive some principles from it—more or less what I've done in this chapter.

Justifications for social activity ought to be drawn from true— reasonable, epistemologically grounded, shareable in common— descriptions of that activity. And the ethical principles governing that activity ought minimally to begin deriving goals from the best actually existing versions of that activity, rather than from a fantastical or idealized projection of that activity. Yes, I know that such a program may leave us short of utopia. But at least for my lifetime, it would be interesting to see if we could get all humanist reason to be as good— as epistemologically and socially powerful, as broadly applicable and useful and shareable—as the very best work that humanist reason has done so far. If we ever get everything to that level, I'm certainly willing to talk about what happens next. There's plenty of work to do in the interim.

My other large-scale claim is that the metadiscourse on humanist reason has had in the past, and has right now, some bad consequences for the humanities.[45] These include accepting, and even emphasizing, the difference between the humanities and the sciences, on for instance the grounds that that the former are oriented toward "interpretation" or "understanding" and the latter toward "explanation"; or that the former are oriented toward "feeling" and the latter toward "doing"; or that the former are fundamentally subjective and the latter objective; or that the former are ethical, ideological, or personal and the latter are morally neutral, objective, and universal. The humanist critique of the ideology of scientific positivism should have made it clear to everyone reading this book how false and dangerous the fantasies describing the right side of the humanities-sciences pairing have been.

But the fantasies describing the left side are just as false and as dangerous, because they radically delimit the field of activity of humanist reason and deny the ways in which its procedures and processes explain things, do things, and make objective, shared knowledge possible.[46] That is why I am describing the work humanists do as a matter of reason, and why a far broader history of human reason of all types, one that would recognize in that history the extraordinary diversity of socially legitimate knowledge-practices (on one scale) as well as the extraordinary commonalities across them (on another), would be necessary in order to produce a complete and unbroken understanding of the emergence of modern humanist reason, as well as the emergence of its metadiscourse.

For now the challenge is this: for the humanities to become responsible for their practice. This taking responsibility will mean abandoning, I am afraid, the residual forms of protection that circle our beloved objects, including the forms of protection that imagine them to be immune to the circulation of violence or of capital (which they most assuredly are not), and to take account therefore of the degree to which idealized forms of being are incompatible (Chakrabarty again) with the evidence given to us by the history of the species. Among other things this means letting go of the centrality of the human to the humanities, which requires us both to recognize the ways in which our experience of the social is subtended by a biological and evolutionary history—and therefore sometimes very much "top-down," in both positive and negative ways—and also to recognize that all beings with minds operate in some kind of a social sphere, and to see that these spheres do not differ in ontological kind from the ones we inhabit. This means that the humanities ought to include as fields of comparable interest many of the subjects and populations currently housed in zoology, and that basic questions of ethical and civic responsibility to other minded beings ought to be part of our general remit (as they already are in the field of animal studies, one subset of the practice of humanist reason from which I learned to think these thoughts).

These changes would also require letting go of the forms of intellectual prejudice that stem from humanist protectionism around its privileged objects, the insistence that some respect for the other requires a thinking of it purely at its level, on its own terms, from the bottom up, and so on. The ethical insistence on flatness, complexity, and ground-up thinking that characterizes humanist metadiscourse would have to give way to a theory of knowledge that recognizes the necessity of concepts for all reason-work, and imagines that conceptualization can be just as much a matter of respect for another as nonconceptualization. At the far end, this would require humanists to be far more open than they have been to large-scale thinking of the structuralist or even computational type, as well as to arguments drawing on such forms of knowledge as biology or medicine, and to do the work of describing epistemologically appropriate practices that use such kinds of evidence—to integrate them, in other words, into the field of humanist reason proper, rather than allowing them to function as a threatening outside. To be clear: This is not an argument that existing practices of humanist scholarship ought to be replaced by such fields, by deterministic models and by the like; it is rather a claim that humanist scholarship will best be able to insist on the value (social and epistemological) of the kinds of close or small-scale forms of attention that it brings to the epistemological table if it, first, stops being so afraid of the so-called violence of syncretic modes of thinking (which it *already uses all the time anyway*), and instead begins to address those modes, to take them on as a matter of practice, and to integrate its practices and experiments in those modes into its more general metadiscourse.

What do the humanities get in return for these changes? An enormous expansion in their field of application. There could and should be humanist thinking in every field, about every kind of object; there should be biologists who tell the story of a single cell, physicists who tell the story of a single atom, and historians of rivers and of continental drift (call them "geologists"). I am not talking about thematizing important social or scientific topics by teaching classes on the "representation" of them. I am not talking about reading five novels featuring poor people and claiming that you have taught a class on poverty. I am saying that the historical and social and economic experience and nature of poverty cannot be understood without humanistic thought, and that a complete understanding of poverty will of necessity involve the humanist investigation of a wide variety of human cultural and economic activity, and lived activity, at any number of scales or in any number of social forms, including those that we call "works of art." And the same for questions of political conflict, for questions of human or group psychology, for questions about humans and their natural or mechanical tools, and so on. And for the history of literariness and aesthetic production more generally, since as we know, humans have *never* lived without dancing, without storytelling, without figurative language, without technological mediations of the mind and of the body, all of which constitute therefore primary (rather than epiphenomenal) matters for the understanding of human life on this planet and in this universe.

Most humanists already believe these things. But we need to see that the consequences of this belief carry us much further forward than they have so far—that they take us out of the comfortable rooms in which we have both thrived and (sometimes) cowered in the face of the rise of the ideologies of scientific positivism and the attacks on humanist reason by right-wing populists and neoliberals.[47] The people who are actively engaged in the attempts, political and cultural, to destroy the institutions of the humanities and to diminish the legitimacy of humanist reason are not trying to do so because those institutions or that reason are socially ineffective; they are trying to destroy them because of all the social work that they have already done. The attacks on the university that come from the right are not actually attacks on the university in general; no one is proposing to get rid of business schools or accounting departments. They are attacks on the humanities disciplines, for which the university serves as a synecdoche.

Though I am wary of repeating here the overblown and almost always too self-aggrandizing claims about the "value" of the humanities (We're critical to democracy! We make animals into people!), I do want to draw your attention to the fact that the enemies of the humanities are as responsible for that discourse as humanists are (their version goes, They're ruining marriage! And America!). I don't think the humanities matter because they're beautiful or because they do left politics. I think the humanities matter because they're a good way of knowing things, and because their way of knowing things has often produced substantial changes in the way all of us think, live our lives, organize our social spheres, and plan for the future. A fundamental rethinking of what it is that humanist scholars do—and a commitment to thinking through, teaching about, and writing with the basic epistemological strengths of our disciplines—will not diminish us. It will extend us.

* * *

That any such extension might be uncomfortable, that it might in fact release the humanities from their institutional shelters, and demand that humanists create newer, different, and more open ones . . . well, this seems to me to be the price we ought to pay for the ideas we already believe in, as well as the consequences of being responsible to their past and future greatness.

IV

CLASSROOMS, UNIVERSITIES, METHODS

1. INSTITUTIONAL QUESTIONS

I have made some effort throughout this book to think of episte-mological questions as fundamentally separate from institutional ones, in order to see if I could grasp the work of humanist reason by generalizing principles that seem to underlie a century's worth of scholarship. Treating those principles as sincerely (if sometimes unconsciously) held, and seeing them as the consequences of individual efforts to say true, valuable, and reasonable things, have helped me understand them as such, with the understanding that nothing ever exists as such, but only in a series of mediating contexts, and that therefore the object perceived "as such" can only be the result of a deliberate heuristic process designed to illuminate some aspects of the social, while necessarily obscuring others.

That is my longwinded way of saying that the production and articulation of humanist metadiscourse are not merely a matter of philosophy, but of institutional work as well. The vast institutional structures that surround and include the modern research univer-sity have shaped, and have been shaped, by humanist metadiscourse in different ways and in different proportions at any given moment of their mutual historical production. This does not mean that humanist reason is therefore—and contra the rest of the content of this book—the epiphenomenal product of some deeper, underlying system of institutional power and prestige. I am simply saying that any effort to separate the practices of reason from the crasser and often depressing (but sometimes also sophisticated and possibility-creating) institutional structures within which they emerge would fail to pass the test of humanist reason itself.

Rather than go back and rewrite the book with that in mind—and because Chad Wellmon, among other historians of the university, has already done the job, so far as the *Methodenstreit* and its aftermath are concerned—it seems now that the institutional question reemerges most forcefully not as a matter of the past I have described, but as a context for the future I have imagined.[1] Simply put: if everything I say is true, and if humanist scholars wish to step across the threshold, what happens next? More specifically: what might the departments, the universities, the journals, or the conferences look like under such conditions?

The changes I propose in this chapter are almost certainly impossible. This is not only because they would involve a great deal of institutional work, the disruption of so many existing structures and administrative units, that the mere fact of their taking place would require years, but also, and mainly, because such changes almost always turn into reasons to reduce the power of faculty governance and to increase the university's reliance on adjunct, precarious teaching labor. We have no model in the modern university, especially in the humanities, for radical institutional revision that is not the product of a financial crisis or part of an attempt to force the work of teaching and learning into a more capitalized model (which means precarious employment for faculty and increased debt for students). So it is difficult to imagine how any change of the type I propose here could take place, except perhaps slowly and piece by piece over a very long time frame.

The change that I am imagining comes down to two intertwined proposals:

1. The undergraduate curriculum in the humanities should not be organized around the institutionalized disciplines.
2. Humanist reason should be found everywhere in the university.

Both proposals stem from the major arguments made about humanist reason in this book: namely, that the separation of humanist epistemological work from the general field of reason (which was then given over to quantitative, scientific, "precise" thought) has restricted the humanities to a field of analysis that is too narrow. In the first case, I would say that the restriction of the humanities to various institutionalized departments has the effect of suggesting to students (and to faculty) that the main reason to get an education in the humanities is to master a disciplinary field: you major in "history" because you want to know how to "do" history, how to marshal the facts and methods of a discipline in particular ways, you major in "English" because you want to learn how to think about literature, or rhetoric, or creative writing, or how to do these things. But if you ask faculty in the humanities what they really want students to get out of their courses, it's rarely something as banal as "a correct understanding of the events and causes of the French Revolution" or "an increased capacity to write about literature." Those might be true, no doubt—they're the stuff that course assessment professionals want to hear, certainly—but, for me at least, I'm trying to teach my students, no matter what class we are in, how to think humanistically, as well as to see how thinking humanistically increases their understanding of the actual functioning of the world and its objects, their capacity to experience beauty and wonder, and their collective interest in being, and ability to be, responsible to their lives and their planet.

The time horizon for that teaching is not the single semester or the course; it's the student's lifetime. And so I don't care too much whether the student remembers anything specific about most of the books they read with me; I care that, in twenty or thirty years, the student will have had a richer and more responsible life, and that the kind of thinking about the world that I helped them learn will have empowered them to do so. I hope, for instance, that they will have gone to one more exhibition or art show than they might have if they had not taken my class, or read one more article on something interesting, or talked to one more stranger, or used their understanding of care and social force to relate to some particular political issue; that they will find their professional and personal lives extended and expanded by the kinds of thinking and knowing they learned with and through and beyond what my teaching made possible. The course content is to some extent incidental to that larger goal.

The undergraduate curriculum has been created by people who have become professional historians, linguists, anthropologists, sociologists, and literature professors. But the vast majority of our undergraduates will not and do not want to become such folks; they do not need a curriculum that prepares them for the subject GRE test. So we shouldn't have a curriculum that organizes itself around the needs and demands of institutionalized disciplines, as though the only reason to study the humanities were to become a professional humanist. We know that's not true! We know we don't care if a student in twenty years remembers the date of something or other; we want this student to understand how historical thinking works, so that they put it to use in their own understanding of the world. Likewise, we don't really care if they remember who wrote some book or other, or what a particular passage of fiction means; we want them to know how to think about the relations between authors and texts, or even the relations between doers and deeds, and we also want them to see the rhetorical and figurative richness of language so they can continue to see it and use it. We want to set their minds on fire.

These days, I can hardly bring myself to tell someone to major in one humanities field over another, as though the best thing you could do with your time was to focus exclusively on one disciplinary field. (Should I major in French, or German, or Chinese? It really doesn't matter; what matters, in terms of your long-term intellectual and personal growth, is learning *any* language at all. Should I study history or sociology? Again, it doesn't matter; you can get where you need to go either way.) In fact, the faculty themselves live this refusal to be restricted to disciplines in their own work. Imagine a professor of history who reads only historians, or a sociologist who reads only sociology. Human life does not organize itself by disciplines, and neither do the faculty. But our undergraduate curriculum reifies that very idea and teaches it to students. In so doing, it conceals what's most exciting about humanist reason: it sees *connections* across the entire fabric of human experience.

So what to do? Probably all the humanities could be collected under the general heading of "history" or "anthropology," so long as one understood that the study of the past or the study of human development included things like sociology, psychology, the artifactual world, natural and social environments, art, literature, music, biology, chemistry, engineering, nursing and care, education, and so on. In fact, this is what we all already believe, even if we know that it takes specialists to do the specific scholarly work needed to make progress in various areas.

Such a system would obviously be institutionally inconvenient; a giant department including all the humanists would be hard to govern. (And of course in general the consolidation of the humanities departments into a single unit is historically an excuse for cutting faculty and programs.) More practically, then, what if faculty in and across the humanities could be associated with two units at once: a graduate program, if appropriate (or a disciplinarily focused research group, if not), and one or more undergraduate programs. *These would not have to be the same thing, or even the same order of thing.* Leaving the disciplines intact at the graduate level (so that we would still have PhDs in history that would inculcate students into the historical discipline of history, with all of its norms of thinking, writing, teaching, and so on), the humanities would then be free to create new undergraduate programs that did not force that disciplinary model onto undergraduate students.

What would take the place of the current undergraduate majors? If I were king of the universe, I would propose that at least one university try replacing the current humanities majors with a much broader set of four-course modules. The modules would be of two types: "skills" modules modules—modules on introductory language learning, on writing (or speaking and writing), and on historical, cultural, and social analysis—and "theme" modules on such topics as Justice, Migration Studies, Translation, Journalism, Poverty, Conflict, Beauty, Television, Society and Technology, and the like. Students could of course combine modules to create majors, including currently existing majors. A student could do modules on Historical Analysis, the History of North America, and Social History, thereby producing a facsimile of the existing History major; or modules on Introductory German, German Literature and Culture, and German for Journalism and the Professions to create a German major. But students could combine one or more modules with a major from outside the humanities as well, such as an Engineering major, plus modules on Urban Design, Poverty, or Spanish, or creating a bespoke humanities major by combining modules on Human Environments, Social Justice, and Writing.

The advantages of moving to such a program would include

- Appealing immediately to students' actual interests/what continues to matter about the humanities; in short, meeting the students where they are, in these historical conditions, rather than lamenting their lack of interest in humanities majors.
- Finding a way to connect to students that does not rely on somewhat uncomfortable models of popularizing (vampire movies) or dumbing down that are often used rhetorically to describe (or justify) changes to the humanities curriculum.
- Allowing students to build an entire educational experience that makes sense to them intellectually and professionally, as well as to explore far more topics than they do when they now pursue a double-major.
- Not forcing students into majors because they need a credential; here the modules serve as the credential, communicating far more clearly than do majors a set of interests, skills, and expertise (to employers as well as others who might be interested, like parents).
- Retaining the possibilities of majoring in the humanities via established/official sequences of three modules (such as Historical Analysis, Labor History, and African-American History) or of pursuing individually developed majors that combine three modules chosen by students themselves.
- Encouraging comparisons of both the geographic/linguistic and historical types, because modules would necessarily be epistemologically comparative. You can't teach someone about poverty or justice or technology without using examples that cross space, language, and time. This has the advantage of moving transnationalism or geographic and linguistic breadth away from being an "angle" that one takes on a topic and toward being a necessary precondition for humanist knowledge.

- Connecting faculty across disciplines as they seek to respond to historical factors and changing situations. Because modules rely to some extent on configurations of existing courses you could (1) get rid of outdated modules after ten to fifteen years and (2) create new modules in response to historical situations or the emergence of new fields of study (environment, animals, or, to go back in time a bit, ethnic/gender studies), all while waiting to see if they develop and grow (in which case you could create a second or third module) or in fact turn out to be not so interesting after all (in which case you could let them go).

Such an approach would liberate departments from the increasingly difficult task of trying to attract students to programs that have become less relevant and overlong (in the modern context) and make it possible for them to engage meaningfully, with a much broader constituency, in order to meet many more student needs. It would also make the functionality (read, also but not only: relevance to future job prospects) of the humanities that much more visible up front, instead of leaving career application to back-end efforts by advisors, word of mouth, or desperation, upon completion of the degree. In short, it would position the humanities in the curriculum by foregrounding their best topics and ideas rather than hiding them behind structures (like the language major or the history major) that no longer function as they used to.

* * *

Putting together a system like this one would involve some complex challenges, to be sure. But it would be nice for humanists to have a chance to imagine curricular change not as a disaster, but as something they could believe in—as something that would in fact improve their teaching and professional experience and allow them to learn and grow in ways that they found exciting.[2]

How could such a change happen? As I see it, the only thing that would make it possible would be for a dean or provost to create the conditions under which the humanities faculty felt free to experiment. Someone needs to say: "I understand that people who feel vulnerable have a hard time taking risks, and I want to you take risks together. With that in mind, here is the average number of tenure-line faculty in the humanities we have had each year over the last twenty years. In order to keep you from wondering whether this is all just an excuse to shut you down, I promise you that a decade from now, we will have about the same number of tenure-line faculty working in these new majors and fields. This is not a trick." Only under these conditions would it be possible for a faculty that has learned through extensive experience that "change" in a university context can only mean cuts, restrictions, and the staving off of disaster to put in the kind of intellectual and institutional work that might be required.

In any case, that's what I would try. I'm not sure it would work, but it seems to me to at least create the conditions for transformational and expansive change. Two happy possible side effects: First, not all universities would have the same undergraduate programs. That seems good! Students might choose to go to one place or another on that basis. And second, these new programs would affect graduate training, both in the crass ways in which prospective faculty orient themselves toward the academic job market and in the more open ways that involve intellectual cross-fertilization, growth, learning, and engagement with new ideas.

In the end, these changes come down to this: If we want to teach our students that human life is not organized into disciplines, then we should not organize our curricula into disciplines. If we want to teach our students to see historical connections across differing conditions of global power, we should not organize our literature departments exclusively around modern languages, which has the effect of reproducing, over and over, all the knowledge and aesthetic work developed during a period of European dominance. If we want to teach our students to use humanist reason to consider problems that they do not think of as humanistic, we should not feel the need to fit topics of political or social justice into our courses on the history of the Ming dynasty or on postcolonial literature, but rather be open about the fact that humanist reason can teach us a great deal about social justice or histories of violence and include courses and majors that have those things right in the name. A new undergraduate curriculum that reflected the remarkable strengths of humanist thought would highlight its astonishing capacity to organize social evidence into patterns, as well as its ability to use those patterns to understand and engage the contemporary world in terms oriented toward the common.

It feels like cheating not to give you some more ideas for possible thematic modules. So here you go: "Wealth and Inequality," "Humans and Their Environments," "Social and Political Justice," "The Problem of God," "What Is Art?", "Minds and Bodies," "Love and Other Feelings," "The Individual and Society," "Sex, Gender, and Sexuality," "How Language Works," "African-American Life," "The Nature of Dominance," "What Is Freedom?", "Literary History," "Ethics," "What Is Human Knowledge?", "War and Conflict," "Culture and Identity" . . . in addition to modules focusing on specific places, languages, times, and other topics, which are easier to imagine, of course, because they're in the curriculum right now ("History of China," "Literature of Germany," etc.). Each of these modules, as I imagine it, would include material from the graduate disciplines of history, literature, linguistics, psychology, economic theory, sociology, philosophy, and others; each of them opens onto a set of questions and problems that cannot restrict themselves to a single discipline or a single type of evidence, or, in most cases, a single set of places and times.

The faculty would have to work during the introductory courses to locate students in a disciplinary context and give them a sense of the broad geographical and historical outlines of their questions—and also remember that just because modules on things like sex and sexuality, Latinx studies, or Chinese history exist doesn't mean that you don't have to include any such material in your discussion of human environments or social justice; the existence of interdisciplinary fields in ethnic studies and women's and gender studies does not mean that the rest of the curriculum is somehow saved from having to address women, gender, or ethnicity. You don't want your curriculum to imply that the study of African Americans happens *over here*, while the study of history "in general" happens *over there*—as though the two things have only something occasional to do with one another.

* * *

So much for reorganizing the existing humanities disciplines. What about expanding the humanities to the rest of the university? Here, the problem will be that the same institutional entrenchments that keep change from happening from within the humanities, for the humanities, will be even more difficult to achieve in departments that may feel like they have no real interest in opening themselves up or losing lines to humanistic disciplines. My model for possible change is therefore slow. It involves a gradual loosening of the hold that a certain model of scientific reason has on both the social and natural sciences, a more widespread recognition of the value of humanist reasoning, and a rejection of the sociocultural imperative to exactitude, precision, and measurability that drives so much of the fetishization of scientific knowledge (and the suspicion felt about its humanist equivalent).

The articles of reason above would take almost no modification to describe the sciences as well. Once you account for the complexity of the social mechanisms governing humanist objects, the gap between so-called scientific and so-called humanist reason closes to almost nothing. Nonetheless the major difference between scientific work of a certain kind and much of what happens in the humanities comes down to analytic scale; or, if one prefers, to the degrees of socially useful meaningfulness that one assigns to a piece of evidence. A single person or poem or historical event takes place at a socially meaningful and essentially normative scale, in the sense that its effects operate largely in the same order of social magnitude as we humans do. A single atom, on the other hand, operates largely at a scale meaningful to other atoms; it's only via the behavior of atoms in general, and specifically of atoms organized at scales that matter to human life, that atoms move into the human social sphere. This at least partly explains why scientists focus on laws that govern large sets of data; the laws are what move the data from a socially meaningless scale to a socially meaningful one (in this way, science too proceeds from the subjective to the objective, in a Weberian sense).

What would science look like if we attempted to make its objects socially meaningful—were we, that is, to approach them in order to reveal not their commonality, but their singularity? What does a physics department get from someone who writes a history of a single atom, or a chemistry department from someone who describes a single chemical reaction? How would the humanist climb up from the singularity of an object to a generality that could be objectively true, interesting, and useful? Would such work ever be considered scholarship, or would it be relegated, with suspicion, to the realm of "popular science" or consigned to the so-called lesser realm of under-graduate teaching?

These are questions for scientists to answer. That said, my guess is that in fact they will in the medium term be answered by humanists, as the most likely professional landing place for a person able to do this kind of work will be a humanities program of some kind. Which would just go to showcase, once again, the humanities' enormous intellectual strength.

2. SO YOU'RE SAYING IT'S OUR FAULT

No, I'm not saying that anything about the current state of the humanities as a set of disciplines and institutional fields is mainly the fault of humanists. I do not believe that the current crisis of the humanities is the result of any significant change in the ways that the humanities are taught, the kinds of content that humanists address, or the theoretical motivations of this or that school of humanist scholarship. The *causes* of the institutional crisis are, to my mind, fairly simple:

(1) They result from the pressures put on social democratic states by capital, and particularly from the attempt made by a variety of state and nonstate actors to reduce all measures of social value to monetizability, in the face of the tremendous body of evidence that no humans have ever really lived, or wanted to live, in that way.

(2) They result, at the same time, from the traffic between that first position (which, in its orientation toward efficiency and monetary value, claims to be politically neutral) and a second, cultural one, in which post-1989 social democratic societies respond to the pressures put on them by immigration and a massive economic slowdown by producing what Bill Bishop calls the "big sort"—a dramatic rise in political polarization that ends up increasing the political valence of nearly everything in the social, from music to food to institutions, including the university.[3] This explains why a majority of Republican and Republican-leaning independents in the United States said,

in a 2017 poll, that colleges and universities have a negative impact on the country.[4] The recent exacerbation of this sorting belongs to a much longer history of the culture wars, with their two recent high points around women's rights and campus culture in the late 1980s and early 1990s (the era of Allan Bloom's *The Closing of the American Mind* and of the rise to fame of Dinesh D'Souza) and more recently (since about 2014) around the same issues, including #MeToo, whose right-wing avatars include alt-right figures like Jordan Peterson and Milo Yiannopoulos.[5]

(3) The final cause is perhaps most direct: it results from a concerted effort by right-wing politicians to combat institutions that they see as supportive of liberal or democratic values—a project that dates, in the major social democracies, mostly from the 1960s, and that involves the creation of para-university structures like institutes or think tanks, as well as funded professorships, in order to produce a counternarrative that is more or less equivalent to the ones that tobacco companies or the makers of Oxycontin created to make it harder for politicians and voters to regulate their products.

Only the third of these causes can remotely be said to respond directly to the kinds of things that humanist faculty do in their classrooms or their publications, where it works by claiming that humanist scholarship is political rather than epistemological, and that therefore the entire apparatus of humanistic work is illegitimate. As I have argued over and over here, this is simply false, false in the sense of being *not true*, and therefore a lie, even if many humanists do think of themselves as oriented toward political goods that the Koch brothers might find unpalatable, or toward the kinds of generalized human flourishing in which, for instance, African Americans or immigrants or transgendered folks actually get to count as people, that will almost certainly result in a loss of cultural prestige and authority for dominant whiteness and masculinity. My argument here is that these orientations, though they may well be subjective in the Weberian sense and therefore frame the kind of scholarship we choose to do or the questions we choose to research, do not necessarily destroy the final demand for the cultural objectivity (and therefore truthfulness) of humanist work, which is itself the product of a shared, and alterable, apparatus of reason that has demonstrated over and over both its reasonable willingness to self-adjust and self-regulate and its tremendous social effectiveness. It is *because* of this effectiveness that so many critics of the humanities are invested in describing the humanities as ineffective. This is the very purpose of the "English BA working at Starbucks" story, which is, unfortunately, a widely believed lie.[6]

So, no, it's not our fault. The causes that I've identified mostly take place at a level well above that of the daily experience of life as a humanist scholar. No devastating critique of the ideological strategies of late capitalism published by a university press is likely to change them—at least not this week, or this month, or even this year. This is why the hiring, enrollment, and funding crisis often makes us feel so helpless. The scale of its operations is political: it calls to us to respond in our capacity as political actors, as voters and activists. And in the absence of strong models of collectivity, many individual political actors feel powerless in relation to the kinds of corporate and governmental power being deployed against them, which explains why, in addition, so much of the work of the political right over the last five decades has been to destroy any existing model of collectivity that might help citizens organize. Having come for the unions, they come now for the university. Every institution that might resist the work of capital or oligarchy is under threat (even if those institutions have, like both unions and universities, sometimes been entirely complicit in the reproduction of capital).

Insofar as the situation of the humanities is also the situation of modern capital and the social democratic welfare state, the proper response to that situation will have to happen at a level of social action quite different from a strong defense of humanist reason. At the same time, we know—once again because of the historical evidence before us—that writing and talking are not politically useless, that ideas can matter and make a difference, that reframing and rearticulating discursive models can work both on the self and on others, at both small, interpersonal scales and larger, mediatic ones. It seems therefore worth remarking, as I have done here, on the ways in which the existing metadiscourse about the humanities, by ceding the ground of reason to the sciences, has made it harder for humanists to make a strong case for their social value.

Too much of humanist metadiscourse is *defensive*. I wanted to write a book that would give us a way to play offense, to be far more assertive that we have been about both the social effectiveness and the epistemological legitimacy of what we do. Whether that discourse will help at larger scales I do not know. But I do know that, at least in the vast experiment in becoming that is an individual life, it has made a difference to me to think this way. Whether my singular experience of its force will be generalizable—and how far—will be answered, at least partially, by the readers of this book.

3. THE HUMANISTIC METHOD

Here is a description of the steps of the scientific method designed for schoolchildren:

1. Ask a question.
2. Gather information and observe (research).
3. Make a hypothesis (guess the answer).
4. Experiment and test your hypothesis.
5. Analyze your test results.
6. Present a conclusion.[7]

And here is Wikipedia's more sophisticated explanation of the process:

> The scientific method is an empirical method of acquiring knowledge that has characterized the development of science since at least the 17th century. It involves careful observation, applying rigorous skepticism about what is observed, given that cognitive assumptions can distort how one interprets the observation. It involves formulating hypotheses, via induction, based on such observations; experimental and measurement-based testing of deductions drawn from the hypotheses; and refinement (or elimination) of the hypotheses based on the experimental findings. These are principles of the scientific method, as distinguished from a definitive series of steps applicable to all scientific enterprises.[8]

Every modern schoolchild learns some version of these ideas. They constitute in many ways the beginning of a transition, natural to most children, from a disorganized or intuitive process of question-asking ("Why is the sky blue?") to an organized one. The elementary and advanced descriptions share a few critical features: observation, an induction-deduction loop that cycles through hypothesis-formation and further observation and "testing," group discussion, and the arrival at a (temporarily) final conclusion.

Although, of course, this description of principles does not carry over fully into scientific practice, and although philosophical critiques of both the principles and the practices in them are legion (see Peter Janich on "measurement," for instance), it nonetheless occurs to me to wonder what it would be like if we had a similarly pithy explanation of something like the humanistic method.[9] It's harder for the humanities, of course, because they have existed for far longer than modern science. Imagine how difficult it would be to describe the "method for understanding things about the natural world" that would unite all classical, medieval, early modern, and modern forms of investigation; what the scientific method has going for it is that it responds mostly to a single episteme.[10] So I begin here with an attempt designed mainly for the modern humanities. One might think of what follows as a set of procedures for moving, as we all do, from a disorganized or intuitive process of asking humanistic questions—Why are people so mean? Why do I have to go to school?—to a more organized, disciplined one:

1. Find a problem, and notice something interesting or unusual about it.
2. Investigate it (research); describe it and understand it on the basis of that investigation. This is tricky in the humanities because, unlike objects of science, humanistic objects are difficult, if not impossible, to isolate from contexts. Describing or delimiting a research object, therefore, may require strategic and essentially temporary decisions about what the object "is" (are Shakespeare's plays just the text of the plays? the plays in performance? and so

on). As a result, much humanistic work cycles through the first two steps a number of times before progressing to steps 3 and 4; the definition of a reasonable object is an important humanist task.

3. Formulate your observations in a way that does not depend too much on the instance that you began with, so that connections to other concepts and ideas can take place; then connect them, inductively, to at least one other general idea.

4. Using that general idea (or ideas), connect and compare your object to other objects that resemble it in critical ways (deciding which ways are critical is part of the problem). There are no pre-set limits on the range or relevance of comparisons; as a result, explaining why these other objects are relevant is an important part of humanist work.

5. Test your generalizations on the basis of these other instances; do not force your instances to conform to the principle, but let things go both ways; the instances ought in almost every case to reshape the generalizations that seem to be "above" them.

6. Loop steps 2 through 5 until you have a general set of claims based on your evidence, as well as a good understanding of how your definition of your object helps make that possible. The distance between your general set of claims and your evidence will serve as a measure of your theory's status as "strong" or "weak"—as something that explains a lot (and in so doing necessarily loses precision), or as something that explains less (but is more precise and nuanced).

7. Present a conclusion and explain how the conclusion fits into existing conclusions about both your general claims and your instances. Your conclusion does not need to be of the "All X are Y" type; rather, it could be focused on what it exceptional in a single instance ("This X is like most Y, except for A") or on patterns or structures that do not resolve themselves into a single law. Indeed, many conclusions in the humanities involve structures of contradiction or of competing tensions or forces that produce different results in different sociohistorical situations.

Or, in paragraph form, in the style of Wikipedia:

> The modern humanistic method is an empirical method of acquiring knowledge that has characterized the development of the humanities since at least the tripartite division of the university into the humanities, social sciences, and sciences, but which draws on methods that go back thousands of years in other forms of humanist practice. It involves careful observation applying rigorous skepticism about what is observed, given that cognitive assumptions can distort how one interprets the observation. It tends to focus on small, complex units of evidence, including historical events, cultural artifacts, and social processes; and to formulate, on the basis of close interpretation and observation of that evidence, both the individual qualities of that evidence and their potential generalizability into larger principles, which might be tested against other complex units. This inductive-deductive looping produces further refinement (or elimination) of generalizations. These are principles of the modern humanistic method, as distinguished from a definitive series of steps applicable to all humanistic enterprises.

A full description of the humanistic method, appropriate for use in schools and universities, would follow these generalizations with specific examples of humanist work. I would begin such a process by showing students some fairly clear-cut instances of empirical success before moving on to models of humanistic work that do not reach, and cannot reach, definitive conclusions. So I would start with the reconstruction of a lost text, the attribution of authorship to a misattributed document, or the reconstruction of a life or historical event (with the emphasis on step 2), before moving to a discussion of a fairly well defined but complex question (How do small-scale social groups differ from large-scale ones? How does the history of media affect such groupings?), and closing with an example of a problem so rich and complex as to defy conclusiveness, or a situation in which eliminating as many wrong answers as possible gets us most of the way to a set of possible right ones, among which decisions cannot be made (What is the meaning, or cultural impact, of the work of W. E. B. DuBois, or Jiang Qing? Can we clearly distinguish between human activity that has an evolutionary purpose and that which is essentially epiphenomenal?). Imagine a world in which this kind of topic was regularly taught in elementary or middle school.

4. TL; DR

The humanities disciplines have been accompanied since at least the late nineteenth century by an epistemological metadiscourse—a series of statements about how humanist scholars think, and should think. It owes its origins at least partly to Immanuel Kant's theorization of the self-legislating qualities of the human being and the theory of beauty that he advances in his *Critique of Judgment*.

This metadiscourse is both philosophically untenable and anthropologically incoherent. That is, it doesn't describe the truth about the objects of humanist attention (novels, historical events, social processes) or the actuality of humanist scholarship. What would be useful, then, is a description of the processes of humanist epistemology, which we will call "humanist reason."

The idea of reason has been thought of too narrowly as scientific—partly because of the tendency in humanist metadiscourse to define humanist thinking in opposition to scientific positivism. Humanist reason, like scientific reason, develops general epistemological principles from the evidence it considers. If we try to describe it, we arrive at the following general principles:

1. *All Human Activity Is Context-Embedded but Not Context-Determined.*
   a. The mediation between contextual determination and freedom is finally undecidable, or decidable only as a function of the needs of a specific epistemological project.
   b. All considerations of historical context must include their non-actualized possibilities.
2. *Human Life Does Not Follow Disciplinary Boundaries; Neither Does Scholarship.*
   a. No humanist scholarship can exist without drawing on history, the arts, literature, philosophy, sociology, anthropology, geography, economics, and other subjects.
   b. The division of the humanities into departments follows a bureaucratic logic, not an epistemological one.

3. *All Social Processes and Artifacts Result from Combinations of Primary and Secondary Causes and Contain Primary and Secondary Information.*
   a. Much humanist work aims to produce explanations for the social activity of secondary forces; these manifest in theories of ideology (at the suprahuman scale) or the unconscious (at the subhuman one), and elsewhere.
   b. The distinction between primary and secondary is not just a matter of scholarly practice, but a critical organizing feature and practice of social life.
4. *Human Social Life Is Not Flat; Scales Are Complex, Overlapping, and Porous.*
   a. The pseudo-poststructuralist prejudice toward flatness and the resistance to hierarchical models is a classic contemporary expression of post-Kantian humanist metadiscourse.
   b. It also tends, because it has a bad theory of concepts, to emphasize concretion over abstraction and reality over thought.
   c. Generalized and abstract concepts, and scalar thinking that recognizes the operation of social forces at various scales, are necessary to humanist reason.
5. *Historical Causality Includes Nondeterministic and Indirect Forces Operating at Multiple Scales.*
   a. Human social life cannot be adequately described by using models from science, no matter how exciting (chaos theory!) or friendly (butterfly effect!) such models may seem.
   b. That is because human causality is both overdetermined and underdetermined, in various ways and in various instances.
   c. And yet humanists regularly make verifiable truth-claims.
6. *Complex Social Systems Do Not Necessarily Follow Statistical or Linear Patterns; Outliers Often Have an Outsized Importance; The Historical Record Makes Epistemological Demands on Concept-Formation; Materiality Is the Limit to Idealism.*
   a. Degrees of social or historical importance do not operate on a linear scale because human beings and human social groups are not motivated on linear scales.
   b. The fact that something happened once means that it must be considered in the formation of a concept of all things.

c. The fact that something has never *not* happened means that we should be very suspicious of either analytic or political concepts that ignore it or present it as a relic.

7. *Fuzziness, Ambiguity, and Contradiction Are Socially Functional; Any Humanist Analysis That Treats Them Necessarily as Problems to Be Resolved Has Misunderstood Its Object.*

   a. A fully paranoid humanist analysis will always fail to confront the actuality of human life, which is in fact not fully determinable.

   b. Therefore, fuzziness, ambiguity, and other structures (including coincidence), all of which actually exist, are necessary targets and sources of humanist scholarship.

8. *Humanist Imagination Is an Epistemologically Necessary Response to the Actuality of Humanist Evidence.*

   a. Humanists don't just make things up.

   b. Humanists need the imagination because the meaning, value, and sociohistorical embeddedness of any given object change over time, actively and in ways that merit continued reconsideration of what humanists already "know."

9. *Humanist Scholarship Values Producing Increased Richness, Making Secondary Information Primary, and Creating Comparative, Transportable Concepts.*

   a. Like the sciences, humanist scholarship can be socially effective; consider how theories of (and laws about, and medical treatments related to) gender and sexuality have changed over the last five decades.

   b. The commitment to what some deride as inclusiveness is in fact a matter of epistemological necessity; this truth has been demonstrated over and over again in the history of humanist scholarship, and constitutes a principle of reason as much as a political commitment.

Abandoning the fetishization of singularity and uniqueness does no damage to humanist reason. Instead, it opens up large new fields of possibility and growth, all of which might involve frightening and significant change. Let's play offense.

NOTES

INTRODUCTION

1. Enrico Spolaore and Romain Wacziarg, "The Diffusion of Development," *Quarterly Journal of Economics*, 124, no. 2 (May 2009), 471.
2. Even though this situation was obviously personally aggravating, the work that Wacziarg and Spolaore did is important for the field of economics, in which the ideology of the rational economic actor has done so much damage. Making economists able to hear that cultural differences matter is a step forward. I should also say that Rogowski was in every other way a nice and wonderful person, and that his entire being should not be judged by this one stupid joke. (Although honestly, it was very annoying and stupid.)
3. Eric Hayot, *The Hypothetical Mandarin: Sympathy, Modernity, and Chinese Pain* (Oxford: Oxford University Press, 2009), 14.
4. For a sense of the ways in which "the university" or "professors" in such books tend to in fact mean "the humanities" (which is fine! many books confuse "the university" with "the sciences," too!), look no further than the shift between the title and the subtitle of Frank Donoghue's *The Last Professors: The Corporate University and the Fate of the Humanities* (New York: Fordham University Press, 2008).
5. To counter arguments that humanists need simply "make the case" for the humanities in order to save the field, see this brilliant piece: Adam Kotsko, "Not Persuasion, but Power: Against 'Making the Case,'" Forum Response, *Boston Review*, May 6, 2020, https://bostonreview.net/forum /higher-education-age-coronavirus/adam-kotsko-not-persuasion-power -against-%E2%80%9Cmaking-case%E2%80%9D.

6. I say this as though the "historical record" were something that existed prior to the exploration, interpretation, and theorization of it. That's not true, as plenty of humanist work has shown.

1. THE RISE OF IDIOGRAPHISM:
OR THE ORIGINS OF HUMANIST METADISCOURSE

1. What was being commemorated? Neither, as Bennett Gilbert notes, the date of the gymnasium's founding (in 1538) nor that of the university (in 1621), but the date "in 1872 on which the old university was incorporated into the Imperial system of Kaiser-Wilhelm Institutes, the date therefore of the school's formal entrance into the rationalized administrative and disciplinary organization and into the power structure of the Prussian system" ("On Wilhelm Windelband's History and Natural Science" [2013], 2).

2. Wilhelm Windelband, *Geschichte und Naturwissenschaft*: Rede . . . (Heitz, 1904), 9; Wilhelm Windelband, "History and Natural Science," trans. Guy Oakes, *History and Theory* 19, no. 2 (February 1980): 173. The latter is also the source for the further references to the Oakes translation in the text.

3. For a longer explanation of the rise of science as the primary culture of the university, see Chad Wellmon, *Organizing Enlightenment: Information Overload and the Invention of the Modern Research University* (Baltimore: Johns Hopkins University Press, 2016).

4. On the history of statistics, see Ian Hacking, *The Taming of Chance* (Cambridge: Cambridge University Press, 1990); Theodore M. Porter, *The Rise of Statistical Thinking, 1820–1900* (Princeton, NJ: Princeton University Press, 1988).

5. Herbert Schnädelbach, *Philosophy in Germany 1831–1933*, trans. Eric Matthews (Cambridge: Cambridge University Press, 1984), 51.

6. Eduard Meyer, Zur *Theorie und Methodik der Geschichte*. Geschichtsphilosophische Untersuchungen (On the theory and methodology of history. Investigations into the history of philosophy) (Halle an der Salle: M. Niemeyer, 1902), 3, https//catalog.hathitrust.org/Record/008904665.

7. Cited in Meyer, *Zur Theorie und Methodik der Geschichte*, 11; Karl Lamprecht, *Zwei Streitschriften den Herren H. Oncken, H. Delbrück, M. Lenz* (H. Heyfelder, 1897), 37.

8. Cited in Schnädelbach, *Philosophy in Germany*, 41–42.

9. Schnädelbach, *Philosophy in Germany*, 43.

10. Leopold von Ranke, *Das politische Gespräch, cited in Fritz Ringer, Max Weber's Methodology: The Unification of the Cultural and Social Sciences* (Cambridge, MA: Harvard University Press, 1998), 11.

11. Ringer, *Max Weber's Methodology*, 13. Knies is perhaps best known today because of Weber's extensive criticism of his work in Max Weber, *Roscher*

and Knies: The Logical Problems of Historical Economics, trans. Guy Oakes (New York: Free Press, 1976).

12. Textual computational analysis dates back decades; in David Lodge's novel *Changing Places: A Tale of Two Campuses*, Morris Zapp, an American professor, dreams of a future in which, using "computers and teams of trained graduate students," he could gradually interpret the entire literary canon down to zero, "spreading dismay through the whole industry, rendering scores of his colleagues redundant" (New York: Penguin Books, 1979, 45). Given new impetus by the digitization of large textual corpora and methods developed in mathematics and linguistics, such analysis has acquired in the last two decades an institutional force out of proportion with its effects—which is a sign that it is speaking in the voice of the "future." On the future of the humanities as a Veblen good, see Paula Krebs, "Wisconsin Is Trying to Segregate Higher Education into the Haves and Have-Nots," *Washington Post*, March 21, 2018, sec. Opinions, https:// www.washingtonpost.com/opinions/wisconsin-is-trying-to-segregate -higher-education-into-the-haves-and-have-nots/2018/03/21/8cd67ac0-2886 -11e8-b79d-f3d931db7f68_story.html.

13. See Franco Moretti, *Distant Reading* (New York: Verso, 2013), 152–53.

14. At no point did he seem to consider whether something nondichotomous (a triangle, a hierarchy) might work; by this point, the institutionalization of knowledge practices had already reified the rift between two types of things, no matter what one calls them.

15. Rudolf A. Makkreel, "Wilhelm Dilthey and the Neo-Kantians: The Distinction of the Geisteswissenschaften and the Kulturwissenschaften," *Journal of the History of Philosophy* 7, no. 4 (1969): 424. As Makkreel shows, Dilthey well understood that he was the target of Windelband's critique, and he responded to the Rectorial Address in an essay, "On Comparative Psychology" (1896).

16. Makkreel, "Wilhelm Dilthey and the Neo-Kantians," 425.

17. The term was developed by Johann Eduard Erdmann in 1870 to describe a position (taken most famously by John Stuart Mill) that logic is a subset of psychology because the latter category governs all mental activity.

18. Guy Oakes, "Value Theory and the Foundations of the Cultural Sciences. Remarks on Rickert," in *Methodology of the Social Sciences, Ethics, and Economics in the Newer Historical School: From Max Weber and Rickert to Sombart and Rothacker*, ed. Peter Koslowski (Berlin/Heidelberg/New York: Springer Verlag, 1997), 66n4.

19. For certain conventional definitions of "happen," of course, which would be destabilized by psychoanalytic theories of *Nachträglichkeit*, by theorists of trauma, or by any theory of figuration or repetition in, for instance, cyclical history. But even then, one might think of each element in a chain of repetitions as unique and distinct, given that it occupies a temporal position unlike that of any other repetition in the chain.

20. Even the choice of "explain" or "understand" as a term to describe the goal of intellectual investigation shades the task toward the nomothetic in the first case, or the idiographic on the other. We have no neutral words for describing our situation, which is simultaneously a matter of epistemological history, social practice, and institutional reification. Indeed, the difference between explanation (for the natural sciences) and understanding (for the cultural ones) was a major point of intellectual ferment during the *Methodenstreit;* see Schnädelbach's discussion of Rickert's critique of Dilthey (*Philosophy in Germany*, 129–31), as well as the extensive discussion in Ringer (*Max Weber's Methodology*, ch. 4).

21. Where this leaves the social sciences is an open question. In fact, it was the ambiguous and complex status of the social sciences within an established division of knowledge between nature and humankind that helped kick off the late-nineteenth-century *Methodenstreit* in the first place—which also explains why Weber was its most internationally influential descendant.

22. To be clear: this is not a restriction imposed on the humanities by the sciences, but by each side on the other, as well as on itself. Would your literature department hire someone who did close readings of single cells, or Foucaultian genealogies of rock formations?

23. For a discussion of this moment in Windelband's philosophy, see Peter Janich, *Was ist Information?* Kritik einer Legende (Frankfurt am Main: Suhrkamp, 2006), 137–38.

24. C. P. Snow, *Two Cultures: And a Second Look*, (New American Library/Mentor, 1964). For two general reconciliations that amount to folding the humanities into a triumphant science, see Steven Pinker, *The Blank Slate: The Modern Denial of Human Nature* (New York: Penguin Books, 2003); Edward Osborne Wilson, *Consilience: The Unity of Knowledge* (New York: Vintage, 1999).

25. A warm smile of recognition for Windelband's "earthy," *Erdgeruch*, whose cognates appear so often in the work of his student's student, Martin Heidegger, and play such an important role in the classic origin text of my field of comparative literature, Erich Auerbach's *Mimesis*. The earthly will have a long career in twentieth-century humanist reason, and the "dirt and rocks" that make it up will make a cameo appearance in chapter 3 of this book.

26. Bennett Gilbert calls it a "sudden ignition of feeling" ("On Wilhelm Windelband's History and Natural Science," 19).

27. All this allows Windelband to make a somewhat charming personal observation: "It has always been painful to me that a people as refined and sensitive as the Greeks," he wrote, "could tolerate one of the doctrines which persists throughout their philosophy"; namely, reincarnation, in which the personality too falls prey to the "periodic recurrence of all things" (*Geschichte und Naturwissenschaft*, 182).

28. Georg Simmel, *Die Probleme der Geschichtsphilosophie*: Eine erkenntnisthe-oretische Studie (Duncker & Humblot, 1892), 43.

29. The notion that "we" inheritors of the Christian worldview believe in a unique history (and its accompanying unique personalities), as opposed to those premoderns and primitives who thought history moved in circles, should be familiar enough; it was after all the principle behind much midt-wentieth-century anthropology of the Mircea Eliade type. See, for instance, Eliade's *The Myth of the Eternal Return: Cosmos and History*, trans. Willard R. Trask (Princeton, NJ: Princeton University Press, 2005). The classic cri-tique of modern time-hegemony appears in Johannes Fabian, *Time and the Other: How Anthropology Makes Its Object*, trans. Matti Bunzl, (New York: Columbia University Press, 2002). See also Peter Osborne, *The Politics of Time: Modernity and Avant-Garde* (London: Verso, 2011).

30. Probably a little narrowly with "criticism," but still. Ted Underwood, *Distant Horizons: Digital Evidence and Literary Change* (Chicago: University of Chicago Press, 2019), 153.

31. I'm speaking for myself, obviously, but also, as far as I can tell, for lots of other folks. Probably not everyone! It may also be that such a feeling is historical, a product of the rise of individualism (if there was such a rise) or of capitalist modernity more broadly. In any case, it seems clear enough to me that lots of people feel this way now, and that feeling this way consti-tutes a problem for all general knowledge-claims that seek to be effective in relation to actually existing people and the ways that they think and feel.

32. Windelband generalizes the example: "a description of the present state of the universe follows from the general laws of nature only if the immedi-ately preceding state of the universe is presupposed. But this state presup-poses the state that immediately precedes it, and so on" (*Geschichte und Naturwissenschaft*, 184).

33. Seize, if you wish, upon a fourth negation: *individual*. Heinrich Rickert would go on to make much of the word's etymology, distinguishing the ordinary individual (some particular person, event, or thing) from what he called the "in-dividual," the particular that cannot be divided, and that thereby constitutes a kind of self-sustaining, insubordinatable whole. In keeping with the generally anthropological orientation of the Heidelberg neo-Kantians, the in-dividual/individual dichotomy "is grounded in a gen-eral fact about human experience that lies within what might be called the universal pragmatics of human life" rather than in any metaphysical claim (Guy Oakes, "Introduction: Rickert's Theory of Historical Knowledge," in Heinrich Rickert, *The Limits of Concept Formation in Natural Science: A Logical Introduction to the Historical Sciences*, trans. Guy Oakes [Cambridge: Cambridge University Press, 1986], xxiv).

34. In this way, the law is, in some respects, the enemy of history. In utopias, no one can, or wants to, break the law; the law has been absorbed fully into

the social, and, as a result, no history can take place. This is why utopian fiction struggles to be narratively interesting; narrative interest—indeed story—comes only from the crack in the utopian law, whether or not that crack ultimately reveals a true opening (*Snowpiercer*, *The Matrix*) or is just the shadow on the wall of a deeper form of control (Yevgeny Zamyatin's *We*, or George Orwell's *1984*).

35. See Meyer, *Zur Theorie und Methodik Der Geschichte*, 5. Compare to Windelband: "all subsumption under general laws is useless" (*Geschichte und Naturwissenschaft*, 184). The phrase also recalls Schnädelbach's description of the late nineteenth century's resistance to idealism: "a priori construction and subordination—whether in the form of subsumption under generalizations as 'a case of . . .' or of deduction from general causes—would reduce the individual to the general and, by making it something completely explicable, annihilate it in its freedom" (*Philosophy in Germany*, 45).

36. Meyer, *Zur Theorie und Methodik Der Geschichte*, 5, 7, 9.

37. Gilbert, "On Wilhelm Windelband's History and Natural Science," 13.

38. John E. Jalbert, "Husserl's Position Between Dilthey and the Windelband-Rickert School of Neo-Kantianism," *Journal of the History of Philosophy* 26, no. 2 (1988): 280.

39. This is where I agree with Paul Reitter and Chad Wellmon, who argue in *Permanent Crisis* (forthcoming) that the "modern humanities" should be broken off socially and structurally from the longer histories of the humanities pursued by scholars like Rens Bod. The kinds of pressure put on those disciplines by the new institutional structure of the post-1800 university seem to institutionalize the humanities in a unique historical formation, which needs some kind of specifying adjective ("modern" is fine; but I would settle for "post-1880" or "capitalist university-oriented").

40. This despite the fact that Windelband rejected, at the beginning of his Rectorial Address, the idea of a substantive dichotomy, preferring to think of idiographic/nomothetic as matters of approach. Nonetheless, the idiographic is justified in the address and elsewhere finally by the fact that history is *ontologically* unique.

41. From Johann Wolfgang von Goethe, *Maximen und Reflexionen*, ed. Gottfried Martin Daiber and Gunter Böhmer (Recklinghausen, Germany: Seemann, 1961), sec. 279, my emphases. That Goethe's line is cited approvingly by both René Wellek, in *A History of Modern Criticism 1750–1950: Volume 1, The Later Eighteenth Century* (Cambridge: Cambridge University Press, 1983, 211), and Pauline Yu, in *The Reading of Imagery in the Chinese Poetic Tradition* (Princeton, NJ: Princeton University Press, 1987, 27), suggests how widely a romantic theory of literature can align itself with Kantian reflecting judgment against its determining counterpart.

42. Bennett Gilbert writes that among philosophers and historians, "none, without exception, has written anything about the back halves of these words," and goes on to argue that for Windelband, "something in the 'colorful world of the senses' has the virtue of reason" ("On Wilhelm Windelband's History and Natural Science," 20).

43. As a description of the division of stylistic and aesthetic labor in the university today, the *tithein-graphein* distinction works awfully well: compare the regulations for research papers in the stylebook of the American Psychological Association, with their confident arrangement of standard sections, to the far looser encouragements of style guides for literary critics, and all their discomfort with rule-following—a reminder, if we ever needed one, that the philosophy of knowledge depends as much on how the research object is related to, as on how that relation eventually gets communicated. See, for instance, American Psychological Association, *Publication Manual of the American Psychological Association* (Washington, DC: American Psychological Association, 2009), or Paul Silvia, *Write It Up: Practical Strategies for Writing and Publishing Journal Articles* (Washington, DC: American Psychological Association, 2014), as against something even as regimented, by literary critical standards, as Gerald Graff and Cathy Birkenstein, *"They Say/I Say": The Moves That Matter in Academic Writing*, 3rd ed. (New York: W. W. Norton, 2014). Or, further afield, look at the experimental prose-forms in the new journal *Thresholds* (http://openthresholds.org/).

44. Ben Etherington, *Literary Primitivism* (Stanford, CA: Stanford University Press, 2017), 162.

45. J. Hillis Miller, *The Ethics of Reading: Kant, De Man, Eliot, Trollope, James, and Benjamin* (New York: Columbia University Press, 1986).

46. Here, one might also think of the problems posed for symbolic logic by something like Bertrand Russell's barber paradox.

47. The scholarly body of literature making this case—in effect denying the possibility of a total ontological or even argumentative separation between particularity and generality, or example and theory adduced from the example—is voluminous. For extended discussions of the problem, see most of the oeuvre of Jacques Derrida, or, in smaller doses, the introductions to Eric Hayot, *The Hypothetical Mandarin: Sympathy, Modernity, and Chinese Pain* (Oxford: Oxford University Press, 2009); or Lisa Gitelman, ed., *"Raw Data" Is an Oxymoron* (Cambridge, MA: MIT Press, 2013).

48. Miller, *The Ethics of Reading*, 24.

49. For a longer discussion of Janich's ideas, see the translators' introduction to Janich, *What Is Information?* For Garfinkel, see Harold Garfinkel, *Ethnomethodology's Program*, ed. Anne Rawls (Lanham, MD: Rowman & Littlefield Publishers, 2002); Harold Garfinkel and Anne Rawls, *Toward a Sociological Theory of Information* (New York: Routledge, 2009). See Anne

Rawls's introduction in the latter volume for an especially clear and useful description of the theory behind Garfinkel's practice.

50. The citation comes from Kumar and Tucker's introduction to a special issue of *New Literary History*, "Writ Large," that addresses questions of scale and generalization in humanist work. Krishnan Kumar and Herbert F. Tucker, "Introduction," *New Literary History* 48, no. 4 (2017): 610.

51. Things don't really work this way, since there is no "raw material" without the categories that govern it, just as there are no categories without phenomena. Ouroboros.

52. Steven Connor, "In Exemplification," in *The State of Theory*, ed. Richard Bradford (New York: Routledge, 1993), 37.

53. See "Conjectures in World Literature," in Moretti, *Distant Reading*, 43–62.

54. Windelband: the nomothetist "is concerned only with the properties of the datum which provide insight into a general nomological regularity"; the idiographer's goal is "to breathe new life into some structure of the past in such a way that all of its concrete and distinctive features acquire an ideal actuality or contemporaneity" (*Geschichte und Naturwissenschaft*, 178). Notice how the difference between the two approaches is described as a matter of the researcher's "goal" or "concern," not as a function of the object per se. This is one of those moments where Windelband vibrates, as he often does, between what feels like a rough philosophical pragmatism and an intensely neo-Kantian orientation toward anthropologically limited metaphysics.

55. The paradox, attributed to the fourth century BCE Greek philosopher Eubulides of Miletus, goes like this: You can pile grains of sand on top of one another until the grains "become" (as measured by some observer) a "heap." But if you remove one grain from that heap, it remains a heap: paradox. Like most paradoxes, it is a paradox only if the solution remains at the same level of the presentation of the problem; paradoxes are, in this sense, simply the name that we give to problems that must be solved at another level than the one at which they are posed.

56. In the study of other universes, such as those abstract universes imagined by mathematicians or logicians, or the worlds of rational actors that economists imagine into being in order to justify their theories, there can be, of course, a kind of pure nomothetism. A history of those imaginations would be in turn, and necessarily, idiographic.

57. But what explains this differential relation to scale? I'll have more to say about that in chapter 3, but for now, here's a guess: the fact that the natural sciences mainly study things without minds.

58. Helen H. Small, *The Value of the Humanities* (New York: Oxford University Press, 2016).

59. Stefan Collini, *Speaking of Universities* (London: Verso, 2018), 225.

60. Underwood, *Distant Horizons*, 152.

61. To pick only one example of many, here is Naomi Schor, in *Reading in Detail: Aesthetics and the Feminine*, ed. Ellen Rooney (New York: Routledge, 2006, 9), attacking the idealist (and masculine) aesthetics of Sir Joshua Reynolds: "The 'selection' procedure Reynolds recommends the painter follow in abstracting the Ideal from brute Nature is not unlike the technique devised by structuralist analysts of myth and folktales to extract the invariant structure of the narrative from its variable concrete manifestations." The opposition between the ground of reality, associated with the variable, the concrete, and the living, and the "extractive" and abstractive industry of the structuralist or the idealist creates a central figure in the rhetoric of idiography. As for critiques of computational literary studies, they are legion, so let me just cite Nan Z. Da's pithy description of the entire discipline of literary criticism as "about *reducing* reductionism" as an absolutely correct statement about the self-conceptualization of the field. See Nan Z. Da, "The Computational Case Against Computational Literary Studies," *Critical Inquiry* 45, no. 3 (March 1, 2019): 638, https://doi .org/10.1086/702594.

62. Cleanth Brooks, *The Well Wrought Urn: Studies in the Structure of Poetry* (Orlando, FL: Mariner, 1956). For a critique of the poststructuralist version of this preference, see Alan Liu, "Local Transcendence: Cultural Criticism, Postmodernism, and the Romanticism of Detail," *Representations*, no. 32 (1990): 75–113.

63. Derek Attridge, *The Singularity of Literature* (New York: Routledge, 2017), 63 (my emphasis). Attridge continues by saying: singularity is not generated by a "core of irreducible materiality . . . but by a configuration of general properties that . . . go beyond the possibilities pre-programmed by a culture's norms." The notion of the singularity of the cultural object as the emblematic expression of the possibility of freedom from norms or "general determination" goes to the heart, I am saying, of the most basic ethico-epistemological imperatives that have defined literary and historical studies as disciplines. That this escape to generalization has so often been conceived of, as Attridge does here, a form of "resisting," also explains why humanistic metadiscourse favors antistatism, anti-institutionalism, and left-liberalism.

64. Stephen Greenblatt, *Shakespearean Negotiations: The Circulation of Social Energy in Renaissance England* (Berkeley: University of California Press, 1989), 1. Questions of exemplarity and close reading as methodological features of literary criticism reached one peak of critical attention in the late 1980s, when Liu, Schor, Connor, and Miller all published their work; this is also the era of Joel Fineman's famous essay on the anecdote, included in Harold Aram Veeser, ed., *The New Historicism* (New York: Routledge, 1989), of Greenblatt's *Shakespearean Negotiations* (1988), and thus the opening strains of the triumph of the New Historicism over deconstruction

(Miller's address as the president of MLA, a major salvo in that engagement, took place in 1986).

65. See the claim/description of method made by a young (!!) Eric Hayot in the introduction to Eric R. J. Hayot, *Chinese Dreams: Pound, Brecht, Tel Quel* (Ann Arbor: University of Michigan Press, 2004).

66. The phrase "listening to the other" appears twice in Jane Gallop, "The Ethics of Reading: Close Encounters," *Journal of Curriculum Theorizing* (Fall 2000, 13–14); the essay's final line argues for "close reading as a means to a more just treatment of others" (17).

2. THE FUTURE OF SINGULARITY: SENTIMENTAL VALUE AFTER KANT

1. Immanuel Kant, *The Critique of the Power of Judgment*, ed. Paul Guyer, trans. Paul Guyer and Eric Matthews (Cambridge: Cambridge University Press, 2000), 66. This is also the source of the further page references in the text.

2. On this topic see Paul Guyer, "The Transcendental Dedution of the Categories," in *The Cambridge Companion to Kant*, ed. Paul Guyer (Cambridge: Cambridge University Press, 1992), 123–60.

3. Guyer and Mathews use italics, as did Kant, to indicate words that he thought of as foreign, and bold to mark words that Kant had originally placed in *Fettdruck*, for emphasis; I have retained that usage here, and noted where I have italicized portions of the citations for emphasis (see "Editor's Introduction," xlix).

4. Guyer and Matthews translate *Zweck*, often given as "purpose," as "end" in order to connect it to Kant's use of the term in his discussion of ethics (see "Editor's Introduction," xlviii); the phrase in their edition thus appears as "purposiveness without end" (translated from *Zweckmäßigkeit ohne Zweck*); I have changed it here to note the connection to the better-known and more mellifluous version of the phrase.

5. Here, we may recall Sianne Ngai's analysis of the aesthetic experience of the "interesting," whose modern articulation of a kind of purposelessness that nonetheless makes some claims on some disinterested intellectual utility seems to occupy a position proximate to, but subtly socially differentiated from, the disinterestedness of the Kantian appreciation of the beautiful. See Sianne Ngai, *Our Aesthetic Categories: Zany, Cute, Interesting* (Cambridge, MA: Harvard University Press, 2015).

6. Connor, "In Exemplification," 39.

7. Connor, "In Exemplification," 51.

8. Readers who know their Kant may be wondering why I have not touched on the section of the third *Critique* that deals most explicitly with problems of analytic scale—namely, the second book, on the "Analytic of the Sublime."

And, of course, it is true that there, especially in the section on the mathematical sublime, Kant addresses scale in its most common-sensical version, writing, "**That is sublime in comparison with which everything else is small**. Here one readily sees that nothing can be given in nature, however great it may be judged to be by us, which could not, considered in another relation, be diminished down to the infinitely small; and conversely, there is nothing so small which could not, in comparison with even smaller standards, be amplified for our imagination up to the magnitude of a world. The telescope has given us rich material for making the former observation, the microscope rich material for the latter" (134). As Kant goes on to say, this merely mathematical set of relations is overcome by our awareness of our incapacity to estimate the true magnitude of things in the world, which "awake[n]s the feeling of a supersensible faculty in us" (134); it is this latter element that connects us to the sublime. But there is for me a crucial difference between the sublime and the beautiful as Kant discusses them, relating particularly to the problem of scale. As you see in the citations given here, the sublime is quite specifically nonscalar; it is constituted not by our laddering up through various mathematical magnitudes to ever-larger numbers, but rather by the rational awareness of our incapacity to grasp totalities at all. Kant writes later that "the systematic division of the structure of the world . . . [represents] to us all that is great in nature as in its turn small"—and therefore the potential "scalar" and relative structuration of our experience of reality—"but," he continues, "*actually representing* our imagination in all its boundlessness, and with it nature, as *paling into insignificance* beside the ideas of reason if it is supposed to provide a presentation adequate to them" (140). In other words, the sublime has to do with the failure of scalar laddering, of sensible experience as oriented around the production of magnitude in *steps* or *levels* in order to grasp reason's capacity to understand totalities. That is why the "feeling of the sublime is thus a feeling of displeasure from the inadequacy of the imagination in the aesthetic estimation of magnitude," and the pleasure that comes from recognizing the law of reason that can—unlike the imagination—"adopt [the absolutely great] alone as the supreme measure of magnitude" (141). In this sense, one might say that the entire analytic of the sublime organizes itself around the difference between *parts* and *wholes*, whereas the analytic of the beautiful orients itself toward the difference between the *singular* and the *universal*, the example and the theory, the particular and the general, the object and its concept, which constitute our subject so far. I have written extensively about the history of part/whole relations as figures of world-thinking elsewhere; see *On Literary Worlds* (Oxford, 2012) and "World Literature and Globalization Studies," *The Routledge Companion to World Literature*, ed. David Damrosch, Theo D'Haen, and Djelal Kadir (Routledge, 2011), esp. 228–30.

9. And indeed, of the romantic theory of the literary work, from which the general romantic justification of the humanities derives. Consider, for instance, Goethe's remarks about allegory, cited in chapter 1. There, the romantic theory of literature aligns itself quite specifically with Kantian reflecting judgment against its determining counterpart.

10. Immanuel Kant, *Groundwork of the Metaphysics of Morals*, rev. ed., ed. and trans. Mary Gregor and Jens Timmerman (Cambridge: Cambridge University Press, 2012), 39. This is the source of further page references in the text.

11. Pheng Cheah fastens onto this moment in Kant, saying that the appearance of a "mercantile" metaphor orients us toward the inevitable tensions (historically) between the theorization of the human being and philosophy's relation to capital (*Inhuman Conditions: On Cosmopolitanism and Human Rights* [Harvard University Press, 2007], 155).

12. Slavoj Žižek, *The Parallax View* (Cambridge, MA: MIT Press, 2009), 10. He continues: "The paradox is thus that one participates in the universal dimension of the 'public' sphere precisely as a singular individual extracted from or even opposed to one's substantial communal identification—one is truly universal only as radically singular, in the interstices of communal identities."

13. David Damrosch and Gayatri Chakravorty Spivak, "Comparative Literature/World Literature: A Discussion with Gayatri Chakravorty Spivak and David Damrosch," *Comparative Literature Studies* 48, no. 4 (2011): 466.

14. Spivak is speaking in a specific interpretive and institutional context—namely, a discussion with David Damrosch, who has been the most prominent advocate for the curricular institutionalization of world literature over the last two decades. For Spivak, the context is, specifically, the teaching and scholarship of literary works in translation and of the teaching of work by nonexperts, both of which undermine the pedagogical and epistemological legitimacy of the practice. The fact that these remarks were spoken to stem the tide of world literature, whose overarching, universalizing point of view Spivak sees as destructive of literature's unique capacity to undermine normativity, reminds us how clearly the ethical resistance to generalization sets itself up as a "radical" rejection of "liberal" ideas. Indeed, it is difficult to know what "radical" and "liberal" could mean in the humanities today absent the structure of difference established by the opposition between homogenization and generalization on the one hand, and singularity on the other.

15. My thoughts here are very much influenced by a history of work in two related subfields, both of which have done so much work to undermine the centrality of the rational, Cartesian being to our descriptions of the meaning, and indeed the actual history, of human life: first, the work done in and around the lives of objects and things, in work from people like

Elaine Scarry or Bill Brown; and second, the work in animal studies and environmental studies done by writers like Sue Donaldson and Will Kymlicka (*Zoopolis: A Political Theory of Animal Rights* [Oxford, 2013]), and Cary Wolfe (*Before the Law: Humans and Other Animals in a Biopolitical Frame* [U of Chicago Press, 2012]).

16. Cited in Franco Moretti, *Far Country: Scenes from American Culture* (New York: Farrar, Straus and Giroux, 2019), 86.

17. Why "Kant"? Because I am not making claims about what Kant *really* thought, nor am I interested in restoring to Kant a coherence that would confirm his status as a great philosopher. "Kant doesn't really think persons are like artworks" is not a defense against the argument here. The argument is that idiographic prejudice exists, that it has roughly the shape I am describing it to have, and that one of the obvious sources for that prejudice is a certain interpretation—largely unconscious, I think—of some things some Kant wrote. This doesn't mean that Kant is the only origin of idiographic prejudice. On the resemblance between Kantian persons and artworks, and the kinds of problems for theories of personhood that emerge from them, see the chapter "Persons and Artworks" in Christopher Williams's *A Cultivated Reason: An Essay on Hume and Humeanism* (Pennsylvania State University Press, 1999).

18. For a counterargument that typifies the Kantian inheritance, and does so by extending it specifically to the privileged realms of the aesthetic and the philosophical that constitute his own habitus as well as the habitus of his primary audiences, see Jean-François Lyotard: "A postmodern artist or writer is in the position of a philosopher: the text he writes, the work he produces are not in principle governed by preestablished rules, and they cannot be judged according to a determining judgment." (*The Postmodern Condition: A Report on Knowledge*, trans. Geoff Bennington and Brian Massumi [Minneapolis: University of Minnesota Press, 1984], 81).

19. Graham Harman, *The Quadruple Object* (Zero Books, 2011), 119.

20. On this subject, see the first few pages of Roberto Esposito, *Persons and Things: From the Body's Point of View* (Malden, MA: Polity, 2015).

21. The difference between people and artworks might be, finally, that people make decisions about how to recognize artworks, and the reverse less so. But of course, a theory of people as ultimately self-legislating, and therefore uniquely individualized, would have to confront the fact that all of us emerge into "circumstances existing already, given and transmitted by the past," as Marx put it in the *18th Brumaire*, and therefore into a world of concepts, things, and institutions (and languages) that put the brakes on full self-legislation.

22. It does not have much of a theoretical life afterward, either. It frequently appears in the same citation that you see here; it also features in German law, where it is used to consider damage, for instance, over and above the

cost of replacing a broken object. The philosopher who makes the most of *Affektionspreis* is Lorenzo Magnani, for whom it serves as a launching pad for his concept of "moral mediators" and whose claims resemble in some ways the ones that I am making here. See Lorenzo Magnani, *Morality in a Technological World: Knowledge as Duty* (Cambridge: Cambridge University Press, 2009); Lorenzo Magnani and Emanuele Bardone, "Distributed Morality: Externalizing Ethical Knowledge in Technological Artifacts," *Foundations of Science* 13, no. 1 (March 1, 2008): 99–108, https://doi.org/10.1007/s10699-007-9116-5.

23. Richard Rorty, *Truth and Progress: Philosophical Papers* (Cambridge: Cambridge University Press, 1998), 212. My copy of this book was—delightfully—delivered to me printed with the pages in reverse order, Taiwan-style, though blessedly with the words still written left to right. Whether reading it this way has made any difference to my understanding of Rorty, I leave as a question for the imaginative reader.

24. This is a simplified way of saying things. As Jacques Derrida points out, the concept of differences of degree, of relativism more broadly, relies (like any other philosophical concept) on a differentiation of kind, insofar as it distinguishes between differences of degree and nondifferences of degree. Derrida refers to this as the "all or nothing" logic of all philosophical concepts and says that it is impossible to form a concept without it. But, he says, one can "think or deconstruct the concept of concept otherwise, think a *différance* which would be neither of nature nor of degree, and of which I say . . . that they are not entirely words or concepts" (Jacques Derrida, *Limited Inc.*, ed. Gerald Graff and trans. Jeffrey Mehlman and Samuel Weber [Evanston, IL: Northwestern University Press, 1988, 117]). So, to translate my relativist argument into slightly different terms: the problem with arguments for differences in degree is almost always that they are not relativist *enough*—and when one turns the relativist claims (which bear some resemblance to the idiographic logic I have been describing so far) back on themselves, one produces precisely the kind of disruption in the concept that Derrida aims for in the deconstructive gesture, for two reasons: first, that the material practice of the relativist critique so often seems to halt at a certain limit that one can clearly place *within* the general sphere of its practice (as is the case with the Kantian attempt to generate an ontological rift between the human and everything else, or as in the case in the geographic critique of scale, where scalar thinking is bad unless one valorizes flatness); and second. because in the effort to make the concept genuinely self-oriented, a wide variety of excluded categories—including categories like the universal or the general—can be made to reappear in the "interior" of the concept, as it were, where they pose (for me) the most important challenges to the elaboration and description of a method that would account for them, a method that would take its place within a conceptual

framework that included (not in any simple way) from the "beginning" the terms it rejected . . . which would make it, then, something not very much like a concept in the "all or nothing" sense. To accept the return of the excluded categories, and to think the study of the humanities within the space of that return, are the major goals of this part of the book.

3. ARTICLES OF REASON:
HOW HUMANISTS REALLY (OUGHT TO?) THINK

1. Max Weber, *The Methodology of the Social Sciences*, trans. Edward A. Shils and Henry A. Finch (Glencoe, IL: Free Press, 1949), 76.
2. Barbara Herrnstein Smith, "What Was 'Close Reading'? A Century of Method in Literary Studies," *Minnesota Review*, no. 87 (2016): 68.
3. Weber, *Methodology of the Social Sciences*, 58.
4. This emphasis on the work of reason as a communicative process echoes some of the work of Jürgen Habermas. If I diverge from him, it is to empha-size to a greater degree than he does the role that contextualization plays as a ground for humanist thought. My argument here is that one can avoid (as Windelband did) most of the facile criticisms of contextualization and relativism by recognizing that the historical context in which reasoning takes place can extend from the very immediate (i.e., a day or two) to the very large (i.e., the entire history of the species), and that the manipula-tion of contextual framework—and the epistemological necessity of being responsible to contexts at a variety of scales—constitute a critical part of the work of what Habermas would call "communicative action."
5. By "rationality," Weber means, and I mean, something as simple as this: how does this person create and live within a shareable and coherent sense of the world?
6. Jürgen Habermas, *Philosophical Introductions: Five Approaches to Communi-cative Reason* (Cambridge: Polity, 2018), 156.
7. One difference between this defense of a certain version of reason (or a claiming and rewriting of the term) and a fully utopian fantasy of its extension to the entire realm of the social (in which everything or every-one would participate in this reason all the time) is that I understand the practice of reason as only one sphere of social life—one that takes part in a more general society that includes spheres that do not include, need, or want reason at all. That is, I do not see reason as a final goal of the species, nor do I imagine that any single mode of thought or of interper-sonal activity could *ever* come to replace all the other modes that coex-ist with it and help make it what it is. Humanist reason, as I describe it here, is the result of a very specific set of historical institutions, intellectual work, and social circumstances that have produced it, and which continue

to produce it because such reason produces social and individual value. This book attempts to clarify that value, as well as the principles that produce it. My understanding of the fundamental problem of describing reason—and, in particular, my interest in encouraging scholars in aesthetic and historical fields to derive a theory of reason from their intellectual practice—draws on the same knot of postwar philosophical difficulties that inspired the work of Habermas and Karl-Otto Apel. My understanding of Apel owes a great deal to Eduardo Mendieta, *The Adventures of Transcendental Philosophy: Karl-Otto Apel's Semiotics and Discourse Ethics* (Lanham, MD: Rowman & Littlefield Publishers, 2002).

8. Habermas, *Philosophical Introductions*, 162.
9. I mean this claim about the universe to apply specifically to *this* universe, with its particular history (14.5 billion human years long) and its particular configuration of physical laws, which I take to be, in their status as quite literally universal, historical facts and not metaphorically or ideally universal ones.
10. Why "almost certainly"? Because the future is long, and may yet surprise us.
11. Together, the entirely of all the contexts that have taken place in human history—the sum total of all the evidence before us, at all its contextual scales—might reveal, if someone could manage to see it, a fairly interesting description of the historical range of context-action relations, which might well provide a rubric for predictions about their future development.
12. Martin Jay, " 'Hey! What's the Big Idea?': Ruminations on the Question of Scale in Intellectual History," *New Literary History* 48, no. 4 (Autumn 2017): 628.
13. Ted Underwood, "A Genealogy of Distant Reading," *DHQ: Digital Humanities Quarterly* 11, no. 2 (2017), http://www.digitalhumanities.org/dhq/vol/11/2/000317/000317.html.
14. D. R. Montello, "Scale in Geography," *International Encyclopedia of the Social and Behavioral Sciences*, ed. N. J. Smelser and P. B. Baltes (Pergamon Press, 2001), 13501–2.
15. If you discover, for instance, that experimental mice react differently in the presence of human male observers (which is true!), you can run the experiment with and without them in the room. See Robert E. Sorge, Loren J. Martin, Kelsey A. Isbester, et al., "Olfactory Exposure to Males, Including Men, Causes Stress and Related Analgesia in Rodents," *Nature Methods*, 11(2014), 629–32.
16. An alternative beginning: Peter Taylor's 1982 essay, "A Materialist Framework for Political Geography" (*Transactions of the Institute of British Geographers* 7, no. 1, 15–34), opens the modern scalar revolution by imagining scales as analogs of the material structures developed in Wallersteinian world-systems theory. I focus on Smith here because his essay pivots

openly, and early, between the tensions of fixed, or ontological scale, and its fluid, more phenomenal cousin, as you shall see.

17. Neil Smith, "Contours of a Spatialized Politics: Homeless Vehicles and the Production of Geographic Scale," *Social Text* 33 (1992), 66. This is also the source of further references in the text.

18. At the limit, you might say that the cognitive ones are more important since the very idea of having the city government report to the regional one, or the idea that certain forces operate (or should operate) only at certain scales, though they do not exactly begin with the idea that the disorganized chaos of the social is actually organized in scalar terms (for ideology does not precede, in any strict sense, social activity), nonetheless orient themselves toward such an idea as a retroactive ground and put it into practice. In this way, the social use of scale differs little from its use by geographers; it is a method of description and interpretation that creates, and builds itself in the image of, its object.

19. Adam Moore, "Rethinking Scale as a Geographical Category: From Analysis to Practice." *Progress in Human Geography* 32, no. 2 (2008), 210.

20. Poststructuralism's continued strength comes partly because, I think, its lessons are so hard to learn, and partly because it aims so directly at the basic processes through which humanists organize their concepts and their work. If it's difficult to think like a poststructuralist, if we find ourselves always being brought up short, and rejuvenated, by the double lessons of the episteme and the supplement, it is because poststructuralism is so very hard to think. Nonetheless we must keep trying, and drawing (if we can) some comfort from the fact that this incomplete task, this pattern of continuous vigilance and continuous forgetting, reproduces something of the Bergsonian philosophy of fluid, diachronic time that captured the interest of so many of poststructuralism's major contributors, offering us thereby another instance of content's return as form. In short: I ♥ *mises-en-abyme*.

21. One may consider geography as a particular of this more general poststructuralist trend, or as a significant node or site in a broader movement of ideas, privileging vertical or horizontal languages in turn. Both cases allow us to recognize that the history of scale in geography will be thought of in terms homologous with those used to describe social scales, which returns inevitably to the problem of the relationship between method and phenomenon.

22. Richard Howitt, "Scale," *A Companion to Political Geography*, ed. John Agnew, Katharyne Mitchell, and Gerard Toal (Blackwell, 2003), 151.

23. Sallie A. Marston, John Paul Jones III, and Keith Woodward, "Human Geography Without Scale," *Transactions of the Institute of British Geographers NS* 30 (2005), 425. This is the source of further references in the text.

24. Edmund Husserl, *The Crisis of European Sciences and Transcendental Phenomenology*, trans. David Carr (Evanston, IL: Northwestern University Press, 1970), 51–52. These remarks echo more general ones Husserl makes a few pages earlier: "But now we must note something of the highest importance that occurred even as early as Galileo: the surreptitious substitution of the mathematically substructured world of idealities for the only real world, the one that is actually given through perception, that is ever experienced and experienceable—our every-day life-world" (48–49).

25. See Martin Heidegger's remarks on the disasters of technology and the modern world-picture in "The Question Regarding Technology" and "The Age of the World Picture," in *The Question Concerning Technology and Other Essays*, trans. William Levitt (New York: Harper, 1977), 3–35 and 115–154, respectively.

26. Husserl, *The Crisis of European Sciences*, 50.

27. Contrast Husserl's emphasis on the historical concealment of the phenomenon by science with the arguments made by Marston et al., which proceed with no real reference to historical activity.

28. Second, because it is the life-world we knew before; first, because in that happy before the life-world needed no revelation—it simply *was*.

29. In fact, I am willing to argue that concretion/abstraction is the mode of relationality for all thinking beings, including nonhuman animals, which must generalize concepts like "danger," "food," "predator," "comfort," and "light" in order to survive.

30. This paragraph cites at length and partially modifies sentences from Jacques Derrida, "And Say the Animal Responded?" trans. David Wills, in *Zootologies: The Question of the Animal*, ed. Cary Wolfe (Minneapolis: University of Minnesota Press, 2003), 127.

31. "The event is what escapes the performative convention": Eric Hayot and Gayatri Chakravorty Spivak, "The Slightness of My Endeavor: An Interview with Gayatri Chakravorty Spivak," *Comparative Literature* 57, no. 3 (2005), 264.

32. "Heterosis, n.," 3: "The tendency of cross-breeding to produce an animal or plant with a greater hardiness and capacity for growth than either of the parents; hybrid vigour." *Oxford English Dictionary*.

33. In this way, I agree with nearly everything Anna Lowenhaupt Tsing says in arguing against the facile use of precision-nested scales, while resisting the opposition between the "living" world and the concept that governs the title of her essay and the rhetoric of her argument. See Anna Lowenhaupt Tsing, "On Nonscalability: The Living World Is not Amenable to Precision-Nested Scales," *Common Knowledge* 18, no. 3 (2012): 505–24.

34. Jacques Derrida, *Limited Inc*, ed. Gerald Graff, trans. Jeffrey Mehlman and Samuel Weber (Evanston, IL: Northwestern University Press, 1988).

35. Judith Butler, *Antigone's Claim* (New York: Columbia University Press, 2002).

36. Mary G. Dietz, "Context Is All: Feminism and Theories of Citizenship," *Daedalus* 116, no. 4 (1987): 1–24; Ngaire Naffine, "Who Are Law's Persons? From Cheshire Cats to Responsible Subjects," *Modern Law Review* 66, no. 3 (2003): 346–67, https://doi.org/10.1111/1468-2230.6603002.

37. Dipesh Chakrabarty, *Provincializing Europe* (Princeton, NJ: Princeton University Press, 2000), 16.

38. By "realism," I do not mean here to refer to a reality that is out there prior to our understanding of it, but rather to a socially functional and actually historically existing reality that is understood and lived through an always essentially ethnocentric (because historical) imaginary—one that we are born into and then shape in various ways for those who come after us. My carefulness on this topic owes something to the work of Richard Rorty, especially the essays in *Truth and Progress* (Cambridge: Cambridge University Press, 1998). But I also recognize the difficulty of being completely rigorous about one's use of terms like "reality," "actuality," and "the world," although I have tried. I am, by saying "realistic," attempting to retain a useful term (rather than abandon it fully to the philosophical realists) and rework it, just as I have been doing with "reason."

39. Here, I merely reinscribe into this set of claims the principle of critical reflexivity that characterizes the work of the Frankfurt School, which James Gordon Finlayson (*Habermas: A Very Short Introduction* [Oxford: Oxford University Press, 2005, 3]) has described as a conceptualization of knowledge "according to which the facts and our theories are part of an ongoing dynamic historical process in which the way we view the world (theoretically or otherwise) and the way the world is reciprocally determine each other."

40. Aijaz Ahmad, "Jameson's Rhetoric of Otherness and the 'National Allegory,'" *Social Text*, no. 17 (Autumn 1987): 23.

41. My emphasis on the social functionality of language comes, as you might have guessed, from my reading of Harold Garfinkel. But one might also refer here to the debate between Heidegger and Ernst Cassirer, in which Cassirer's position involved, as Andrew Hines points out, gently suggesting to Heidegger that his insistence on the opacity of language probably ought to account for the fact that most of us understand each other most of the time (Andrew Hines, "How Do We Understand Each Other? The Contemporary Relevance of Cassirer's and Heidegger's Historic Disputation at Davos," *Blog of the Journal of the History of Ideas*, February 6, 2019, https://jhiblog.org/2019/02/06/how-do-we-understand-each-other-the-contemporary-relevance-of-cassirers-and-heideggers-historic-disputation-at-davos/).

42. Studying the humanities makes individuals into more empathetic people or more informed citizens; these things then produce social value by a process of aggregation or agglomeration. The assumption is that the main product of humanist knowledge is humanist teaching, and the main

product of humanist teaching is a kind of *Verstand*-oriented person, a sensitive cosmopolitan. For an extensive critique of these claims, see Helen H. Small, *The Value of the Humanities* (Oxford: Oxford University Press, 2014).

43. I am thinking here of the debates around both computational methods (characterized often as the battle between close and distant reading) and symptomatic, Marxist criticism (which almost always begin by referring to Eve Sedgwick's essay on paranoid reading, in *Touching Feeling: Affect, Pedagogy, Performativity* [Durham: Duke University Press, 2003]).

44. More generally, we might think of the resistance to transactability that we see in Kant—the attempt to reserve against the market some special set of objects that cannot be exchanged for one another—an attempt to think through the social category of "uniqueness," to imagine the unique as that which is essentially unexchangeable. This position is of a piece with the Windelbandian emphasis on the demands placed on scholarship by the "unique" qualities of the historical moment—which will never happen in the same way again, by virtue of its time-boundedness—and the resistance to the "reduction" or "subordination" of that event to a series, and thus to a kind of epistemological transactability.

45. It also has had some very good ones! But I think that one can have the good ones—or most of them, anyway—without the bad ones.

46. To be clear: The actual practice of natural science is far more epistemologically sophisticated than the metadiscourse that describes it, and many scientists have a far richer sense of the work of scientific reason than the common-sense one that appears in the ideology of scientific positivism. But I am not describing the practices of actual scientists, or indeed the beliefs of all scientists; rather, I am describing and attacking the more generalized ideology of knowledge that produces the fetishization of scientific positivism and the denigration of humanist reason, an ideology widely shared and widely operant across all fields of the social, including the humanities themselves.

47. See, for instance, this overview of the global right-wing war on universities, where "universities" almost always means the humanities: Jack Stripling, "How Far Will Higher Ed's Culture Wars Go?" *Chronicle of Higher Education*, March 17, 2020, https://www.chronicle.com/article/How-Far-Will-Higher-Ed-s/248254.

4. CLASSROOMS, UNIVERSITIES, METHODS

1. Chad Wellmon, *Organizing Enlightenment: Information Overload and the Invention of the Modern Research University* (Baltimore: Johns Hopkins University Press, 2016).

2. This entire module concept was developed in conversation with Sandra Berman, Lutz Koepnik, Françoise Lionnet, Thomas Seifrid, and Helmut Müller-Sievers, and draws on language we wrote together for a departmental review in January 2020.

3. On the economic slowdown, see Thomas Piketty, *Capital in the Twenty-First Century*, trans. Arthur Goldhammer (Cambridge, MA: Harvard University Press, 2014); Bill Bishop, *The Big Sort: Why the Clustering of Like-Minded America Is Tearing Us Apart* (Boston: Mariner, 2009).

4. Pew Research Center, "Sharp Partisan Divisions in Views of National Institutions," July 10, 2017, https://www.people-press.org/2017/07/10/sharp-partisan-divisions-in-views-of-national-institutions/.

5. D'Souza, who in the interim was convicted of campaign finance violations (and then was pardoned by President Donald Trump), served as a kind of elder statesman of the whole farce. The intentional echo of Bloom's title in Jonathan Haidt's *The Coddling of the American Mind* also gives us a sense of the ways in which the parallel between the 2015–2020 period and the 1988–1994 one is being deliberately used and/or manufactured.

6. Benjamin Schmidt, "The Humanities Are in Crisis," *The Atlantic*, August 23, 2018, accessed June 26, 2020, https://www.theatlantic.com/ideas/archive/2018/08/the-humanities-face-a-crisisof-confidence/567565/.

7. "Kids Science: Learn About the Scientific Method," Ducksters, accessed May 1, 2019, https://www.ducksters.com/science/scientificmethod.php.

8. "Scientific Method," Wikipedia, April 19, 2019, https://en.wikipedia.org/w/index.php?title=Scientific_method&oldid=893175270. But the Wikipedia definition misses the importance (both historical and philosophical) to all this of peer review, of the kinds of skepticism that involve communities of scholars, and thus of the radically social nature of this form of knowledge-production.

9. Peter Janich, *Das Maß der Dinge: Protophysik von Raum, Zeit und Materie* (Frankfurt am Main, Germany: Suhrkamp, 1997).

10. For a sense of the diversity of humanist method, as well as a list of basic principles (some of which are opposed to one another, and therefore constitute variations in practice or cyclical patterns of rejection and return), see Rens Bod, *A New History of the Humanities: The Search for Principles and Patterns from Antiquity to the Present.* (Oxford: Oxford University Press, 2016).

WORKS CITED

Ahmad, Aijaz. "Jameson's Rhetoric of Otherness and the 'National Allegory.'" *Social Text*, no. 17 (Autumn 1987): 3–25.

American Psychological Association. *Publication Manual of the American Psychological Association*, 6th ed. Washington, DC: American Psychological Association, 2009.

Attridge, Derek. *The Singularity of Literature*. New York: Routledge, 2017.

Bishop, Bill. *The Big Sort: Why the Clustering of Like-Minded America Is Tearing Us Apart*. Boston: Mariner, 2009.

Bod, Rens. *A New History of the Humanities: The Search for Principles and Patterns from Antiquity to the Present*. Reprint ed. Oxford: Oxford University Press, 2016.

Brooks, Cleanth. *The Well Wrought Urn: Studies in the Structure of Poetry*. Orlando, FL: Mariner, 1956.

Butler, Judith. *Antigone's Claim*. New York: Columbia University Press, 2002.

Cheah, Pheng. *Inhuman Conditions: On Cosmopolitanism and Human Rights*. Cambridge, MA: Harvard University Press, 2007.

Chakrabarty, Dipesh. *Provincializing Europe*. Princeton, NJ: Princeton University Press, 2000.

Collini, Stefan. *Speaking of Universities*. London: Verso, 2018.

Connor, Steven. "In Exemplification." In *The State of Theory*, ed. Richard Bradford, 27–41. New York: Routledge, 1993.

Da, Nan Z. "The Computational Case Against Computational Literary Studies." *Critical Inquiry* 45, no. 3 (March 1, 2019): 601–39. https://doi.org/10.1086/702594.

Damrosch, David, and Gayatri Chakravorty Spivak. "Comparative Literature/World Literature: A Discussion with Gayatri Chakravorty Spivak and David Damrosch." *Comparative Literature Studies* 48, no. 4 (2011): 455–85.

Derrida, Jacques. "And Say the Animal Responded?" Trans. David Wills. In *Zoontologies: The Question of the Animal*, ed. Cary Wolfe. Minneapolis: University of Minnesota Press, 2003.

——. *Limited Inc*. Ed. Gerald Graff, trans. Jeffrey Mehlman and Samuel Weber. Evanston, IL: Northwestern University Press, 1988.

Dietz, Mary G. "Context Is All: Feminism and Theories of Citizenship." *Daedalus* 116, no. 4 (1987): 1–24.

Donoghue, Frank. *The Last Professors: The Corporate University and the Fate of the Humanities*. New York: Fordham University Press, 2008.

Ducksters. "Kids Science: Learn About the Scientific Method." Accessed June 26, 2019. https://www.ducksters.com/science/scientificmethod.php.

Eliade, Mircea. *The Myth of the Eternal Return: Cosmos and History*. Trans. Willard R. Trask. Princeton, NJ: Princeton University Press, 2005.

Esposito, Roberto. *Persons and Things: From the Body's Point of View*. Malden, MA: Polity, 2015.

Etherington, Ben. *Literary Primitivism*. Stanford, CA: Stanford University Press, 2017.

Fabian, Johannes. *Time and the Other: How Anthropology Makes Its Object*. Trans. Matti Bunzl. New York: Columbia University Press, 2002.

Finlayson, James Gordon. *Habermas: A Very Short Introduction*. Oxford: Oxford University Press, 2005.

Gallop, Jane. "The Ethics of Reading: Close Encounters." *Journal of Curriculum Theorizing*, Fall 2000, 7–17.

Garfinkel, Harold. *Ethnomethodology's Program*. Ed. Anne Rawls. Lanham, MD: Rowman & Littlefield, 2002.

Garfinkel, Harold, and Anne Rawls. *Toward a Sociological Theory of Information*. New York: Routledge, 2009.

Gilbert, Bennett. "On Wilhelm Windelband's History and Natural Science," 2013.

Gitelman, Lisa, ed. *"Raw Data" Is an Oxymoron*. Cambridge, MA: MIT Press, 2013.

Goethe, Johann Wolfgang von. *Maximen und Reflexionen*. Ed. Gottfried Martin Daiber and Gunter Böhmer. Recklinghausen, Germany: Seemann, 1961.

Graff, Gerald, and Cathy Birkenstein. *"They Say/I Say": The Moves That Matter in Academic Writing*. 3rd ed. New York: W. W. Norton, 2014.

Greenblatt, Stephen. *Shakespearean Negotiations: The Circulation of Social Energy in Renaissance England*. Berkeley: University of California Press, 1989.

Habermas, Jürgen. *Philosophical Introductions: Five Approaches to Communicative Reason*. Cambridge: Polity, 2018.

Hacking, Ian. *The Taming of Chance*. Cambridge: Cambridge University Press, 1990.

Harman, Graham. *The Quadruple Object*. Alfresford, UK: Zero Books, 2010.

Hayot, Eric R. J. *Chinese Dreams: Pound, Brecht, Tel Quel*. Ann Arbor: University of Michigan Press, 2004.

——. *The Hypothetical Mandarin: Sympathy, Modernity, and Chinese Pain*. Oxford: Oxford University Press, 2009.

Hayot, Eric, and Gayatri Chakravorty Spivak. "The Slightness of My Endeavor: An Interview with Gayatri Chakravorty Spivak," *Comparative Literature* 57, no. 3 (2005), 256–72.

Heidegger, Martin. "The Age of the World Picture." In *The Question Concerning Technology and Other Essays*, trans. William Levitt, 3–35. New York: Harper, 1977.

——. "The Question Concerning Technology." In *The Question Concerning Technology and Other Essays*, trans. William Levitt, 115–154. New York: Harper, 1977.

Hines, Andrew. "How Do We Understand Each Other? The Contemporary Relevance of Cassirer's and Heidegger's Historic Disputation at Davos." *Blog of the Journal of the History of Ideas*, February 6, 2019. Accessed June 26, 2020. https://jhiblog.org/2019/02/06/how-do-we-understand-each-other-the-contemporary-relevance-of-cassirers-and-heideggers-historic-disputation-at-davos/.

Howitt, Richard. "Scale." In *A Companion to Political Geography*, ed. John Agnew, Katharyne Mitchell, and Gerard Toal, 138–57. Malden, MA: Blackwell, 2003.

Husserl, Edmund. *The Crisis of European Sciences and Transcendental Phenomenology*. Trans. David Carr. Evanston, IL: Northwestern University Press, 1970.

Jalbert, John E. "Husserl's Position Between Dilthey and the Windelband-Rickert School of Neo-Kantianism." *Journal of the History of Philosophy* 26, no. 2 (1988): 279–96.

Janich, Peter. *Das Maß der Dinge: Protophysik von Raum, Zeit und Materie*. Frankfurt am Main, Germany: Suhrkamp, 1997.

——. *Was Ist Information? Kritik einer Legende*. Frankfurt am Main, Germany: Suhrkamp, 2006.

Jay, Martin. " 'Hey! What's the Big Idea?' Ruminations on the Question of Scale in Intellectual History." *New Literary History* 48, no. 4 (Autumn 2017): 617–31.

Kant, Immanuel. *The Critique of the Power of Judgment*. Ed. Paul Guyer, trans. Paul Guyer and Eric Matthews. Cambridge: Cambridge University Press, 2000.

——. *Groundwork of the Metaphysics of Morals*. Rev. ed. Ed. and trans. Mary Gregor and Jens Timmerman. Cambridge: Cambridge University Press, 2012.

Kotsko, Adam. "Not Persuasion, but Power: Against 'Making the Case.' " *Boston Review*, May 6, 2020. Accessed June 26, 2020. https://bostonreview.net/forum/higher-education-age-coronavirus/adam-kotsko-not-persuasion-power-against-%E2%80%9Cmaking-case%E2%80%9D.

Krebs, Paula. "Wisconsin Is Trying to Segregate Higher Education into the Haves and Have-Nots." *Washington Post*, March 21, 2018, Opinions. Accessed June 26, 2020. https://www.washingtonpost.com/opinions/wisconsin-is-trying-to-segregate-higher-education-into-the-haves-and-have-nots/2018/03/21/8cd67aco-2886-11e8-b79d-f3d931db7f68_story.html.

Kumar, Krishnan, and Herbert F Tucker. "Introduction." *New Literary History* 48, no. 4 (2017): 609–16.

Lamprecht, Karl. *Zwei Streitschriften den Herren H. Oncken, H. Delbrück, M. Lenz.* H. Heyfelder, 1897.

Liu, Alan. "Local Transcendence: Cultural Criticism, Postmodernism, and the Romanticism of Detail." *Representations*, no. 32 (1990): 75–113.

Lodge, David. *Changing Places: A Tale of Two Campuses.* 2nd ed. New York: Penguin, 1979.

Lyotard, Jean-Francois. *The Postmodern Condition: A Report on Knowledge.* Trans. Geoff Bennington and Brian Massumi. Minneapolis: University of Minnesota Press, 1984.

Magnani, Lorenzo. *Morality in a Technological World: Knowledge as Duty.* Cambridge: Cambridge University Press, 2009.

Magnani, Lorenzo, and Emanuele Bardone. "Distributed Morality: Externalizing Ethical Knowledge in Technological Artifacts." *Foundations of Science* 13, no. 1 (March 1, 2008): 99–108. https://doi.org/10.1007/s10699-007-9116-5.

Makkreel, Rudolf A. "Wilhelm Dilthey and the Neo-Kantians: The Distinction of the Geisteswissenschaften and the Kulturwissenschaften." *Journal of the History of Philosophy* 7, no. 4 (1969): 423–40.

Marston, Sallie A., John Paul Jones III, and Keith Woodward. "Human Geography Without Scale." *Transactions of the Institute of British Geographers* 30, no. 4 (2005), 416–32.

Mendieta, Eduardo. *The Adventures of Transcendental Philosophy: Karl-Otto Apel's Semiotics and Discourse Ethics.* Lanham, MD: Rowman & Littlefield Publishers, 2002.

Meyer, Eduard. *Zur Theorie und Methodik Der Geschichte. Geschichtsphilosophische Untersuchungen.* Halle an der Salle: M. Niemeyer, 1902. Accessed June 26, 2020. https//catalog.hathitrust.org/Record/008904665.

Miller, J. Hillis. *The Ethics of Reading: Kant, De Man, Eliot, Trollope, James, and Benjamin.* New York: Columbia University Press, 1986.

Montello, D. R. "Scale in Geography." In *International Encyclopedia of the Social and Behavioral Sciences*, ed. N. J. Smelser and P. B. Baltes (Pergamon Press, 2001), 13501–2.

Moore, Adam. "Rethinking Scale as a Geographical Category: From Analysis to Practice." *Progress in Human Geography* 32, no. 2 (2008), 203–25.

Moretti, Franco. *Distant Reading.* New York: Verso, 2013.

——. *Far Country: Scenes from American Culture.* New York: Farrar, Straus and Giroux, 2019.

Naffine, Ngaire. "Who Are Law's Persons? From Cheshire Cats to Responsible Subjects." *Modern Law Review* 66, no. 3 (2003): 346–67. https://doi.org/10.1111/1468-2230.6603002.

Ngai, Sianne. *Our Aesthetic Categories: Zany, Cute, Interesting.* Cambridge, MA: Harvard University Press, 2015.

Oakes, Guy. "Introduction: Rickert's Theory of Historical Knowledge." In Heinrich Rickert, *The Limits of Concept Formation in Natural Science: A Logical*

Introduction to the Historical Sciences, vii–xxx. Trans. Guy Oakes. Cambridge: Cambridge University Press, 1986.

——. "Value Theory and the Foundations of the Cultural Sciences. Remarks on Rickert." In *Methodology of the Social Sciences, Ethics, and Economics in the Newer Historical School: From Max Weber and Rickert to Sombart and Rothacker*, ed. Peter Koslowski. New York: Springer Verlag, 1997.

Osborne, Peter. *The Politics of Time: Modernity and Avant-Garde*. London: Verso, 2011.

Pew Research Center, "Sharp Partisan Divisions in Views of National Institutions." July 10, 2017, https://www.people-press.org/2017/07/10/sharp-partisan-divisions -in-views-of-national-institutions/.

Piketty, Thomas. *Capital in the Twenty-First Century*. Trans. Arthur Goldhammer. Cambridge, MA: Harvard University Press, 2014.

Pinker, Steven. *The Blank Slate: The Modern Denial of Human Nature*. New York: Penguin, 2003.

Porter, Theodore M. *The Rise of Statistical Thinking, 1820–1900*. Princeton, NJ: Princeton University Press, 1988.

Ringer, Fritz. *Max Weber's Methodology: The Unification of the Cultural and Social Sciences*. Cambridge, MA: Harvard University Press, 1998.

Rorty, Richard. *Truth and Progress: Philosophical Papers*. Cambridge: Cambridge University Press, 1998.

Schmidt, Benjamin. "The Humanities Are in Crisis." *The Atlantic*, August 23, 2018. Accessed June 26, 2020. https://www.theatlantic.com/ideas/archive/2018/08 /the-humanities-face-a-crisisof-confidence/567565/.

Schnädelbach, Herbert. *Philosophy in Germany 1831–1933*. Trans. Eric Matthews. Cambridge: Cambridge University Press, 1984.

Schor, Naomi. *Reading in Detail: Aesthetics and the Feminine*. Ed. Ellen Rooney. New York: Routledge, 2006.

"Scientific Method." In *Wikipedia*, April 19, 2019. https://en.wikipedia.org/w /index.php?title=Scientific_method&oldid=893175270.

Sedgwick, Eve Kosofsky. *Touching Feeling: Affect, Pedagogy, Performativity*. Durham, NC: Duke University Press, 2003.

"Sharp Partisan Divisions in Views of National Institutions | Pew Research Center," July 10, 2017. Accessed June 26, 2020. https://www.people-press.org /2017/07/10/sharp-partisan-divisions-in-views-of-national-institutions/.

Silvia, Paul. *Write It Up: Practical Strategies for Writing and Publishing Journal Articles*. Washington, DC: American Psychological Association, 2014.

Simmel, Georg. *Die Probleme der Geschichtsphilosophie: Eine erkenntnistheoretische Studie*. Duncker & Humblot, 1892.

Small, Helen H. *The Value of the Humanities*. Oxford: Oxford University Press, 2013.

——. *The Value of the Humanities*. Paperback ed. Oxford and New York: Oxford University Press, 2016.

Smith, Barbara Herrnstein. "What Was 'Close Reading'? A Century of Method in Literary Studies." *Minnesota Review*, no. 87 (2016): 57–75.

Smith, Neil. "Contours of a Spatialized Politics: Homeless Vehicles and the Production of Geographic Scale." *Social Text* 33 (1992), 54–81.

Snow, C. P. *The Two Cultures: And a Second Look*. New American Library/Mentor, 1964.

Sorge, Robert E., Loren J. Martin, Kelsey A. Isbester, et al., "Olfactory Exposure to Males, Including Men, Causes Stress and Related Analgesia in Rodents." *Nature Methods, 11* (2014), 629–32.

Spolaore, Enrico, and Romain Wacziarg. "The Diffusion of Development." *Quarterly Journal of Economics*, May 2009, 469–529.

Stripling, Jack. "How Far Will Higher Ed's Culture Wars Go?" *Chronicle of Higher Education*, March 17, 2020, https://www.chronicle.com/article/How -Far-Will-Higher-Ed-s/248254.

Taylor, Peter. "A Materialist Framework for Political Geography." *Transactions of the Institute of British Geographers* 7, no. 1 (1982), 15–34.

Tsing, Anna Lowenhaupt. "On Nonscalability: The Living World Is not Amenable to Precision-Nested Scales." *Common Knowledge* 18, no. 3 (August 1, 2012): 505–24.

Underwood, Ted. *Distant Horizons: Digital Evidence and Literary Change*. Chicago: University of Chicago Press, 2019.

——. "A Genealogy of Distant Reading." *DHQ: Digital Humanities Quarterly* 11, no. 2 (2017). Accessed June 26, 2020. http://www.digitalhumanities.org/dhq /vol/11/2/000317/000317.html.

Veeser, Harold Aram. *The New Historicism*. New York: Routledge, 1989.

Weber, Max. *The Methodology of the Social Sciences*. Trans. Edward A. Shils and Henry A. Finch. Glencoe, IL: Free Press, 1949.

——. *Roscher and Knies: The Logical Problems of Historical Economics*. Trans. Guy Oakes. New York: Free Press, 1976.

Wellek, René. *A History of Modern Criticism 1750–1950. Volume 1: The Later Eighteenth Century*. Cambridge and New York: Cambridge University Press, 1983.

Wellmon, Chad. *Organizing Enlightenment: Information Overload and the Invention of the Modern Research University*. Baltimore: Johns Hopkins University Press, 2016.

Williams, Christopher. *A Cultivated Reason: An Essay on Hume and Humeanism*. University Park: Pennsylvania State University Press, 1999.

Wilson, Edward Osborne. *Consilience: The Unity of Knowledge*. Reprint ed. New York: Vintage, 1999.

Windelband, Wilhelm. *Geschichte und Naturwissenschaft: Rede . . .* Heitz, 1904.

——. "History and Natural Science." Trans. Guy Oakes. *History and Theory* 19, no. 2 (February 1980): 165–68.

Yu, Pauline. *The Reading of Imagery in the Chinese Poetic Tradition*. Princeton, NJ: Princeton University Press, 1987.

Žižek, Slavoj. *The Parallax View*. Cambridge, MA: MIT Press, 2009.

INDEX